Optimal Tourism Development

Optimal Tourism Development

Editor

Juan A. Campos-Soria

MDPI • Basel • Beijing • Wuhan • Barcelona • Belgrade • Manchester • Tokyo • Cluj • Tianjin

Editor
Juan A. Campos-Soria
Universidad de Málaga
Spain

Editorial Office
MDPI
St. Alban-Anlage 66
4052 Basel, Switzerland

This is a reprint of articles from the Special Issue published online in the open access journal *Sustainability* (ISSN 2071-1050) (available at: https://www.mdpi.com/journal/sustainability/special_issues/optimal_tourism).

For citation purposes, cite each article independently as indicated on the article page online and as indicated below:

LastName, A.A.; LastName, B.B.; LastName, C.C. Article Title. *Journal Name* **Year**, *Article Number*, Page Range.

ISBN 978-3-03943-691-0 (Hbk)
ISBN 978-3-03943-692-7 (PDF)

Contents

About the Editor

Juan A. Campos-Soria is an Associate Professor of Economics and Tourism Economics at the University of Málaga, Spain. He has led different seminars on tourism economics at the Christel Dehaan Tourism and Travel Research Institute (University of Nottingham, UK). He has participated in international research projects for the Department for Culture, Media and Sport (UK) and the World Travel and Tourism Council (WTTC), as well as numerous national projects for public and private institutions. He has published papers in leading journals, such as *Annals of Tourism Research*, *Tourism Management*, *Journal of Sustainable Tourism*, *Journal of Travel Research*, *International Journal of Hospitality Management*, *Tourism Economics*, and *Applied Economics*, among others, and collaborated with well-known researchers in tourism economics, such as professors M. T. Sinclair, A. Blake, and J. L. Eugenio-Martín. He has been a working Editorial Board Member of various journals, such as *Tourism Economics*, *Tourism Analysis*, and *Tourism & Management Studies*, in recent years. He has also collaborated on different book chapters, among which are several published in *Recent Developments in the Economics of Tourism* (Edward Elgar Publishing), edited by Professors L. Dwyer and N. Seetaram. His main current lines of research are the economic analysis of tourism, gender economics, and the labour market.

Preface to "Optimal Tourism Development"

This work comprises a selection of papers that have significantly advanced the study of sustainable tourism from different perspectives. The papers have been selected for their theoretical and empirical contributions as well as their contribution to informed policy making. Some articles represent advances in the area of tourist supply and demand modelling from an environmental approach, paying attention to tourism planning and development. This collection of papers will have particular appeal to researchers, graduate students, and tourism economists in the private sector, as well as to policy-making organizations for improving sustainable tourism.

Juan A. Campos-Soria
Editor

Article

Perceived Sustainable Destination Image: Implications for Marketing Strategies in Europe

Arminda Almeida-Santana [1],* and Sergio Moreno-Gil [2]

[1] Research Group in Business Management (Gide), University of León (ULE), 24007 León, Spain
[2] Institute of Tourism and Sustainable Economic Development, Universidad Las Palmas de Gran Canaria, 35001 Las Palmas de Gran Canaria, Spain; sergio.moreno@ulpgc.es
*   Correspondence: aalms@unileon.es

Received: 30 October 2019; Accepted: 15 November 2019; Published: 17 November 2019

Abstract: There is currently a growing concern about the consequences of tourism activity on the environment. In this regards, sustainable management is understood as a key element that can help destination marketing organizations (DMOs) to improve a tourist destination's competitiveness. This study provides some clues about the best way to develop the image and branding of a destination using the concept of sustainable image. Through an analysis of 28,947 tourists from 18 European countries, this paper studies what sociodemographic, cultural, and behavioral characteristics of tourists influence their perception of sustainable destination. The results of the binomial logit analysis show that destination primary and secondary images, motivations, cultural background of tourists, and sociodemographic characteristics are determinant factors explaining the perception of sustainable destination image (SDI). Thus, the fundamental role of segmentation to positioning a destination as a sustainable destination is suggested. The study provides interesting recommendations for DMOs in order to be able to design better marketing strategies focused on destination image.

Keywords: sustainable destination; destination image; marketing strategies; communication; segmentation

---

1. Introduction

A concern of academics over the last couple of decades has been that of destination image [1], with it becoming one of the key topics among researchers. Although there have been many attempts to understand the concept of the image of a destination [1–3], it can be thought of as the accumulated perception of both cognitive and affective evaluations [4–6]. Almeida-Santana and Moreno-Gil (2018) [7] pointed out that the image's cognitive component concerns the beliefs and information in respect to a destination's attributes which are retained by tourists, whereas emotional feelings or responses to the characteristics of a place represent the affective component. Destination image has been defined by Bigne, Sanchez, and Sanchez (2001) [8] as the subjective interpretation of reality within the tourist's mind.

There is no doubt that tourists' profiles have undergone a significant change in recent years. Previous studies indicate a greater awareness of tourists on how their activity can impact on the destination's environment, society, and culture [9]. Thus, it can be said that sustainable tourist behavior is an extant and thriving field of study [9,10]. Some authors [11–13] dare to indicate that more and more tourists make purchases with an eye to the environmental, social, and economic quality of products. There is a growing trend towards the consumption of sustainable brands that influences the destination choice [14–17]. Therefore, currently, destinations are more concerned with sustainability in their response to adapt to the new demands of tourists [18]. Destination marketing organizations (DMOs) must be able to convey a sustainable destination image if they want to improve their levels of competitiveness.

Notable efforts have been made within the literature to investigate factors which have an influence on image [18,19]; however, no research has undertaken analyses on the factors which determine a tourist's perception of an image of sustainable destination (SDI). Thus, the aim of this study is to understand whether tourists' sociodemographic, cultural, and behavioral characteristics influence their perception of a destination as being sustainable.

2. Literature Review

2.1. Sustainable Destination Image

A greatly explored construct within tourism literature is that of destination image [1,20,21]. Since its inception into the academic studies in the early 70s, scholars have sought to clearly define this concept. Fakeye and Crompton (1991) [10] defined destination image as the mental representation based on a group of images chosen by the tourist from the large amount of images available through different information sources. The concept of a subjective, personal perception of the tourists was added latter by other researchers [8,22].

Sustainable destination has been defined by past studies as a destination which provides economic development, a higher level of standard of living, ecological preservation, and social and cultural heritage preservation [23,24]. However, SDI may be differently perceived by visitors.

Destination image research attempts to conceptualize the concept of destination image and to identify its dimensions [25–27]. These destination image researchers endeavor to unravel the components of this concept in order to facilitate DMOs in shaping strategies regarding customer segments. Thus, Echtner and Ritchie (1991) [19] claim a need for more research that will aim to provide an improved understanding of the destination image, further conceptualizing it in terms of an accumulation of attributes. Besides the more holistic impressions, it would also be important to measure the cognitive and affective images with the consideration immersed within the characteristics of the destination and the personal perception of the tourists [20,28]. Thus, the primary image is formed via acquisition of information through visitation of the destination [20], while information sources that are organic, induced, and autonomous form the secondary image [29].

Past research assumes that environmental and socioeconomic aspects of a location exhibit a direct linkage to the image of the destination [30], highlighting the importance of sustainability as a destination's positioning strategy. Consequently, Souza et al. (2014) [30] have claimed that the concepts of sustainability and image have a grounding in common basic aspects. However, past studies include sustainability as a component of cognitive image [27,31,32]. Given this prominence that sustainability is taking today, its association with the affective and general image of the destination is crucial.

2.2. Motivations

Motivations, as one of the key influences that guides the development of a destination image, are included in the models of destination choice and image formation [33]. These motivations can be grouped with respect to push and pull factors [34]. For Dann (1977) [35], what can be termed as internal (push) motives are linked to tourists' wishes and include such aspects as desires to escape or rest and to acquire prestige, adventure, and social interaction. Pull factors, on the other hand, are connected with a destination's attractiveness and resources. Previous research has shown that an individual's internal motivations significantly affects the formation of destination image [20,25]. For instance, Baloglu (2000) [36] found the relationship between motivations to relax, escape, and gain knowledge to be statistically significant.

In current tourism literature, motivation has often been used as a criterion of segmentation [37–39] with this method being suggested as one of the most effective [34,40]. Easy categorization of heterogeneous groups of tourists via these motivational factors has been shown to be possible by numerous empirical studies [41–43]. Thus, an expansion of knowledge on the various motivations of tourists is important for the positioning of brands in differing markets [44,45]; however, previous literature has not paid special attention to the relationship between motivations to travel and SDI. Thus, the contribution of this study resides in a better understanding of this relationship. This can help DMOs in their choice of content to be communicated according to the motivations of tourists.

2.3. Cultural Background

A considerable volume of research has utilized national culture as a rationale for market segmentation [45–47], and thus, it is felt to be an appropriate basis for segmentation. Nationality has received growing attention in research studies since Hofstede (1980) [48], as it has been argued to be one of the most influential aspects that affects tourism behavior [49–52] and influences destination image [53–57]. Furthermore, national culture plays a key role in the way tourists from different countries interpret the sustainability and, in consequence, as a fundamental element on the sustainability image of tourism destinations [30].

Nevertheless, extant research on the manner in which national culture affects consumer behavior [58] and specially perceived destination image [59] is still not sufficiently conclusive. Researchers are seeking further studies on segmentation which utilize geographical criteria [60,61] that better guide the development of more improved, efficient marketing strategies [45,62].

Considering that which has been mentioned so far, the purpose of this paper is to initiate debate on the relationship between the image of tourism destination sustainability and the tourists' countries of origin. There is importance, both with respect to the academic realm and for practitioners, to have clarity in understanding how the national culture of tourists might cause SDI to differ. Through this, the design of better marketing strategies will be possible, which will lead to a more appropriate positioning of sustainable tourism destinations within different cultures.

2.4. Sociodemographic Characteristics

Consumer behavior research has traditionally been linked to sociodemographic characteristics, and these have been frequently used as segmentation criteria [63]. The incorporation of sociodemographic variables as factors influencing the perception of a destination's image has occurred in most image formation models [31,64]. Studies have identified that there are differences in image perceptions by gender, age, and level of education [31,65].

Given the changes in consumer behavior in relationship with sustainability, there is a need for the development of further research on SDI from the perspective of market segmentation. It is feasible that segmentation criteria that has a basis in sociodemographic characteristics may not be fully aligned with the profile of sustainable tourists.

3. Methodology

3.1. Population

Generating greater than half of the yearly international arrivals, Europe represents the world's largest outbound region with respect to tourist flow [66]. Therefore, tourists aged 16 or over who, within the last two years, had gone abroad and who had made use of the Internet to plan their trip were the target population for this research. Tourists from the 18 major European countries, in tourist terms, were utilized for this study: Germany, Austria, Belgium, Denmark, Spain, Russia, Finland, France, Netherlands, Ireland, Italy, Luxembourg, Norway, Poland, Portugal, United Kingdom, Czech Republic, and Sweden.

3.2. Sample Selection

This research was progressed through the use of a computer-assisted web interview (CAWI). A sample from the 18 countries was considered and was yielded from a database of panelists residing in each of these countries. It was to maintain the representativeness of the sample with respect to the population of each country. In order to achieve this, a random selection of the sample was undertaken, with this being based on the variables of stratification of the geographical area and province, on the one hand, and of the criteria of gender and age, on the other. Participation in the research by the selected sample was sought by sending them a personalized e-mail, with a personalized link being embedded in the e-mail that led them to an online survey. To achieve the expected quantity of completed surveys, two reminders were sent during the three months of fieldwork in the countries so as to encourage response. This culminated in the final sample consisting of 28,947 tourists.

Visits to the Canary Islands (Spain) was the focus of the analysis of the results, in particular with respect to the sustainable perceived image of this destination. In addition to the reason of convenience, the Canary Islands were chosen as the specific case due to it being a leading destination in Europe which enjoys a well-known brand throughout the continent. Given that it receives approximately 15 million tourists annually and has a complex economic ecosystem [7], these are factors which make it a perfect subject for consideration of the topic of sustainability. One of the 17 autonomous communities of Spain, the group of Canary Islands is formed as an archipelago located in the Atlantic Ocean.

Island destinations face specific challenges regarding tourism development [67]. The Canary Islands are highly relevant as a place of research, due to steady discussions about tourism development and growth [68] and the islands' character as an experimental zone for sustainable tourism in the context of an overflowing capacity of tourism growth [69]. Thus, sustainability in the Canary Islands destination has been the subject of a great amount of recent studies [70–73].

3.3. Questionnaire, Quality Control, and Data Analysis

The questionnaire was translated into the languages of each of the 18 countries. The survey was undertaken once the questionnaire had been pre-tested in the languages of the potential tourists and questions that had raised difficulties in comprehension had received pertinent corrections. Upon completion of the necessary programming, the online system undertook a review of all of the conducted surveys. This included detecting the amount of time that respondents had taken to complete the survey, and any survey answered in less than 5 minutes was deemed as not valid. A binomial logit analysis was performed after completion of the fieldwork. A logit model based on the theory of random utility was chosen for this research. In utilizing this model, robustness in the estimated results is guaranteed, along with fulfilment of the properties of the conventional utility functions as established by the theory of the consumer.

With respect to the variables included in the model, tourists were invited to answer how sustainable they perceived the Canary Islands destination. A score of 1 indicates very unsustainable and 7 indicates very sustainable. For the statistical treatment of this variable, following the study of Almeida-Santana and Moreno Gil (2018) [7], it was necessary to dichotomize it, understanding that tourists who marked a 6 or 7 out of 7 were considered to perceive the destination as sustainable, while we understand that those who gave values between 1 and 4 do not perceive the Canary Islands destination as sustainable. Table 1 shows the description of all the variables included in the estimated model.

Table 1. Description of the variables included in the model.

Category	Variables	Definition
Sociodemographic and geographic variables	Age	A continuous variable that explains the age of the individuals in years
	Gender	Dichotomic variables that take 0 as a value when the individual is male and 1 when is female
	Years of study	Number of years of study
	Germany, Austria, Belgium, Denmark, Spain, Russia, Finland, France, Netherlands, Ireland, Italy, Luxembourg, Norway, Poland, Portugal, United Kingdom, Czech Republic, Sweden	Dichotomic variables that take 0 as a value when the individual does not belong to one of the nationalities under study and 1 when they do
Motivation variables	Fodness Scale (1994) [74]. See Table 2	Scale of 1 to 7 (very negative image to very positive image)
Behavioral characteristics (Primary and secondary images)	Number of times a destination is visited	A continuous variable that explains the number of visits to Canary Islands
	Last year visited	Number of years since the last visit
	Has seen advertising about the destination	Dichotomic variables that take 0 as a value when the individual has seen advertising about the destination and 1 when they have not
Endogenous	Sustainable Destination Image (SDI)	Dichotomic variables that take 0 as a value when the individual has not perceived a sustainable image and 1 when they have

Table 2. Motivation factor analysis.

Variables	MOT1	MOT2	MOT3	MOT4	Cronbach´s Alpha
To go to places that are fashionable	0.738				
To look for entertainment and fun	0.688				0.560
To enjoy and spend time with friends	0.479				
To rest and relax		0.772			
To spent time in a destination with good beaches and pleasant climate		0.654			0.623
To enjoy and spend time with family		0.611			
To go to comfortable places		0.495			
To do sports			0.834		
To be in contact with nature			0.692		0.692
To do watersports			0.636		
To do exciting things			0.487		
To know new and different places				0.780	0.413
To escape from daily routine				0.545	
Cronbach´s alpha					0.768
% Explained variance: 55.933					
KMO: 0.806					
Bartlett: 49379.541					
Significance: 0.000					

4. Results

Below, in order to fulfil the aim of this study, a binomial logit model has been estimated with the perception of a sustainable destination image (SDI) as dependent variable. The model explored the existence of a relationship between SDI and sociodemographic, cultural, and behavioral characteristics of tourists.

A factor analysis was undertaken prior to estimating the model so as to examine the motivations' dimensions. The aim for this was to affect a reduction in their dimensions and an appropriate identification of the determining factors. With due regard to the criteria addressed in the literature, each item has been classified in respect to the higher loading. With the majority of the factor loadings being greater than 0.40, this is an indication of a good correlation between the items as well as the factor grouping to which they belong [75,76]. The validity of these analyses was further supported by the outcome of Pearson correlation coefficient calculations for each of the variables and factors.

Completion of the factor analysis on the motivations revealed four dimensions that explain 55.93% of the variance. As portrayed in Table 2, the first factor incorporates 3 items which we have labelled as "Fashion, Fun, and Friends". Four items are collected together for the second factor, namely "Sun, Beach, Relax, and Family". The third factor also holds 4 items, in this instance, related to "Sports and Nature". Lastly, 2 items comprise the fourth factor named "Knowledge". Regarding the findings of the Cronbach's alpha calculations, it is necessary to consider that MOT4's low value could feasibly be consequential to this factor only consisting of 2 items, given that Cronbach's alpha is known to be sensitive to the number of items in a scale [68]. It can be said that these findings are largely in accordance with the literature [18,55,77,78].

Table 3 summarizes the results of the estimation for the proposed model. Regarding the consumer's previous experience as a tourist in a specific destination, it was unsurprisingly found that the greater the number of times a destination is visited, the greater is the likelihood of SDI being evident ($\beta = 0.004$; $p < 0.01$). Furthermore, it is also not surprising that a tourist having had a recent travel to the Canary Islands increases the probability of perception of SDI ($\beta = 0.200$; $p < 0.01$). These findings align with the argument that primary sources of information influence the perceived destination image, as suggested by Beerli and Martín (2004) [20].

As for advertising, tourists having seen advertisements about the destination have a positive influence on SDI ($\beta = 0.187$; $p < 0.05$), and thus, this portrays the importance of this tool being utilized by destinations (as secondary sources of information) for enhancing the image of sustainable destination.

Furthermore, the motivations related to going to places that are fashionable, to looking for entertainment and fun, and to enjoying and spending time with friends have positive effects on SDI ($\beta = 0.365$; $p < 0.01$). In the light of the results of our study, those tourists are 40% more likely to perceive the destination as sustainable. The motivations of rest and relaxation, of spending time in a destination with good beaches and pleasant climate, of enjoying and spending time with family, and going to comfortable places all positively influence SDI ($\beta = 0.244$; $p < 0.01$). They are 27.7% more likely to perceive SDI. The motivations of doing sports and being in contact with nature ($\beta = 0.205$; $p < 0.01$) also has a positive effect on the tourist perceiving SDI. These are the tourists with the minor probability to perceive SDI. However, the motivations to know new and different places and to escape from the daily routine do not have an influence on SDI.

Furthermore, the relationship between the nationality of the tourists and their perception of SDI was analyzed. Here, positive relations were revealed with the majority of the markets: Germany, Austria, Belgium, Spain, Russia, France, Netherlands, Ireland, Italy, Luxembourg, Norway, Poland, Portugal, United Kingdom, and Czech Republic. Therefore, the Canary Islands are more likely to be perceived as an SDI by tourists from these countries, whereas the nationalities of Denmark, Finland and Sweden were found to be nonsignificant. Attending to the differences between countries, it could be confirmed that the nationalities with a minor perception of sustainability are the Austrians, the Dutch, and those from Luxembourg. However, the Russians are those who, only because they are of this nationality, are more likely to perceive the destination as sustainable. The greatest value in the case of Russians can be explained by the fact that Russia could be considered as not being a typical European country and, further, that the preferences and experience of Russian tourists differ strikingly from those of tourists of the other European countries [79]. Those results give weight to the concept that national culture influences the way tourists from different countries interpret the sustainability and its fundamental role in the formation of sustainability image of tourism destinations [30].

The results found that age and level of studies determine SDI. The results show, in line with Baloglu and McCleary (1999) [31] and Calantone et al. (1989) [65], that the older a person is, the greater is the likelihood that the individual will perceive SDI ($\beta = 0.163$; $p < 0.01$). On the other hand, the relationship between the mean studies level of a tourist and SDI is negative ($\beta = 0.140$; $p < 0.01$).

Table 3. Estimated binomial logit model.

	Sustainable Destination Image		
	β	ε	Percent Change in the Odds
Number of times a destination is visited	0.004 ***	0.001	0.4
Last year visited	0.200 ***	0.023	22.1
Has seen advertising about the destination	0.187 ***	0.061	20.5
MOT1: Fashion, Fun, and Friends	0.365 ***	0.033	44.0
MOT2: Sun, Beach, Relax, and Family	0.244 ***	0.031	27.7
MOT3: Sports and Nature	0.205 ***	0.031	22.7
MOT4: Knowledge	-	-	-
Germany	0.753 ***	0.160	112.4
Austria	0.457 **	0.185	57.9
Belgium	0.867 ***	0.184	138.0
Denmark	-	-	-
Spain	2.171 ***	0.171	776.9
Russia	2.637 ***	0.312	1296.4
Finland	-	-	-
France	0.906 ***	0.203	147.4
Netherlands	0.452 ***	0.168	57.1
Ireland	1.262 ***	0.168	253.1
Italy	1.814 ***	0.205	513.7
Luxembourg	0.592 **	0.259	80.8
Norway	0.822 ***	0.172	127.6
Poland	1.745 ***	0.234	472.6
Portugal	1.836 ***	0.214	526.9
United Kingdom	1.102 ***	0.163	201.0
Czech Republic	0.973 ***	0.239	164.5
Sweden	-	-	-
Age	0.163 ***	0.029	17.7
Gender	-	-	-
Education	−0.140 ***	0.031	−13
Constant	−1.690 ***	0.197	
−2 Log likelihood	6815.447		

Note: *** 0.01%; ** 0.05%.

5. Discussion

The theoretical implication of this study lies in presenting a comprehensive understanding of factors influencing an SDI. More specifically, the model uses destination primary and secondary images, motivations, cultural background of tourists, and sociodemographic characteristics to explain the perception of SDI. Those variables are crucial in fully understanding the perception of SDI. This means that destination marketing organizations should adjust their strategies to different market segments, attending to the mentioned variables. As far as we are aware, no other researchers have investigated this relationship prior to us.

The more intense the previous experience (primary image) in the destination, the more likely are travelers to have an SDI. This study further suggests that a key determinant of SDI is a destination secondary image. Thus, destination marketing organizations should consider these findings when designing their marketing strategies. The secondary image of a destination could be affected by destinations and the companies operating in the sector through various sources of information such as magazines, tour operators, travel agencies, social media, and so on [80]. DMOs must be able to design strategies in which an image of a sustainable destination is projected since, according to the results of our study, the information that the tourist receives through these sources will influence their perception of a sustainable destination and, consequently, their decision of whether to visit the destination. Those results are in line with the study of Lian and Yu (2019) [81], who highlighted the influence of online information sources in the decision to travel.

Furthermore, the results suggest that three motivational factors ("Fashion, Fun, and Friends", "Sun, Beach, Relax, and Family", and "Sports and Nature") are statistically significant for SDI. Whilst we had hypothesized that a traveler's motivation to know new and different places and to escape from the daily routine would have a positive effect on the SDI, our findings have revealed that this is not supported. Therefore, destination marketing organizations should project the SDI according to tourists' motivations [33,82]. Thus, the content used to promote the SDI should be adapted to match tourism motivations. In this way, the possible congruence that exists between the message and the specific motivations of the target market could determine better results [45]. Either way, developing a professional social command centre in charge of managing the social content of the destination seems to be an interesting strategy to foster SDI.

Our findings also suggest that the cultural background of a tourist is an important factor determining SDI. More specifically, our findings reveal that national culture influences the way tourists from different countries interpret sustainability and its fundamental role on the sustainability image of tourism destination formation [30]. This sheds lights on the usefulness of using the nationality as a segmentation criterion, helping marketers to tier customers. DMOs should pay special attention to the markets of The Netherlands, Austria, and Luxembourg, since they are those that have a lower probability of perceiving the destination as sustainable. In markets such as Russia, Spain, Portugal, and Italy, efforts must be aimed at maintaining or even improving the SDI. This is in accordance with the Almeida-Santana et al. (2018) [45] study, which suggests nationality as being a relevant factor when seeking to comprehensively understand the behavior of travelers when choosing their holiday destination.

Furthermore, the results also determined that age and level of studies determine SDI. The results show, in line with Baloglu and McCleary (1999) [31] and Calantone et al. (1989) [65], that the older a person is, the more likely they are to perceive SDI. The negative relationship between the mean study levels expressed by the tourists and SDI is demonstrated. Destination marketing organizations should consider those results in order to better design their marketing strategies. Younger tourists have a lower perception of a sustainable destination, so marketing campaigns aimed at this younger segment should place greater emphasis on the projection of a sustainable destination image. The same approach could be applied to the segment with a high level of studies.

Finally, some limitations of this research are given. This study considers SDI only in respect to the Canary Islands. However, it could be applied to other destinations. SDI could also be further analyzed, with introduction to the model of other factors influencing SDI.

6. Conclusions

This study has focused on seeking to explain the factors that influence the perception of a sustainable destination image by tourists. The importance of carrying out this research is justified by the growing concern shown by tourists about the impact of their activity [83]. DMOs must adapt to the new demands of tourists and design strategies that allow them to position themselves as a sustainable destination if they want to remain competitive in this day and age in which sustainability is fundamental [83].

In order to achieve the aims of this study, information was collected from tourists from 18 European countries who have visited the Canary Islands. This is presented as an appropriate destination to study sustainability [70–73].

The findings of this research confirm that the primary and secondary images of the destination, the travel motivations of tourists, and their nationality, as well as their age and level of studies influence their perception of SDI. This gives emphasis to the importance of segmentation in the design of destination marketing strategies to position the destination as sustainable.

Author Contributions: All authors made a proportional contribution.

Funding: This research received no external funding.

Acknowledgments: This research and the APC was funded by the Ministerio de Economía, Industria y Competitividad ECO2017-82842-R and by the Canarian Agency for Research, Innovation, and Information Society (ACIISI) cofinanced by the European FEDER Fund under project 2017010116.

Conflicts of Interest: The authors declare no conflict of interest.

References

1. Költringer, C.; Dickinger, A. Analyzing destination branding and image from online sources: A web content mining approach. *J. Bus. Res.* **2015**, *68*, 1836–1843. [CrossRef]
2. Gallarza, M.G.; Saura, I.G.; García, H.C. Destination image: Towards a conceptual framework. *Ann. Tour. Res.* **2002**, *29*, 56–78. [CrossRef]
3. Moreno-Gil, S.; Martín-Santana, J.D. Understanding the image of self-contained and serviced apartments: The case of sun and beach destinations. *J. Hosp. Tour. Res.* **2015**, *39*, 373–400. [CrossRef]
4. Baloglu, S.; Mangaloglu, M. Tourism Destination Images of Turkey, Egypt, Greece, and Italy as Perceived by US-Based Tour Operators and Travel Agents. *Tour. Manag.* **2001**, *22*, 1–9. [CrossRef]
5. Carballo, M.M.; Araña, J.E.; León, C.J.; Moreno-Gil, S. Economic valuation of tourism destination image. *Tour. Econ.* **2015**, *21*, 741–759. [CrossRef]
6. Kim, D.; Perdue, R.R. The Influence of Image on Destination Attractiveness. *J. Travel Tour. Mark.* **2011**, *225–239*, 225–239. [CrossRef]
7. Almeida-Santana, A.; Moreno-Gil, S. Understanding tourism loyalty: Horizontal vs. destination loyalty. *Tour. Manag.* **2018**, *65*, 245–255. [CrossRef]
8. Bigne, J.E.; Sanchez, M.I.; Sanchez, J. Tourism image, evaluation variables and after purchase behaviour: Inter-relationship. *Tour. Manag.* **2001**, *22*, 607–616. [CrossRef]
9. Pulido-Fernández, J.; López-Sánchez, Y. Are tourists really willing to pay more for sustainable destinations? *Sustainability* **2016**, *8*, 1240. [CrossRef]
10. Weeden, C. *Responsible and Ethical Tourist Behaviour*; Routledge: London, UK, 2013.
11. Miller, G. Consumerism in sustainable tourism: A survey of UK consumers. *J. Sustain. Tour.* **2003**, *1*, 17–39. [CrossRef]
12. Yeoman, I. *Tomorrow's Tourist: Scenarios & Trends*; Elsevier: Oxford, UK, 2008.
13. Boniface, B.; Coope, C. *Worldwide Destinations Casebook—The Geography of Travel and Tourism*; Elsevier Butterworth-Heinemann: Burlington, MA, USA, 2005.
14. Rheem, C. *PhoCusWright's Going Green: The Business Impact of Environmental Awareness on Travel*; PhocusWright: Sherman, CT, USA, 2008.
15. Adlwarth, W. Corporate social responsibility: Customer expectations and behavior in the tourism sector. In *Trends and Issues in Global Tourism 2010*; Conrady, R., Buck, M., Eds.; Springer: Heidelberg/Berlin, Germany, 2010.
16. Dodds, R.; Graci, S.R.; Holmes, M. Does the tourist care? A comparison of tourists in Koh Phi Phi, Thailand and Gili Trawangan, Indonesia. *J. Sustain. Tour.* **2010**, *18*, 207–222. [CrossRef]
17. Hedlund, T. The impact of values, environmental concern, and willingness to accept economic sacrifices to protect the environment on tourists' intentions to buy ecologically sustainable tourism alternatives. *Tour. Hosp. Res.* **2011**, *11*, 278–288. [CrossRef]
18. Edgel, S.D.L. *Managing Sustainable Tourism: A Legacy for the Future*; Haworth Hospitality Press: New York, NY, USA, 2006.
19. Echtner, C.M.; Ritchie, J.B. The meaning and measurement of destination image. *J. Tour. Stud.* **1991**, *2*, 2–12.
20. Beerli, A.; Martin, J.D. Factors influencing destination image. *Ann. Tour. Res.* **2004**, *31*, 657–681. [CrossRef]
21. Pike, S. Destination image analysis—A review of 142 papers from 1973 to 2000. *Tour. Manag.* **2002**, *23*, 541–549. [CrossRef]

22. Kim, S.S.; Morrison, A.M. Changes of images of South Korea among foreign tourists after the 2002 FIFA World Cup. *Tour. Manag.* **2005**, *26*, 233–247. [CrossRef]
23. Blažević, B.; Peršić, M. *Turistička Regionalizacija u Globalnim Procesima*; Fakultet za Turistički i Hotelski Menadžment: Opatija, Croatia, 2009.
24. Pearce, D. Destination management in New Zealand: Structures and functions. *J. Destin. Mark. Manag.* **2015**, *4*, 112. [CrossRef]
25. San Martín, H.; Del Bosque, I.A.R. Exploring the cognitive–affective nature of destination image and the role of psychological factors in its formation. *Tour. Manag.* **2008**, *29*, 263–277. [CrossRef]
26. Hallmann, K.; Zehrer, A.; Müller, S. Perceived destination image: An image model for a winter sports destination and its effect on intention to revisit. *J. Travel Res.* **2015**, *54*, 94–106. [CrossRef]
27. Stylidis, D.; Shani, A.; Belhassen, Y. Testing an integrated destination image model across residents and tourists. *Tour. Manag.* **2017**, *58*, 184–195. [CrossRef]
28. Moreno Gil, S.; Ritchie, B.J.; Almeida-Santana, A. Museum tourism in Canary Islands: Assessing image perception of Directors and Visitors. *Mus. Manag. Curatorship* **2019**, 1–20. [CrossRef]
29. Phelps, A. Holiday destination image—The problem of assessment: An example developed in Menorca. *Tour. Manag.* **1986**, *7*, 168–180. [CrossRef]
30. de Souza, A.G.; de Farias, S.A.; de Brito, M.P. Cultural dimensions and image: An essay on the impacts of masculinity and individualism on the interpretation of the sustainability of tourism destinations. *Rev. Bras. Pesqui. Em Tur.* **2014**, *8*, 238–260.
31. Baloglu, S.; McCleary, K.W. A model of destination image formation. *Ann. Tour. Res.* **1999**, *26*, 868–897. [CrossRef]
32. Wehrli, R.; Priskin, J.; Schaffner, D.; Schwarz, J.; Stettler, J. *Do Sustainability Experienced Travellers Prefer a More Rational Communication of the Sustainability of a Tourism Product*; Hochschule Luzern-Wirtschaft, ITW Institut für Tourismuswirtschaft: Luzern, Switzerland, 2013.
33. Li, M.; Cai, L.A.; Lehto, X.Y.; Huang, J. A missing link in understanding revisit intention—The role of motivation and image. *J. Travel Tour. Mark.* **2010**, *27*, 335–348. [CrossRef]
34. Crompton, J.L. Motivations for pleasure vacation. *Ann. Tour. Res.* **1979**, *6*, 408–424. [CrossRef]
35. Dann, G.M. Anomie, ego-enhancement and tourism. *Ann. Tour. Res.* **1977**, *4*, 184–194. [CrossRef]
36. Baloglu, S. A path analytic model of visitation intention involving information sources, socio-psychological motivations, and destination image. *J. Travel Tour. Mark.* **2000**, *8*, 81–90. [CrossRef]
37. Bieger, T.; Laesser, C. Market segmentation by motivation: The case of Switzerland. *J. Travel Res.* **2002**, *41*, 68–76. [CrossRef]
38. Chen, G.; Bao, J.; Huang, S. Segmenting Chinese backpackers by travel motivations. *Int. J. Tour. Res.* **2014**, *16*, 355–367. [CrossRef]
39. Sung, Y.K.; Chang, K.C.; Sung, Y.F. Market segmentation of international tourists based on motivation to travel: A case study of Taiwan. *Asia Pac. J. Tour. Res.* **2016**, *21*, 862–882. [CrossRef]
40. Park, D.B.; Yoon, Y.S. Segmentation by motivation in rural tourism: A Korean case study. *Tour. Manag.* **2009**, *30*, 99–108. [CrossRef]
41. Awaritefe, O.D. Destination environment quality and tourists' spatial behaviour in Nigeria: A case study of third world tropical Africa. *Int. J. Tour. Res.* **2003**, *5*, 251–268. [CrossRef]
42. Awaritefe, O.D. Destination image differences between prospective and actual tourists in Nigeria. *J. Vacat. Mark.* **2004**, *10*, 264–281. [CrossRef]
43. Keng, K.A.; Cheng, J.L.L. Determining tourist role typologies: An exploratory study of Singapore vacationers. *J. Travel Res.* **1999**, *37*, 382–390. [CrossRef]
44. De Mooij, M.; Hofstede, G. Cross-cultural consumer behavior: A review of research findings. *J. Int. Consum. Mark.* **2011**, *23*, 181–192.
45. Almeida-Santana, A.; Moreno-Gil, S.; Boza-Chirino, J. The paradox of cultural and media convergence. Segmenting the European tourist market by information sources and motivations. *Int. J. Tour. Res.* **2018**, *20*, 613–625. [CrossRef]
46. Budeva, D.G.; Mullen, M.R. International market segmentation: Economics, national culture and time. *Eur. J. Mark.* **2014**, *48*, 1209–1238. [CrossRef]
47. Tkaczynski, A.; Rundle-Thiele, S.R.; Beaumont, N. Segmentation: A tourism stakeholder view. *Tour. Manag.* **2009**, *30*, 169–175. [CrossRef]

48. Hofstede, G. Culture and organizations. *Int. Stud. Manag. Organ.* **1980**, *10*, 15–41. [CrossRef]
49. Crotts, J.C.; Erdmann, R. Does national culture influence consumers' evaluation of travel services? A test of Hofstede's model of cross-cultural differences. *Manag. Serv. Qual. Int. J.* **2000**, *10*, 410–419. [CrossRef]
50. Hudson, S.; Wang, Y.; Gil, S.M. The influence of a film on destination image and the desire to travel: A cross-cultural comparison. *Int. J. Tour. Res.* **2011**, *13*, 177–190. [CrossRef]
51. Muskat, B.; Muskat, M.; Richardson, A. How do Europeans travel in Australia? Examining cultural convergence in travel behaviour. *J. Vacat. Mark.* **2014**, *20*, 55–64. [CrossRef]
52. Thrane, C.; Farstad, E. Nationality as a segmentation criterion in tourism research: The case of international tourists' expenditures while on trips in Norway. *Tour. Econ.* **2012**, *18*, 203–217. [CrossRef]
53. Frías, D.M.; Rodríguez, M.A.; Alberto Castañeda, J.; Sabiote, C.M.; Buhalis, D. The formation of a tourist destination's image via information sources: The moderating effect of culture. *Int. J. Tour. Res.* **2012**, *14*, 437–450. [CrossRef]
54. Kim, B. Prideaux Marketing implications arising from a comparative study of international pleasure tourist motivations and other travel-related characteristics of visitors to Korea. *Tour. Manag.* **2005**, *26*, 347–357. [CrossRef]
55. Kozak, M. Comparative assessment of tourist satisfaction with destinations across two nationalities. *Tour. Manag.* **2001**, *22*, 391–401. [CrossRef]
56. Andersen, O.; Øian, H.; Aas, Ø.; Tangeland, T. Affective and cognitive dimensions of ski destination images. The case of Norway and the Lillehammer region. *Scand. J. Hosp. Tour.* **2018**, *18*, 113–131. [CrossRef]
57. de la Hoz-Correa, A.; Muñoz-Leiva, F. The role of information sources and image on the intention to visit a medical tourism destination: A cross-cultural analysis. *J. Travel Tour. Mark.* **2019**, *36*, 204–219. [CrossRef]
58. Ko, S.; Lee, T.; Yoon, H.; Kwon, J.; Mather, M. How does context affect assessments of facial emotion? The role of culture and age. *Psychol. Aging* **2011**, *26*, 48. [CrossRef]
59. Lee, G.; Lee, C.K. Cross-cultural comparison of the image of Guam perceived by Korean and Japanese leisure travelers: Importance–performance analysis. *Tour. Manag.* **2009**, *30*, 922–931. [CrossRef]
60. Min, K.S.; Martin, D.; Jung, J.M. Designing advertising campaigns for destinations with mixed images: Using visitor campaign goal messages to motivate visitors. *J. Bus. Res.* **2013**, *66*, 759–764. [CrossRef]
61. Obenour, W.; Lengfelder, J.; Groves, D. The development of a destination through the image assessment of six geographic markets. *J. Vacat. Mark.* **2005**, *11*, 107–119. [CrossRef]
62. Agarwal, J.; Malhotra, N.K.; Bolton, R.N. A cross-national and cross-cultural approach to global market segmentation: An application using consumers' perceived service quality. *J. Int. Mark.* **2010**, *18*, 18–40. [CrossRef]
63. Cleveland, M.; Papadopoulos, N.; Laroche, M. Identity, demographics, and consumer behaviors: International market segmentation across product categories. *Int. Mark. Rev.* **2011**, *28*, 244–266. [CrossRef]
64. Baloglu, S. The relationship between destination images and sociodemographic and trip characteristics of international travellers. *J. Vacat. Mark.* **1997**, *3*, 221–233. [CrossRef]
65. Calantone, R.; Di Benetton, C.; Hakam, A.; Bojanic, D. Multiple multinational tourism positioning using correspondence analysis. *J. Travel Res.* **1989**, *28*, 25–32. [CrossRef]
66. World Tourism Organization. *International Tourism Highlights*, 2019 ed. UNWTO: Madrid, Spain, 2019. [CrossRef]
67. Bramwell, B. Mass Tourism, Diversification and Sustainability in Southern Europe's Coastal Regions. In *Coastal Mass Tourism: Diversification and Sustainable Development in Southern Europe*; Bramwell, B., Ed.; Channel View: Bristol, UK, 2004; pp. 1–31.
68. Jimenez, F.; García Quesada, M.; Villoria, M. Corruption in Paradise: The puzzling case of Lanzarote. In Proceedings of the XXII Pisa World Congress of Political Science, Canary Islands, Spain, 9 July 2012.
69. Santana-Talavera, A.; Fernández-Betancort, H. Times of Tourism: Development and Sustainability in Lanzarote, Spain. In *Tourism as an Instrument for Development: A Theoretical and Pracitcal Study*; Fayos-Solà, E., Ed.; Emerald: Bingley, UK, 2014; pp. 241–264.
70. Eckert, C.; Pechlaner, H. Alternative product development as strategy towards sustainability in tourism: The case of Lanzarote. *Sustainability* **2019**, *11*, 3588. [CrossRef]
71. González-Morales, O.; Talavera, A. CSR as a strategy for public-private relationships in protected island territories: Fuerteventura, Canary Islands. *Isl. Stud. J.* **2019**, *14*. [CrossRef]

72. Pérez, F.; Martín, R.; Trujillo, F.; Díaz, M.; Mouhaffel, A. Consumption and Emissions Analysis in Domestic Hot Water Hotels. Case Study: Canary Islands. *Sustainability* **2019**, *11*, 599. [CrossRef]

73. Uche-Soria, M.; Rodríguez-Monroy, C. An Efficient Waste-To-Energy Model in Isolated Environments. Case Study: La Gomera (Canary Islands). *Sustainability* **2019**, *11*, 3198. [CrossRef]

74. Fodness, D. Measuring tourist motivation. *Ann. Tour. Res.* **1994**, *21*, 555–581. [CrossRef]

75. Hair, J.; Babin, B.; Money, A.; Samouel, P. *Fundamentos de Métodos de Pesquisa em Administração*; Bookman Companhia Ed: Sao Paulo, Brazil, 2005.

76. Meyers, L.S.; Gamst, G.; Guarino, A.J. Data screening. In *Applied Multivariate Research-Design and Interpretation*; SAGE: Newcastle upon Tyne, UK, 2006.

77. Beerli, A.; Martín, J.D. Tourists' characteristics and the perceived image of tourist destinations: A quantitative analysis—A case study of Lanzarote, Spain. *Tour. Manag.* **2004**, *25*, 623–636. [CrossRef]

78. Chen, R.S.; Tsai, C.C. Gender differences in Taiwan university students' attitudes toward web-based learning. *Cyberpsychol. Behav.* **2007**, *10*, 645–654. [CrossRef] [PubMed]

79. Whang, H.; Yong, S.; Ko, E. Pop culture, destination images, and visit intentions: Theory and research on travel motivations of Chinese and Russian tourists. *J. Bus. Res.* **2016**, *69*, 631–641. [CrossRef]

80. Marine-Roig, E.; Ferrer-Rosell, B. Measuring the gap between projected and perceived destination images of Catalonia using compositional analysis. *Tour. Manag.* **2018**, *68*, 236–249. [CrossRef]

81. Lian, T.; Yu, C. Impacts of online images of a tourist destination on tourist travel decision. *Tour. Geogr.* **2019**, 1–30. [CrossRef]

82. Hernández-Mogollón, J.; Duarte, P.; Folgado-Fernández, J. The contribution of cultural events to the formation of the cognitive and affective images of a tourist destination. *J. Destin. Mark. Manag.* **2018**, *8*, 170–178. [CrossRef]

83. Hanna, P.; Font, X.; Scarles, C.; Weeden, C.; Harrison, C. Tourist destination marketing: From sustainability myopia to memorable experiences. *J. Destin. Mark. Manag.* **2018**, *9*, 36–43. [CrossRef]

 *sustainability*

Article

A Model for the Development of Innovative Tourism Products: From Service to Transformation

Margarida Custódio Santos [1], Ana Ferreira [2], Carlos Costa [3] and José António C. Santos [1,*]

[1] Research Centre for Tourism, Sustainability and Well-Being, and School of Management, Hospitality and Tourism, University of Algarve, 8005-139 Faro, Portugal; mmsantos@ualg.pt
[2] CIDEHUS—Interdisciplinary Center for History, Cultures and Societies, University of Évora, 7000-645 Évora, Portugal; amferreira@uevora.pt
[3] Department of Economics, Management, Industrial Engineering and Tourism, University of Aveiro, 3810-193 Aveiro, Portugal; ccosta@ua.pt
* Correspondence: jasantos@ualg.pt; Tel.: +35-1289-800-136

Received: 29 April 2020; Accepted: 22 May 2020; Published: 26 May 2020

Abstract: This study sought to develop a conceptual model of innovative tourism product development, because the existing models tend to provide an incomplete framework for these products' development. The models presented to date focus on either the resources needed, the tourism experiences to be provided, or development processes. These models also tend to see the overall process as linear. The proposed model gives particular importance to the development process's design, as well as stressing a dynamic, nonlinear approach. Based on the new services or products' concept, project managers identify tourism destinations' core resources, select the stakeholders, and design transformative tourism experiences. This framework can be applied to innovative tourism products or re-evaluations of existing products in order to maintain tourism destinations' competitiveness. Thus, the model is applicable to both destination management companies and the private tourism sector.

Keywords: product innovation model; transformative tourism experience; development process design; core resource identification; tourism product development

---

1. Introduction

Competition among tourism destinations has increased substantially, intensified by changes in tourism demand, major markets' saturation, and the emergence of new information and communication technologies [1,2]. A wide range of studies have emphasised that the only way for tourism destinations to maintain their ability to compete internationally, especially as mature tourist destinations, is through innovation. While researchers explicitly acknowledge the need to innovate—in particular through new tourism product development—thus far, models for this type of development are surprisingly quite scarce [3]. Therefore, more research is needed on this topic [4].

Contrary to the industrial sector, in which the process of developing new products has been intensively studied [5,6], research in the services sector is much scarcer [7]. Steven and Dimitriadis [8] point out that this situation is unjustifiable given the service sector's growing importance in more developed economies. Researchers have confirmed that substantial differences exist between physical products and services, which are necessarily reflected in the way new service development has to be conducted. Menor et al. [9] argue that this lack of systematic research stems from how new services are thought to appear spontaneously as a result of intuition, flair or simply luck rather than being the result of properly organised development processes. The absence of structured procedures, weaknesses in preparatory work and the lack of customer involvement throughout these processes may also explain the high failure rate of new service development [10,11]. With regard to tourism, only a few studies have sought to model how new tourism products or services are developed [4,12]. In addition, most models to date complement each other but lack sophistication and correspond to a large extent to the models for new service development created in the 1980s.

In this context, the present research's objective was to build a model of innovative tourism product development and thus to contribute to closing the aforementioned gap in tourism research. The proposed framework (see Figure 1) for the development of new tourism products is based on three fundamental components: (1) identifying destinations' core resources on which innovative tourism products should be based, (2) determining the transformative experiences provided by these products, and (3) establishing the design of product development processes.

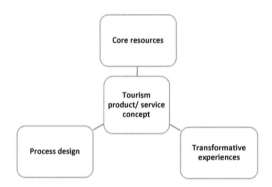

Figure 1. Framework for new tourism product development.

2. From Tangible Products to Transformative Experiences

An extensive literature exists on innovation models of tangible product development. These models' main aim is to present a sequence of steps whose primary purpose is to guide the process of developing new products in order to reduce the uncertainty inherent in innovation and help developers make the right decisions about continuing or abandoning projects. Rothwell [13] observes that, in the industrial sector, the models developed during the 1950s and until the mid-1960s were called linear models, reflecting the widespread conviction that innovation was a linear process starting with technological development and ending with market introduction. This first generation of innovation models was clearly driven by technological development and based on the conviction that more investment in research and development would result in a higher number of successful new products [14,15].

From the second half of the 1960s to the early 1970s, economic and social change contributed to an emphasis being placed on demand-related factors. This second generation of linear models was driven by the market, which, in turn, was perceived as the source of new ideas in product development. Research and development took on an overt reactive function. However, these models had various shortcomings. First, innovation was always triggered by fundamental research. Second, researchers failed to consider the possibility of technological knowledge preceding empirical knowledge. Third, models were hampered by an absence of feedback or interactions that occur throughout development processes. Last, these models did not consider design's fundamental importance in new products' effectiveness and success [16]. The early 1970s were marked by high constraints on demand, which drove companies to seek to understand more accurately how to carry out successful innovation with the least possible waste of resources. This quest was accompanied by intense research into new product development models. The resulting models suggest nonlinear approaches, and these frameworks characteristically present a sequence of functionally distinctive steps—but with high levels of interaction and interdependence [13]. The number of steps tends to differ between models, yet essentially they all aim to obtain and process simultaneously technical and market-related information, with innovation conceptualised as a complex process of interaction between agents involved in the processes' different stages. Among the many models developed in the 1970s, Kline and Rosenberg's [16] chain-link or interactive model most closely represents the complex structures and diverse patterns that innovation processes involve. This framework provides an understanding of how to encourage continuous innovation, that is, how to apply old or new knowledge to satisfy individual or collective demands. In this decade, another model was developed by Cooper [17], which was known as the stage-gate model and which was an attempt to provide companies with a tool to minimise the risks inherent in developing new products. This model recognises that each phase encompasses various activities and progressing to the next phase is conditioned by passage through a 'door' that functions as a controlling entity. During the course of each step, information is collected that facilitates decisions about whether to move forward with the process, interrupt it or go back to the previous stage and reassess the situation. All company departments are called upon to comment on the process and confirm that the information collected is enough to make a safe decision possible. Based on a set of software development methodologies known as Agile, Cooper and Sommer [18] propose the Agile-stage-gate model, which is an improvement of the previous stage-gate model by introducing speed, agility, and productivity into the model and thus accelerating product cycles of new product development. According to Cooper and Sommer [18], the benefits of this hybrid Agile-stage-gate model are: "increased design flexibility; improved productivity, communication, and coordination among project team members; better focus on projects, resulting in better prioritization of time and effort; and raised team morale" (p. 20).

2.1. New Service Development Processes

Johne and Storey [19] conducted an extensive review of the literature on new product development and found that this term is often used as a synonym for 'new service development' [20,21]. In reality, the overwhelming majority of prior studies have focused on tangible product development. Although the terminology used can cover both tangible products and services, various authors have acknowledged that quite significant differences exist between the development of tangible products and services [10,19,20]. These divergences essentially arise from the characteristics attributed to services such as intangibility, heterogeneity, inseparability, and perishability [10,15,19,21]. Despite agreeing with this analysis, Sampson and Froehle [22] present an extremely critical view of how services are defined and categorised, arguing that what is or is not a service should not be determined by the aforementioned four characteristics but instead by information gathered from the perspective of customer involvement. The cited authors argue that the process of developing new services is only clearly differentiated from that of developing tangible products through clients' role in the process. Sampson and Froehle [22] argue that, in all services, customers provide quite significant inputs to service production, which can include clients' physical, mental, and emotional involvement, as they are always present in services that involve co-production. The inputs may further result from the tangible goods belonging to customers or clients' provision of information. Kitsios and Kamariotou [11] also report that customers are involved in co-creation during the service innovation process, because their ideas are often more creative and valuable than the innovations developed within organisations. In addition, Andreassen et al. [23] observe that innovation in service design is crucial for improving both customer satisfaction and service quality. Effective communication with clients helps providers understand their customers' needs and allows clients to participate indirectly in innovation processes, as well as reducing the time needed to introduce new services into the market [11,24,25]. Although differences have been found between how new tangible products and services are developed, a more careful examination of the available models of new service development did not reveal significant differences from the existing models of new product development since their structure and proposed stages are extremely similar [9,21]. Thus, Scheuing and Johnson's [26] model—often referred to as an example of a model of innovative service development [15,27,28]—does not differ substantially from Booz, Allen, and Hamilton's [29,30] model of new product development. More specifically, in the initial versions presented in 1968, models consisted of five stages. However, Johnson et al.'s [31] model introduces some innovation by representing innovative service development in a circular way, thereby conveying the nonlinear and highly interactive character of this process. The cited model also emphasises that the main stages of the process of developing new services centre around service concept design and configuration and explicitly recognises the fundamental importance of specific features such as teams and tools throughout innovative service development. Therefore, despite the growing number of publications, new service development remains an immature field that requires further research [11].

2.2. New Tourism Product Development

Regarding the process of developing new tourism products, researchers commonly refer to a better understanding of this process as a way to avoid failure and increase both companies and destinations' competitiveness [32]. Nonetheless, relatively little progress has been made in this direction. According to Walder [28], advanced models of new tourism product development are rare, which led the cited author to create a model composed of 12 stages. Walder's [28] model offers an advance on previous research by recognising the process's nonlinearity and contemplating the need to return to previous phases to reassess the innovation. The cited author also admits the possibility that the development process can begin with ideas generated within companies or in their interactions with customers, suppliers or other partners. Pechlaner and Döpfer [33] proposed another approach to new tourism product development based on the assumption that innovation cannot be implemented in an ad hoc manner but instead is the result of a process involving various stages. Based on Scheuing and Johnson's [26] model, Pechlaner and Döpfer [33] identified three fundamental phases in new tourism product development: invention, adoption and diffusion. These phases can in turn be subdivided into a total of 14 steps. This model presents some shortcomings, namely, failing to clarify different actors' involvement in the process's stages and to acknowledge more explicitly the importance of service design phases. Haahti and Komppula's [34] work confirms these shortcomings, showing that a substantial part of research into tourism product development has focused on technical properties rather than on overall customer experience. The cited authors thus argue that methodologies should be developed that encompass design into the process of creating experiences that generate value for clients.

Benur and Bramwell [4] more recently contributed to this field by developing two conceptual frameworks for analysing relationships and strategic options related to tourism product development, such as primary products' concentration and diversification and their advantages and disadvantages for destinations. However, these frameworks are not centred around the process of new tourism product development. A related study by Divisekera and Nguyen [2] in an Australian context generated a model that examines the relationship between innovation inputs and institutional factors. The cited researchers concluded that the most important innovation inputs are collaboration, human capital, information technology and funding and that the most significant institutional factors are foreign ownership, market competition, firm size and business environment. Divisekera and Nguyen's [2] model of innovation in tourism products does not take tourists' experiences into consideration.

After reviewing the literature on new product and service development, the present study went on to create a model of innovative tourism product development. On the one hand, this model has the capacity to differentiate between tourism destinations in the maturity phase and their competitors. On the other hand, the proposed approach helps generate unique, memorable experiences for clients, thereby reinforcing destinations' competitiveness [35].

3. Model of New Tourism Product Development

Various authors have observed that tourism product development is especially complex due to the different levels at which companies need to think through the development process. In addition, unlike other sectors in which producers can focus essentially on either generating tangible or intangible components of products, tourism product development must take into account both types of components. Given the new requirements created by tourists' demand and tourism destinations need to differentiate their offer from that of their most direct competitors, providers should also ensure that the products made available are perceived as enriching, memorable experiences [36–41].

The present study's literature review revealed that the proposed model of tourism product development had to include the following elements. The first is the resources necessary for product development [33,42–45]. The second element is an accurate determination of customers' needs so that the products developed correspond to what clients need and expect [10,34]. Last, based on the previous elements, the process should include design in the process of developing new products [33,34,42,43,45].

3.1. Core Resources Needed for New Tourism Product Development

In tourism planning contexts, Inskeep [46] asserts that attractions are the basis of tourism development as these are the most essential components of tourism products and they reflect the intrinsic cultural and environmental features that make tourism destinations distinctive and unique. That is, attractions are these destinations' differentiating elements. Swarbrooke [47] further points out that attractions are at the core of tourism products, motivating most tourists' trips. Gunn [48] has a quite similar opinion since the cited author's functional tourism model gives attractions a prominent place. Benur and Bramwell [4] report that primary tourism products that attract tourists to visit destinations consist of physical, environmental, and sociocultural characteristics. This set of attributes, which varies between destinations and constitutes their core resources, is crucial for the competitiveness of tourism destinations; [49] argue that new tourism product development should be based on these core resources. Pechlaner et al. [45] also point out that tourism products have a particularity that distinguishes them from other products. Unlike financial or other services, tourism product development requires a physical stage in the form of mountains, beaches, or infrastructure created on purpose (e.g., theme parks). Tourism products are thus linked to specific locations, so customers have to travel physically to those places to enjoy these products. Tourism product development is not only influenced by the actors involved in the process but also destinations' characteristics that give distinctive features to the tourism products developed. Similar to core competencies, only resources that have been identified simultaneously by the different actors involved in the development process (i.e., public institutions, companies, and residents) should be considered valid resources [43]. Once core resources have been identified using the methodology described above, thematisation can be carried out, according to Pechlaner and Döpfer [33] and Pechlaner et al. [43], based on the core competencies or, as in the present case, the core resources. In this way, the themes for developing core products are derived and defined by destinations' strengths. These core products should be understood as intangible services linking the core resources identified to the final tourism products. Themes can and should have specific connections with tourism sites and consist of natural, cultural, or social components. The present study took the position, however, that themes need to develop out of a combination of natural features with cultural or social components.

According to Gupta and Vajic [50], thematisation's application in Pine and Gilmore's [39] work is less clear. While the examples mentioned by the cited authors, such as Planet Hollywood, the Hard Rock Café, or the Rainforest Café are well-defined themes, this type of thematisation is limited to the physical environment, without considering the central activity. Gupta and Vajic [49] argue that this kind of thematisation is nothing more than themed entertainment provided for customers eating their meals. The cited authors suggest that the diminished success that some of these types of companies have begun to experience is not due to their inability to refresh periodically the products offered, as Pine and Gilmore [39] propose, but more essentially due to these firms' failure to anchor their thematisation in a central activity in which clients could be fully involved. Smith [51] presents a model of tourism products combining five elements represented as circles with a physical facility or resource in the centre. These elements are supported by services and hospitality from the destination or service provider's side and freedom of choice and involvement from the clients' side. Smith's [51] model shows clearly that tourism products consist of a combination of elements. In this sense, the Austrian government's

Amt der NÖ Landesregierung—Abteilung Wirtschaft, Tourismus und Technologie maintains that a route or trail, even if duly marked, does not yet constitute a tourism product. A product exists only when a chain of services is properly integrated, including car parks, equipment rental where applicable, reception areas, security in the form of necessary information, rest areas, guided tours properly planned, tourist attractions and gastronomy. These services are what transform routes or trails into tourism products [52].

As can be seen from the above example, no one organisation can provide all the elements needed to constitute a tourism product structured around an activity that involves customers and give them genuine experiences. Thus, those involved in tourism product development must determine which organisations are able to provide the essential elements of each product. To ensure that the products to be developed meet target market segments' needs, Haahti and Komppula [34] assert that the clients' needs at the heart of tourism products must be previously identified, around which different service providers can be associated. Various authors state that these needs should be defined based on collaboration in buyer–supplier relationships and be fulfilled in socially, environmentally, and economically responsible ways [53].

The present study's analysis up to this point focused on the resources on which the development of new tourism products should be based. In addition, tourism product development must involve a considerable number of actors or stakeholders [54], who contribute other types of resources, such as specific knowledge or skills. The need to add other types of resources to physical assets was previously confirmed by Froehle and Roth [42], who consider intellectual and organisational resources fundamental in business contexts. In the course of the current literature review, the conclusion was reached that new tourism products with the capacity to provide memorable experiences can rarely be developed without relying on networking within business clusters or other similar organisational structures [34,41,43–45]. Since these resources are inherent to the actors involved in tourism product development networks, Pechlaner et al. [45] suggest that integration into clusters requires specific organisational competencies, such as epistemic, heuristic, relational, and integrative skills.

The next step in the present study's elaboration of a model of innovative tourism product development thus took into consideration that the processes involved in the creation of each product or service module needs to be centred around the value created for customers by providing memorable experiences that meet clients' needs and expectations. This research, therefore, proceeded to analyse the concept of experience and, more specifically, sought to understand what memorable tourist experiences are, how they are created, and how they can be evaluated.

3.2. Transformative Tourism Experiences

According to Brunner-Sperdin [55], customers today want not only to consume tourism products but also to feel them and actively participate in their staging. The question of experiences has always been an extremely significant topic within tourism studies, because experiences are the essence of tourism [56] and tourism is an industry that sells experiences [57–60]. All situations in tourism can be seen as constituting experiences [61,62], even mass tourism based on sun and sea [63]. Stamboulis and Skayannis [63] suggest that more recent approaches to tourist experiences take into account that tourist experiences can be designed, intentionally produced (i.e., staged), organised, planned, calculated and, in many cases, sold. Scott et al. [64] also mention that human nature dictates that individuals constantly have a diverse set of experiences that are both positive and negative. However, a distinction needs to be made between 'wild' or unplanned experiences, which are usually serendipitous and the result of happy discoveries and fruit of chance or favourable, unexpected events and which produce different feeling in each individual, and 'staged' experiences that contain design elements. The latter experiences are in line with the approaches of Mathisen [65], Pikkemaat et al. [66], Rickly and McCabe [67], and Stamboulis and Skayannis [63] advocate regarding new tourist experience development. Peric and Dragicevic [68] suggest that there is a need to distinguish, on the one hand, between highly individualized experiences and general experiences like the ones related to entertainment, and on the other hand, between special experiences that are dependent on the outcome of special events like sports events and the "guaranteed" experiences like the ones provided by amusement parks.

Given the existence of so many ways of approaching tourism experiences, Ritchie and Hudson [69] carried out an extensive review of the literature in order to understand and make more explicit the diverse perspectives in analyses of tourists' experiences. The cited authors applied a chronological approach to each stream. However, the present study sought to achieve more pertinent results by analysing the concept of tourism experience in terms of researchers' perspective, that is, how different areas of knowledge tend to analyse these experiences. Quan and Wang [70] and Volo [71] observe that research related to tourism experiences can fit into two distinct approaches, namely, social science versus management and marketing approaches. Volo [71] states that the former approach includes research related to motivations, activities, interests, meanings, attitudes, searches for authenticity. and analyses of subjective experiences. Management and marketing-related disciplines, in turn, focus on tourists and examine tourists' experiences from the perspective of consumer behaviours linked to designated supportive experiences. The latter experiences result from contact with different suppliers of tourism products and services, transport companies and accommodation and catering units, as well as other tourism services [71]. Regarding the methodologies used to evaluate experiences, Volo [71] reports that structured questionnaires, travel diaries, structured or semi-structured interviews, participant observation, travel narratives, and memory reports are traditional methodologies, but more recently—especially in the environmental sciences—video recordings, sensory devices, and global positioning systems have been used. These diverse methodologies clearly indicate that the field of study and its position regarding the chosen paradigm dictates the most appropriate methodologies. In addition, part of the literature on investigations of tourism experiences mentions that this research is based on a phenomenologist paradigm [72,73], which tends to favour qualitative methodologies. In contrast, the approaches related to management and marketing studies tend to rely on quantitative methodologies [12,36]. In psychology, experiences can be considered private incidents that occur in response to stimuli, involve the entire human nature, and often result from direct participation in and/or observation of real, surreal, or virtual events [74,75]. Müller and Scheurer [74] argue that researchers unanimously accept that experiences can be triggered by both internal stimuli such as physiological sensations and changes in the environment, which are captured by sensory organs and cognitive processes such as evaluation. The involvement of multiple senses in experiences contributes to richer sensory experiences and to destination loyalty [76]. However, experiences do not depend only on stimuli as they are equally conditioned by each person's intrinsic characteristics and "can be defined as anything that stimulates the senses, heart and mind" [77] (p. 7). The determining factors are made up of physical and mental states, for example, motivations or physical conditions, and personality traits and other individual characteristics such as gender, age, and previous experiences [74]. Although experiences cannot be 'produced,' specific devices can be developed that create an external framework conducive to positive experiences for customers and/or tourists [74].

The management and marketing approach to experiences is associated with the concept of the experience economy. Pine and Gilmore [39] traced the evolution of different economic sectors in industrialised countries, concluding that, as economies mature, the highest growth rates are related to the consumption of experiences. Competition between companies and their efforts to ensure high quality products and services have led to a decrease in differentiation between products or services. This trend has forced companies to attach added value to their services or products by incorporating elements that provide unique, memorable experiences to customers or even have the ability to involve clients in ways that create these experience [78,79]. This interaction results in a transformation in the consumer. Pine and Gilmore [39] argue that, as goods and services have become increasingly undifferentiated, customers' appetite for experiences that play a fundamental role in generating value has grown, becoming a distinct market offering both goods and services. For companies to be able to design, stage, distribute, and communicate experiences more effectively, firms must gain more knowledge about the nature of experiences.

Within the experience economy, Pine and Gilmore [39] define experiences as events that involve individuals personally at an emotional, physical, intellectual, or even spiritual level. These events have four distinct dimensions defined along two axes. The horizontal axis is the degree of customers' participation in and influence on the unfolding of experiences, which can go from totally passive participation, for example, attending a show or sport event, up to an extremely active level of participation, such as playing a sport. The vertical axis represents how deeply customers get involved with the environment and context in which events develop, which ranges from simple absorption to total immersion. In this context, absorption means capturing clients' attention by bringing the experience into their minds, and immersion is understood as physically or virtually integrating customers into the experience. The combination of these two axes highlights four distinct types of experiences: entertainment, educational, escapist, or aesthetic. These experiences can be understood and communicated individually, but, according to Oh et al. [61], in tourism and leisure contexts, the boundaries between these four experiences are sometimes quite blurred. For instance, offers of edutainment also exist in which museums dedicated mainly to science combine knowledge transmission (i.e., education) with entertainment components. According to Pine and Gilmore [39], optimal experiences are the result of a simultaneous combination of the four different dimensions. Entertainment experiences probably constitute the oldest format and the most highly developed and prevalent. This type of experience consists of capturing and maintaining individuals' attention through their senses and occurs, for example, when clients watch a show, sport event, television show, or movie. Individuals are only passive participants limited to absorbing and apprehending the experiences' elements and reacting to stimuli [39]. Despite being an extremely common experience, in tourism, entertainment assumes a significant role, with many destinations offering different events, such as the classical music festivals that take place annually in Salzburg or Bayreuth. The latter is dedicated exclusively to Richard Wagner's operas. This type of offer is not limited to classical music as destinations currently organise festivals of all kinds of music ranging from the erudite to the traditional. Entertainment events are also linked to specific sport activities. These offers have the common denominator of involving spectators through experiences that are essentially entertainment [55]. Another more recent tourism product related to entertainment is theme parks such as the Disneyland Resort or Legoland Theme Parks.

In educational experiences, customers absorb events as they unfold through active mental participation or intellectual education, for example, by participating in seminars or activities simultaneously involving the mind and body such as skiing, horse-riding, or yoga courses. This type of experience is absolutely crucial to tourism as an increasing number of tourists consider learning something new during their holidays extremely important. Knowledge acquisition can be related to destinations' culture or may focus only on a particular topic [80,81]. Another aspect of educational experiences is visits to places where, for example, villages of particular historical periods are recreated so that visitors become aware of the way of life and activities specific to those times [61].

Escapist experiences, in turn, presuppose clients and/or tourists' partial or even total immersion in events and customers' involvement in activities that enable these individuals to influence performances or occurrences, whether in the real or virtual world. Tourism research has a strong tradition of investigations focused on these experiences because various authors suggest that the act of travel translates into a form of escape from daily life and routines imposed by professional and/or family obligations. Many tourists seek physical and mental regeneration, chances to reencounter and gain a fuller understanding of other modes of existence or direct, deep contact with the natural world [82]. Given the multiple motivations for going on trips that involve a form of escape from everyday life, a huge variety of tourism experience offers have been developed to satisfy these motivations. These products include, among others, participating in religious ceremonies [63], doing extreme sports and taking trips to inhospitable places [83], as well as encounters with different cultures and ways of life considered exotic [84]. The present discussion is not intended to be exhaustive but only to illustrate—based on tourism experience studies' findings—some of the aspects that fit within the escapist dimension. The literature shows a general acceptance that one of the main motivations for travelling is the need to escape daily routines and for physical and mental rest. However, some researchers, as mentioned previously, argue that the theory of compensation, according to which people seek to do something different or even opposite to what they do in their daily lives during their leisure time, may not be the only valid theory. Evidence has been found that some people tend to engage in leisure activities similar to those they do in their work [85]. Richards's [86] research corroborated this idea, revealing that surveys of cultural tourists have shown that many prefer activities related to these visitors' professional duties. For instance, people who work in museums are the most likely to visit museums during their holidays, and musicians often attend concerts during vacations or leisure time.

According to Banner [85], any spillover or continuity and similarity between work activities and leisure pursuits may translate only into extremely ingrained habits. Nonetheless, studies conducted by Csikszentmihalyi [87] of musicians, athletes, chess players, and surgeons clearly show that people tend to occupy themselves with the activities they love most, simply for the pleasure of performing these tasks. Based on observations of these people's feelings while engaged in their favourite activities, the cited author developed the concept of flow—a state reached by being so absorbed by an activity that nothing else matters. During these periods, all notion of time and space is lost, and the activity is performed continually even if this is associated with some kind of sacrifice. In this state, individuals feel an intense euphoria and deep sense of pleasure that are remembered for a long time afterward, becoming the standard against which they measure what their life should be [86]. In addition, according to Csikszentmihalyi [87], these rare moments are composed of optimal experiences during which happiness is achieved. Thus, the escapist dimension needs to include the possibility of clients' and/or tourists' total absorption in activities so that customers' experiences become the best possible, as illustrated by Csikszentmihalyi's [87] subjects.

The last dimension mentioned by Pine and Gilmore [39] is aesthetic experiences in which clients and/or tourists merge into the surrounding environment without interfering with or altering any features. These experiences have always been a decisive component of tourism as many tourists travel to specific destinations only for a particular landscape, building, or built environment's aesthetic value [61]. For tourism destinations, natural and cultural elements should be considered the stage and scenario where aesthetic experiences occur [45]. Any components that can diminish the quality of these places, that is, have a negative impact on the environment, are obstacles to the successful development of this important type of tourism experience. When purchasing a car or other objects, customers are indifferent to the aesthetic dimension of the space in which they are produced because clients do not have to go to that place to take possession of the acquired object. In contrast, tourists have to travel to destinations to acquire tourism services and/or experiences. According to Pechlaner et al. [45] and Theiner and Steinhauser [41], this means that tourists evaluate experiences holistically, including the aesthetics of the surrounding environment of accommodations and destinations in general [88]. This aspect is also highlighted by Müller and Scheurer [74], who report that, from the point of view of tourists' demand, the cost of transport, accommodations, and food can be regarded as the payment made to gain access to specific aesthetic environments that characterise destinations. In addition, research conducted by Pikkemaat et al. [12] concentrated on the way in which visitors following wine routes evaluate their experiences in five different destinations and found that the dimension most valued by tourists is aesthetics.

Pine and Gilmore's [39] model had previously considered tourists' total immersion in experiences, opening the way for tourism researchers to explore the older theoretical construct of co-creation in terms of consumers' physical and psychological involvement in their experiences. Prebensen and Xie consider that psychological co-creation is more important than physical co-creation in enhancing perceived experience value in tourism [89]. As a marketing concept, co-creation consists of 'creating an experience environment in which consumers can have active dialogues and co-construct personalised experiences' [90] (p. 8). In tourism, co-creation is specifically about integrating tourists as active partners in designing their experiences together with their hosts, with the ultimate goal of achieving tourists' overall well-being [91]. Co-creation can thus involve tourists' participation in the design, production, and consumption of experiences [58]. This approach can also be defined as tourism product development in collaboration with users [92]. Therefore, co-creation in tourism is about being open to new ideas, experiences, and concepts proposed by clients, but this strategy can only be effective if providers are open to innovative ideas, changes, adaptations, and viewpoints [92].

Another construct mentioned by Pine and Gilmore [39] is transformative tourism experiences, which is based on previous studies of transformative learning theory. Kirilova [93] suggests that transformative tourism experiences must be personally meaningful and conducive to self-actualisation. The cited author reports that these experiences involve a process of meaning making triggered by the experiences and continue after tourists return to their home environment, bringing new meaning to their lives [93]. Various authors have observed that peak tourism experiences elicit strong emotions, increase self-awareness, and lead to existential transformations by causing visitors to question personal values and re-evaluate their existential priorities [94]. In addition, Kirillova et al. [94] affirm that "transformative experiences are those especially extraordinary events that not only trigger highly emotional responses but also lead to self-exploration, serve as a vehicle for profound intra-personal changes, and are conducive to optimal human functioning" (p. 498). According to the cited authors, peak, extraordinary, and transcendent experiences can potentially lead to transformative experiences, which are triggered by introspection, unity with nature, unity with others, self-development, aesthetic experiences, or spontaneity and novelty [94].

Given the above findings, the present model was based on a management perspective because the ultimate goal is to 'stage' tourism experiences according to various authors [12,39,44,63,66,78,80]. Zatori, Smith, and Puczko [95] report that, through higher-quality interactions, interactive experience environments and customisable services, service providers can create favourable external environments in which deeper, more memorable experiences can occur. Müller and Scheurer [74] developed a model of how to stage tourism experiences in a given environment, which assumes that, although experiences cannot be 'produced,' their occurrence can be triggered and influenced by planned events. This model focuses on how visitors' experiences are triggered by environmental stimuli in a given context and can be positive or negative [74]. The way different people perceive particular events or situations is strongly influenced by determining factors inherent to each person and their personal involvement in experiences [95]. Thus, different people perceive the same situation in totally different ways, and the resulting experiences are equally diverse.

The totality of environmental stimuli in specific contexts generates specific emotional impacts, which Müller and Scheurer [74] designate as atmosphere. The cited authors also suggest that these stimuli can be shaped or influenced by staging, that is, through the planning and developing given offers. This principle is also promoted in Pine and Gilmore [39] and Schmitt's [75] work. However, certain environmental stimuli cannot be manipulated, such as climate or atmospheric conditions [74]. More specifically, Müller and Scheurer [74] state that staging involves seven different strategies that can be used to stage offers of particular tourism products. The theme is the guiding strategy, which is a decisive factor in ensuring products' consistency and which makes making the products appealing to different market segments. These themes must be authentic and rooted in destinations' culture, history, legends, or myths. In tourism destinations, managers should be able to identify a large number of relevant topics that can later be ordered hierarchically and interconnected with a core theme. The remaining staging elements are developed to fit that theme. Using thematisation in product or service development to provide memorable experiences is also advocated by several authors [33,39,43,75]. The second strategy is staging, namely, planning and coordination, whose main function is to harmonise the other elements. The first step is analysing the target market segments to understand their expectations, behaviours, and needs. The remaining staging elements require strategic and operational planning. This strategy also provides an excellent platform on which to coordinate the different actors involved in order to optimise the staging of experiences. Haahti and Komppula [34] also argue that the entire process of developing tourism products should start with an analysis of the target tourists' needs and characteristics and that the entire process of service development must be based on the findings.

Attractions and activities constitute the third strategy, which serves as the triggering element. Based on various attractions and activities, events can be created that facilitate experiences that should be appropriate in terms of the theme and visitors' expectations and needs and be supported by the remaining staging elements. This strategy appears to be closely related to the four dimensions of experiences discussed earlier from Pine and Gilmore's [39] perspective and complemented with other authors' views on the scope of tourism experiences. The fourth strategy is scenery or the aesthetic dimension of tourism destinations, which is greatly influenced by the stimuli generated by the natural environment, such as the landscape, atmospheric conditions, and light. However, architecture, lighting, interventions in the landscape, and urban built environments can also contribute to improving or destroying tourism scenarios. Visitor management is a fifth strategy that consists of an adequate regulation of tourist flows mainly by providing information and signs. These flows can also be driven through created elements, for example, the placement of access doors, resting places, or viewpoints, which must be compatible with visitors' well-being. In tourism research, this aspect of product development is often discussed in the context of carrying capacity, and its significant impact on tourism destinations' competitiveness [96–98] needs to be highlighted. However, according to Müller and Scheurer [74], visitor management should also be considered a fundamental element in the development of tourism experiences. Visitors' well-being or support strategy is considered by Müller and Scheurer [74] to be the sixth strategy in this context because experiences are more likely to receive positive evaluations if customers feel good. Basic physiological and safety needs must always be ensured in tourism settings. Managing tourists' well-being involves planning bathrooms' locations, providing places for visitors to purchase food and drinks, and the necessary tranquility to take pictures. In all situations, this strategy is closely linked to the management of visitor flows. Visitors are the last strategy as they provide the component of evaluation and tourists determine whether the events provided are great or memorable experiences. Visitors have needs that change from segment to segment and different expectations induced by the selected theme that must be matched or exceeded through activities and attractions, scenery, flow management, and well-being. Managers also need to bear in mind that visitors sometimes integrate their own attractions and activities and even have the ability to influence event performance, as mentioned previously in relation to certain types of experiences. Müller and Scheurer [74] suggest that the order in which these strategies are implemented should not be regarded as rigid, especially since this last element can initiate the entire staging process.

3.3. Process of Developing Innovative Tourism Products

Before conducting an analysis of how the process of innovative tourism product development can be managed and staged so as to encourage the creation of memorable and transformative experiences, Johnson et al.'s [31] work deserves further discussion. According to the cited authors, the development process's design is substantially different depending on the type of innovation. That is, incremental innovations require less attention and allocation of resources in the development and launch phases and less attention in the planning and analysis phase. In contrast, radical innovations need intensive investment during development, and the planning phase is extremely important, requiring an in-depth study of the resources essential to their development.

As mentioned previously, one of the present research's objectives was to propose a model of new tourism product development, which can also be used to reassess existing tourism products and, at a more fundamental level, to *reevaluate* the design of processes through which these products are made available to customers. In the first case, innovation takes place in products and, in the second case, innovation involves processes. Both cases may require introducing innovation at the organisational structure level as this is where new tourism products are developed. Innovation can also occur in the channels used for disseminating or introducing new tourism products to the market.

The present literature review covered the literature on the development of both tangible and intangible products and, more specifically, the staging of tourism products in order to induce memorable experiences. Based on the discussed results, the proposed model of new tourism product development has the following configuration (see Figure 2).

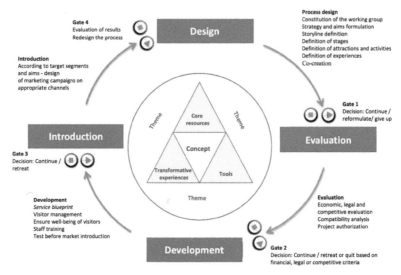

Figure 2. Model of new tourism product development.

3.4. Results

The model's centre consists of the concept of service, which must always keep in mind that the goal is to provide the necessary framework based on staging that provides the ideal conditions for memorable and transformative tourism experiences. According to Goldstein et al. [99], how service is conceptualised plays a central role in the process of developing new services. This concept not only defines the form or 'how' and the content or 'what' of service design, but also ensures the necessary integration between form and content and mediates as needed between companies' strategic intentions and customers' needs. Goldstein et al. [99] assert that one of the reasons for services' failure is the mismatch between what organisations intend to provide (i.e., strategic intention) and what customers need and expect (i.e., customer needs). This gap can be the result of inappropriate marketing or development processes that have not taken into account clients' needs. Edvardsson [100] offers a similar perspective, highlighting the concept of service's importance in terms of establishing the link between primary and secondary customer needs and the central and support services offered. Based on Edvardsson [100], Goldstein et al. [99] and Johnson et al.'s [31] research, the present study defined the concept of service as the integration of customers' needs with destinations' resources. These are both tangible resources such as built heritage, museums, monuments, beaches, mountains, and intangible resources such as image, identity, lifestyle, atmosphere, narrative, creativity, equipment, and other resources necessary for services or particular themes' development. Once the concept of service incorporates clients' needs, the destination resources available, and the selected theme, the development process can be designed. In this first phase (i.e., the design phase), the working group and objectives to be achieved must be defined, and the storyline must be developed so that this narrative can be used to guide all stakeholders and ensure that they develop the remaining service components within the spirit of that narrative.

3.5. Design Phase Process

Some authors [13,101] highlight the importance of involving different stakeholders in all phases of new product development. However, this perspective is not commonly found in the literature on new product or service creation or in models that have served as a reference point for innovative tourism product development (e.g., Scheuing and Johnson's [26] model). The question of involving different stakeholders or defining project teams to develop new products is not explicitly addressed. However, Müller and Scheurer [74] suggest that, in the first phase of staging tourism experiences, a working group that can coordinate the entire development process should be formed. In addition, the cited authors assert that the project team needs to involve all stakeholders who can contribute to the process. If a single organisation is able to carry out the product's full development process, the identification of relevant departments and employees is easier. When several organisations are needed to develop the tourism product, establishing the working group is much more complex, potentially involving public and private sector organisations. In all cases, the process leadership should be clearly defined, and external experts need to be recruited who can contribute specific know-how and coordinate the overall process [74].

Regarding the definition of strategies and objectives, Scheuing and Johnson [26] observe that these two steps are decisive because they drive and direct the entire service innovation process and infuse this with the required effectiveness and efficiency. The other topics listed under the design phase of the tourism product development process were proposed for the present study, including the definition of the storyline, scenarios, attractions and activities and dimensions of the experiences to be achieved. These items are not usually present in models of tangible product or service development, because they do not focus on how products or services can generate memorable and transformative experiences for customers. At this point in the process, the level of costumer involvement and co-creation should be analysed and addressed.

Various authors such as Trott [15] agree that stage-gate models do not have to be applied to new service development, arguing that their sequential nature is a limitation, as "each stage of the process is needed to be completed before proceeding to the subsequent stage" (p. 535). However, the present study found that applying stage-gate and Agile-stage-gate [18] models' principles can offer added value to tourism product development that depends on several independent entities during the creation process. Formal meetings with all stakeholders involved in the project can be used to analyse the information collected and the measures taken during the previous phase, as well as providing support for decision-making regarding sending the project on to the next stage. Notably, stakeholders may also want to consider retreating to the previous phase for re-evaluation or even abandoning the project. If the decision is made to move on to the next stage, these meetings will also serve to define the tasks each intervener should carry out during the subsequent phase [102]. Thus, the present proposed model includes that the process's design phase needs to end with a formal meeting of stakeholders, in which they deliberate on the process's evolution and the tasks to be accomplished in the next stage, namely, the information to be collected.

3.6. Evaluation Phase

This phase is part of most existing models, regardless of whether they focus on the development of tangible products, services, or tourism products [28,31,42,102], but the components integrated in this phase can vary between models. Johnson et al. [31] and Scheuing and Johnson [26] assert that the analysis phase should include business or economic analysis and project authorisation, while Cooper and Kleinschmidt [102] subdivide this phase into a preliminary evaluation and a more detailed assessment. The preliminary evaluation includes a rapid appraisal of the project's technical, financial, legal, and market aspects, and the detailed assessment consists of a definition and justification of the product, as well as a description of the project plan, market research, and competitive, technical, production, and financial analyses.

The final decision to move on to the development phase is based on financial criteria. As Johne and Storey [19] point out, a good idea is not in itself a guarantee that the new service will succeed, so the current proposed model followed Cooper and Kleinschmidt [102], Johnson et al. [31], and Scheuing and Johnson's [26] suggestion that this phase should include an analysis of the project's economic viability. According to Cooper and Kleinschmidt [102], an analysis must also be conducted of the legal constraints that may affect the project's development, in addition to competitive analysis, in order to verify that no similar products exist in the market. The present study's model further adds an analysis of how the new product can be integrated into existing products, given that Tax and Stuart [103] consider understanding new products and services' potential impacts on the existing offers important at this stage. The last topic listed within the proposed model's evaluation phase is the project's authorisation, which can be done in a formal meeting with the characteristics mentioned in the preceding paragraph. In addition, the decision to authorise the project's transition into the development phase must be based on the information collected during this phase on legal and competitive aspects, as well as the assessment of the project's economic viability.

3.7. Development Phase

Shostack [104] argues that, although processes can be reduced to steps and stages, these should be understood as interdependent and interactive systems and not as disconnected or isolated parts. The researchers are in agreement that specific techniques can make analyses of the process of new service development more objective and enable more effective and efficient management. According to Shostack [104], one useful approach to visualising service systems is a mapping technique called 'service blueprint,' which is also advocated by other authors [9,15,74,103]. In essence, a service blueprint is a diagram that shows all the elements that constitute the service under study and whose main purpose is to facilitate more objective analyses of the service process. This technique documents all the steps and points of divergence in a specific service, identifying weaknesses and anticipating the occurrence of any problems that may have a negative impact on the way customers will perceive that service [104,105]. The results can provide important insights into how best to manage tourist or visitor flows and ensure their comfort and well-being. Shostack [104] notes that service blueprints must not be generic but rather quite specific, as a separate blueprint needs to be prepared for each service. In addition, Laws [105] states that the service should be mapped based on clients' explicit actions that allow them to receive the service and that the blueprint needs to include the moments of contact between people and internal procedures for providing the service.

Services in general and tourism in particular are characterised by an inseparability of consumption and production, clients and/or tourists' close involvement throughout service processes, and the issue of spatiality. Therefore, the necessary elements for staging experiences must also be present at this stage (i.e., clearly defined scenarios, attractions, and activities and dimensions of experience). According to Müller and Scheurer [74], these aspects need to be dealt with both strategically and operationally. The relevant strategies should be implemented in the process's design phase, and the development phase should focus on the operational side of the process. At a more advanced stage of the development phase, training needs to be offered to employees in direct contact with clients [21,26,28,31,103], that is, service providers who interact with customers in the co-production of experiences. Direct experience with the tourism sector also suggests that employees involved in selling these products should also receive special training after the prelaunch test and before the new products are introduced to the market. Destination management organisations and tour operators customarily invite key personnel to visit the destination and experience new products directly, especially people who are linked to outgoing travel agencies, so that they can become more at ease with selling these services. Tour operator representatives begin their training at the destination by watching and participating in all products sold to customers (e.g., excursions or theme park tickets) in order to be able to explain to clients the types of experiences that the products can provide.

The development phase ends with a prelaunch test [21,26,28,31,103]. However, this test is not always conducted, but, according to Tax and Stuart [103], it may be performed in different configurations, such as surveys or experimental offers in selected branches.

3.8. Market Introduction

Before moving on to the launch phase, the proposed model requires another formal meeting with all relevant participants. Based on analyses of the information collected during the development phase, in particular the service blueprint and the prelaunch test of the service—if this has been run—the decision is made to move forward or go back to the previous stage to reassess possible weaknesses [102].

The last phase consists of the market launch. Depending on the target tourist segments, the project team selects the most appropriate distribution channels [33,43]. Despite the decisive importance that this phase has in new products' or services' success or failure, the planning, execution, and launch of marketing campaigns fell outside the scope of the present study, so they were not subjected to further analysis. After the launch, the working group needs to meet again to re-evaluate the entire process. Following Johnson et al.'s [31] lead, the proposed model emphasises the circular nature of the process (see Figure 2 above), as a main objective of the current study was to demonstrate the dynamic nature of new tourism product development and the constant need to re-evaluate these products. Contrary to Johnson et al. [31], however, the arrow linking the launch and design phases cannot be represented as dashed as this would indicate only a possibility of redesigning the process. The entire process of developing new products is based on destinations' resources and customers' needs, which are both constantly changing, so an accurate model of innovative tourism product development must include continuous re-adaptations of these services.

4. Conclusions

This article sought to offer a comprehensive explanation of the different components that need to be integrated in an accurate model of new tourism product development. This study differs from other studies on the development of new tourism products by proposing a circular and not a linear model and by offering an innovative approach built around the design, evaluation, development, and introduction of innovative tourism products in a way that the new tourism product can be continuously re-evaluated, improved, or discontinued. Furthermore, the process is based on the core resources of the destination.

The starting point is the concept of service, that is, the type of products that should be developed or re-evaluated, in order to identify the resources required to create the new services, which must correspond as much as possible to destinations' core resources. Concurrently, project managers have to define the needs of customers for whom the products are intended.

The development process must ensure that the new services do not present shortcomings, although considering only the products' quality is not a guarantee that they will provide memorable experiences, because customers in many situations will take for granted that the service quality will be flawless. Thus, the working group should deliberately proceed with designing scenarios and ensuring indispensable conditions for visitors' well-being to ensure that new products exceed customers' expectations and foster unique, memorable, or transformative experiences. Contrary to what has been repeatedly stated elsewhere, experiences cannot be created as these occur within each individual and they are influenced by multiple factors related to personalities, previous experiences or expectations.

After the resources on which products are based are determined and customers' needs are identified, the design of the process of new tourism product development begins, respecting the information gathered in each phase and always taking into account that the process is nonlinear. Sometimes, the project team must return to previous stages to conduct reformulations that more fully respect the assumptions made in order to validate the project's continuation. The process does not end with the new or re-engineered products' introduction into the market because, after every launch, an evaluation must be carried out and, based on the results, the development process then restarts.

This model fills a gap in the existing literature, providing destination management companies and private businesses with a comprehensive conceptual framework for innovative tourism product development, which is urgently needed to ensure interfirm and destination competitiveness.

This study's main limitation is that the proposed model of innovative tourism product development has not yet been tested empirically. This will be a challenge for future research.

Author Contributions: Conceptualization, M.C.S.; formal analysis, J.A.C.S.; funding acquisition, J.A.C.S.; methodology, M.C.S.; supervision, A.F. and C.C.; writing—original draft, M.C.S.; writing—review and editing, J.C.S. All authors have read and agreed to the published version of the manuscript.

Funding: This paper is financed by National Funds provided by FCT—Foundation for Science and Technology through project UIDB/04020/2020.

Conflicts of Interest: The authors declare no conflict of interest. The funders had no role in the design of the study, collection, analyses, interpretation of data, writing of the manuscript, and decision to publish the results.

References

1. Dinis, M.G.F.; Costa, C.M.M.; Pacheco, O.M.R. Composite Indicators for measuring the online search interest by a tourist destination. In *Big Data and Innovation in Tourism, Travel, and Hospitality Managerial Approaches, Techniques, and Applications*; Sigala, M., Rahimi, R., Thelwall, R., Eds.; Springer: Berlin, Germany, 2019; pp. 1–19.
2. Divisekera, S.; Nguyen, K. Determinants of innovation in tourism evidence from Australia. *Tour. Manag.* **2018**, *67*, 157–167, . [CrossRef]
3. Hall, M.C.; Williams, A.M. *Tourism and Innovation*; Routledge: Abingdon, UK, 2019.
4. Benur, A.M.; Bramwell, B. Tourism product development and product diversification in destinations. *Tour. Manag.* **2015**, *50*, 2013–2224. [CrossRef]
5. Hauschildt, J. Dimensionen der Innovation. In *Handbuch Technologie-und Innovationsmanagement: Strategie—Umsetzung—Controlling*; Sönke, A., Gassmann, O., Eds.; Gabler Verlag: Wiesbaden, Germany, 2005; pp. 23–39.
6. Page, A.L.; Schirr, G.R. Growth and development of a body of knowledge: 16 years of new product development research, 1989–2004. *J. Prod. Innov. Manag.* **2008**, *25*, 233–248. [CrossRef]
7. Biemans, W.G.; Griffin, A.; Moenaert, R.K. New service development: How the field developed, its current status and recommendations to move the field forward. *J. Prod. Innov. Manag.* **2016**, *33*, 382–397. [CrossRef]
8. Steven, E.; Dimitriadis, S. New service development through the lens of organisational learning: Evidence from longitudinal case studies. *J. Bus. Res.* **2004**, *57*, 1074–1084. [CrossRef]
9. Menor, L.J.; Tatikonda, M.V.; Sampson, S.E. New service development: Areas for exploitation and exploration. *J. Oper. Manag.* **2002**, *20*, 135–157. [CrossRef]
10. Alam, I.; Perry, C. A Customer-oriented new service development process. *J. Serv. Mark.* **2002**, *16*, 515–534. [CrossRef]
11. Kitsios, F.; Kamariotou, M. Mapping new service development: A review and synthesis of literature. *Serv. Ind. J.* **2019**, 1–23. [CrossRef]
12. Pikkemaat, B.; Peters, M.; Weiermair, K. *Innovationen im Tourismus—Wettbewerbsvorteile Durch Neue Ideen und Angebote*; Erich Schmidt Verlag: Berlin, Germany, 2006.
13. Rothwell, R. Towards the fifth-generation Innovation Process. *Int. Mark. Rev.* **1994**, *11*, 7–31. [CrossRef]
14. Wonglimpiyarat, J.; Yuberk, N. In support of innovation management and Roger's innovation diffusion theory. *Gov. Inf. Q.* **2005**, *22*, 411–422. [CrossRef]
15. Trott, P. *Innovation Management and New Product Development*, 6th ed.; Pearson: Harlow, UK, 2017.
16. Kline, S.J.; Rosenberg, N. An overview of innovation. In *The Positive Sum Strategy: Harnessing Technology for Economic Growth*; Landau, R., Rosenberg, N., Eds.; National Academy Press: Washington, WA, USA, 1986; pp. 275–306.
17. Cooper, R.G. The new product process: A decision guide for managers. *J. Mark. Manag.* **1988**, *3*, 238–255. [CrossRef]
18. Cooper, R.G.; Sommer, A.F. Agile—Stage-Gate for manufacturers. *Res.-Technol. Manag.* **2018**, *61*, 17–26. [CrossRef]
19. Johne, A.; Storey, C. New service development: A review of the literature and annotated bibliography. *Eur. J. Mark.* **1998**, *32*, 184–251. [CrossRef]

20. Bitran, G.; Pedrosa, L. A structured product development perspective for service operations. *Eur. J. Mark.* **1998**, *16*, 169–189. [CrossRef]

21. Tsai, W.; Verma, R.; Schmidt, G. New service development. In *Handbook of New Product Development Management*; Loch, C., Kovadias, S., Eds.; Butterworth-Heinemann: Oxford, UK, 2008; pp. 495–525.

22. Sampson, S.E.; Froehle, C.M. Foundations and implications of a proposed unified services theory. *Prod. Oper. Manag.* **2006**, *15*, 329–343. [CrossRef]

23. Andreassen, T.W.; Kristensson, P.; Lervik-Olsen, L.; Parasuraman, A.; McColl-Kennedy, J.R.; Edvardsson, B.; Colurcio, M. Linking service design to value creation and service research. *J. Serv. Manag.* **2016**, *27*, 121–129. [CrossRef]

24. Ordanini, A.; Parasuraman, A. Service innovation viewed through a service-dominant logic lens: A conceptual framework and empirical analysis. *J. Serv. Res.* **2011**, *14*, 3–21. [CrossRef]

25. Weyers, M.; Louw, L. Framework for the classification of service standardisation. *Serv. Ind. J.* **2017**, *37*, 409–425. [CrossRef]

26. Scheuing, E.E.; Johnson, E.M. A Proposed model for new service development. *J. Serv. Mark.* **1989**, *3*, 25–34. [CrossRef]

27. Frehse, J.; Toedt, M. Innovationen in der Hotelbetrieblichen Praxis: Webbasiertes Customer Relationship Management bei ArabellaSheraton. In *Erfolg Durch Innovationen—Perspektiven Für den Tourismus-und Dienstleistugssektor*; Pechlaner, H., Tschurtschenthaler, P., Peters, M., Pikkemaat, B., Fuchs, M., Eds.; Deutscher Universitäts-Verlag: Wiesbaden, Germany, 2005; pp. 445–460.

28. Walder, B. *Tourismus—Management von Innovationen*; Tectum Verlag: Marburg, Germany, 2007.

29. Booz, Allen & Hamilton, Inc. *Management of New Products*; Booz, Allen & Hamilton, Inc.: New York, NY, USA, 1968.

30. Booz, Allen & Hamilton, Inc. *New Product Management for the 1980s*; Allen & Hamilton, Inc.: New York, NY, USA, 1982.

31. Johnson, S.P.; Menor, L.J.; Roth, A.V.; Chase, R.B. A Critical evaluation of the new service development process. In *Creating Memorable Experiences*; Fitzsimmons, J.A., Fitzsimmons, M.J., Eds.; Sage Publications: Thousand Oaks, CA, USA, 2000; pp. 1–32.

32. Ottenbacher, M.; Gnoth, J.; Jones, P. Identifying determinants of success in development of new high-contact services—Insights from the hospitality industry. *Int. J. Serv. Ind. Manag.* **2006**, *17*, 344–363. [CrossRef]

33. Pechlaner, H.; Döpfer, B.C. Strategische Produktentwicklung im Tourismus—Durch Systematisches Management zur Produktinnovation. In *Strategische Produktentwicklung im Standortmanagement—Wettbewerbsvorteile für den Tourismus*; Pechlaner, H., Fischer, E., Eds.; Erich Schmidt Verlag: Berlin, Germany, 2009; pp. 153–176.

34. Haahti, A.; Komppula, R. Experience Design in Tourism. In *Tourism Business Frontiers—Consumers, Products and Industry*; Buhalis, D., Costa, C., Eds.; Butterworth-Heinemann: Oxford, UK, 2006; pp. 101–110.

35. Cetin, G.; Bilgihan, A. Components of cultural tourists' experiences in destinations. *Curr. Issues Tour.* **2016**, *19*, 137–154. [CrossRef]

36. Brunner-Sperdin, A.; Peters, M. What influences guests' emotions?—The case of high-quality hotels. *Int. J. Tour. Res.* **2009**, *11*, 171–183. [CrossRef]

37. Fitzsimmons, J.A.; Fitzsimmons, M.J. *Creating Memorable Experiences*; Sage Publications: Thousand Oaks, CA, USA, 2000.

38. Hudson, S.; Ritchie, J.R.B. Branding a memorable destination experience. The case of "Brand Canada". *Int. J. Tour. Res.* **2009**, *11*, 217–228. [CrossRef]

39. Pine, B.J.; Gilmore, J.H. *The Experience Economy—Work Is Theatre & Every Business a Stage*; Harvard Business School Press: Boston, UK, 1999.

40. Richards, G.; Wilson, J. Developing creativity in tourist experiences: A solution to the serial reproduction of culture? *Tour. Manag.* **2006**, *27*, 1209–1223. [CrossRef]

41. Theiner, B.; Steinhauser, C. *Neue Erlebnisse im Tourismus*; Tectum Verlag: Marburg, Germany, 2006.

42. Froehle, C.M.; Roth, A.V. A Resource-process framework of new service development. *Prod. Oper. Manag.* **2007**, *16*, 169–188. [CrossRef]

43. Pechlaner, H.; Fischer, E.; Hammann, E.-M. Innovationen in Standorten—Perspektiven für den Tourismus. In *Strategische Produktentwicklung im Standortmanagement—Wettbewerbsvorteile für den Tourismus*; Pechlaner, H., Fischer, E., Eds.; Erich Schmidt Verlag: Berlin, Germany, 2009; pp. 9–29.

44. Pechlaner, H.; Fischer, E.; Priglinger, P. Die Entwicklung von Innovationen in Destinationen—Die Rolle der Tourismusorganisationen. In *Innovationen im Tourismus—Wettbewerbsvorteile Durch Neue Ideen und Angebote*; Pikkemaat, B., Peters, M., Weiermair, K., Eds.; Erich Schmidt Verlag: Berlin, Germany, 2006; pp. 121–136.

45. Pechlaner, H.; Hammann, E.-M.; Fischer, E. Leadership und Innovationsprozesse: Von der Kernkompetenz zur Dienstleistung. In *Erfolg durch Innovationen—Perspektiven für den Tourismus-und Dienstleistungssektor*; Pechlaner, H., Tschurtschenthaler, P., Peters, M., Pikkemaat, B., Fuchs, M., Eds.; Van Nostrand Reinhold: New York, NY, USA, 2005; pp. 63–85.

46. Inskeep, E. *Tourism Planning—An Integrated and Sustainable Development Approach*; Van Nostrand Reinhold: New York, NY, USA, 1991.

47. Swarbrooke, J. *The Development and Management of Visitor Attractions*; Butterworth-Heinemann: Oxford, UK, 2002.

48. Gunn, C. *Vacationscape—Designing Tourist Regions*; Van Nostrand Reinhold: New York, NY, USA, 1988.

49. Estêvão, C. Tourism sector competitiveness in Portugal: Applying Porter's Diamond. *Tour. Manag. Stud.* **2018**, *14*, 30–44. [CrossRef]

50. Gupta, S.; Vajic, M. The contextual and dialectical nature of experiences. In *Creating Memorable Experiences*; Fitzsimmons, J.A., Fitzsimmons, M.J., Eds.; Sage Publications: Thousand Oaks, CA, USA, 2000; pp. 33–51.

51. Smith, S. The tourism product. *Ann. Tour. Res.* **1994**, *24*, 582–595. [CrossRef]

52. Amt der NÖ Landesregierung—Abteilung Wirtschaft, Tourismus und Technologie. *Kursbuch Tourismus*; Amt der Niederösterreichischen Landesregierung: St. Pölten, Germany, 2006.

53. Ampe-Nda, L.D.; Payne, B.A.; Spake, R.I.; Sharpe, S.; Arona, A. Buyer-supplier relationships: Role of collaboration, sustainability, and technology. In *Sustainable Innovation: Trends in Marketing and Management*; Arora, A.S., Bacouel-jentjens, S., Sapheri, M., Arora, A., Eds.; Palgrave Macmillan: Cham, Switzerland, 2020; pp. 47–58.

54. Ratten, V.; Braga, V.; Álvarez-García, J.; Rio-Rama, M.C. *Tourism Innovation: The Role of Technology, Sustainability and Creativity*; Routledge: New York, NY, USA, 2020.

55. Brunner-Sperdin, A. *Erlebnisprodukte in Hotellerie und Tourismus—Erfolgreiche Inszenierungen und Qualitätsmessung*; Erich Schmidt Verlag: Berlin, Germany, 2008.

56. Ritchie, J.R.B.; Tung, V.W.S.; Ritchie, R.J.B. Tourism experience management research: Emergence, evolution, and future directions. *Int. J. Contemp. Hosp. Manag.* **2010**, *23*, 419–438. [CrossRef]

57. Buhalis, D.; O'Connor, P. Information communication technology. In *Tourism Business Frontiers Consumers, Trends, Management and Tools*; Buhalis, D., Costa, C., Eds.; Butterworth-Heinemann: Oxford, UK, 2006; pp. 196–209.

58. Campos, A.C.; Mendes, J.; Valle, P.O.; Scott, N. Co-creation of tourist experiences: A literature review. *Curr. Issues Tour.* **2018**, *21*, 369–400. [CrossRef]

59. Ihamäki, P. Geocachers: The creative tourism experience. *J. Hosp. Tour. Tech.* **2012**, *3*, 152–175. [CrossRef]

60. Kim, J.-H. Determining the factors affecting the memorable nature of travel experiences. *J. Travel Tour. Mark.* **2010**, *27*, 780–796. [CrossRef]

61. Oh, H.; Fiore, A.M.; Jeoung, M. Measuring experience economy concepts: Tourism applications. *J. Travel Res.* **2007**, *46*, 119–132. [CrossRef]

62. Walls, A.R.; Okumus, F.; Wang, Y.; Kwun, D.J.-W. An epistemological view of consumer experiences. *Int. J. Hosp. Manag.* **2011**, *30*, 10–21. [CrossRef]

63. Stamboulis, Y.; Skayannis, P. Innovation strategies and technology for experience-based tourism. *Tour. Manag.* **2003**, *24*, 35–43. [CrossRef]

64. Scott, N.; Laws, E.; Boksberger, P. The marketing of hospitality and leisure experiences. *J. Hosp. Mark. Manag.* **2009**, *18*, 99–110. [CrossRef]

65. Mathisen, L. Staging natural environments: A performance perspective. *Adv. Hosp. Leis.* **2013**, *9*, 163–183. [CrossRef]

66. Pikkemaat, B.; Peters, M.; Boksberger, P.; Secco, M. The staging of experiences in wine tourism. *J. Hosp. Mark. Manag.* **2009**, *18*, 237–253. [CrossRef]

67. Rickly, J.M.; McCabe, S. Authenticity for tourism design and experience. In *Design Science in Tourism. Tourism on the Verge*; Fesenmaier, D., Xiang, Z., Eds.; Springer: Cham, Germany, 2017; pp. 55–68.

68. Peric, M.; Dragicevic, N.W.D. Suggesting a service research agenda in sports tourism: Working experience(s) into business models. *Sport Bus. Manag.* **2017**, *7*, 58–76. [CrossRef]

69. Ritchie, J.R.B.; Hudson, S. Understanding and meeting the challenges of consumer/tourist experience research. *Int. J. Tour. Res.* **2009**, *11*, 111–126. [CrossRef]

70. Quan, S.; Wang, N. Towards a structural model of the tourist experience: An illustration from food experiences in tourism. *Tour. Manag.* **2004**, *25*, 297–305. [CrossRef]

71. Volo, S. Conceptualizing experience: A tourist based approach. *J. Hosp. Mark. Manag.* **2009**, *18*, 111–126. [CrossRef]

72. Chan, J.K.L. The consumption of museum service experiences: Benefits and value of museum experiences. *J. Hosp. Mark. Manag.* **2009**, *18*, 173–196.

73. Hayllar, B.; Griffin, T. The precinct experience: A phenomenological Approach. *Tour. Manag.* **2005**, *26*, 517–528. [CrossRef]

74. Müller, H.; Scheurer, R. *Tourismus-Destinationen als Erlebniswelten*; Forschungsinstitut für Freizeit und Tourismus der Universität Bern: Bern, Germany, 2007.

75. Schmitt, B.H. *Experiential Marketing: How to Get Customers to Sense, Feel, Think, Act, Relate*; The Free Press: New York, NY, USA, 1999.

76. Agapito, D.; Pinto, P.; Mendes, J. Tourists' memories, sensory impressions and loyalty: In loco and post-visit study in Southwest Portugal. *Tour. Manag.* **2017**, *58*, 108–118. [CrossRef]

77. Meaci, L.; Liberatore, L. A senses-based model for experiential tourism. *Tour. Manag. Stud.* **2018**, *14*, 7–14. [CrossRef]

78. Coelho, M.F.; Gosling, M.F. Memorable tourism experience (MTE): Scale proposal and test. *Tour. Manag. Stud.* **2018**, *14*, 15–24. [CrossRef]

79. Dalilis Escobar-Rivera, D.; Casadesús-Fa, M.; Sampaio, P.A.C.A.; Simon-Villar, A. Exploring the role of service delivery in remarkable tourism experiences. *Sustainability* **2019**, *11*, 1382. [CrossRef]

80. Hudson, S. *Tourism and Hospitality Marketing—A Global Perspective*; SAGE Publications: London, UK, 2008.

81. Kozak, M.; Andreu, L. *Progress in Tourism Marketing*; Elsevier: Amsterdam, The Netherlands, 2006.

82. Uriely, N. The tourist experience—Conceptual Developments. *Ann. Tour. Res.* **2005**, *32*, 199–216. [CrossRef]

83. Laing, J.H.; Crouch, G.I. Myth, adventure and fantasy at the frontier: Metaphors and imagery behind an extraordinary travel experience. *Int. J. Tour. Res.* **2009**, *11*, 127–141. [CrossRef]

84. McIntosh, A.J. Tourists' appreciation of Maori culture in New Zealand. *Tour. Manag.* **2004**, *25*, 1–15. [CrossRef]

85. Banner, D.K. Towards a theoretical clarification of the 'spillover' and 'compensatory' work/leisure hypotheses. *OMEGA-Int. J. Manag. Sci.* **1985**, *13*, 13–18. [CrossRef]

86. Richards, G. *Cultural tourism: Global and Local Perspectives*; The Haworth Hospitality Press: Birghamton, NY, USA, 2006.

87. Csikszentmihalyi, M. *Flow: The Psychology of Optimal Experience*; Harper and Row: New York, NY, USA, 1990.

88. Rigall-I-Torrent, R.; Fluvià, M. Managing tourism products and destinations embedding public good components: A hedonic approach. *Tour. Manag.* **2011**, *32*, 244–255. [CrossRef]

89. Prebensen, N.K.; Xie, J. Efficacy of co-creation and mastering on perceived value and satisfaction in tourists' consumption. *Tour. Manag.* **2017**, *60*, 166–176. [CrossRef]

90. Prahalad, C.K.; Ramaswamy, V. Co-creation experiences: The next practice in value creation. *J. Interact. Mark.* **2004**, *18*, 5–14. [CrossRef]

91. Correia, A.; Kozak, M.; Gnoth, J.; Fyall, A. *Co-Creation and Well-Being in Tourism*; Springer: Cham, Germany, 2017.

92. Proebstl-Haider, U.; Lampl, R. From conflict to co-creation: Ski-touring on groomed slopes in Austria. In *Co-Creation and Well-Being in Tourism*; Correia, A., Kozak, M., Gnoth, J., Fyall, A., Eds.; Springer: Cham, Germany, 2017; pp. 69–82.

93. Kirilova, K.A. Existential Outcomes of Tourism Experience: The Role of Transformative Environment. Ph.D. Thesis, Purdue University, ProQuest, Ann Arbor, MI, USA, 2015.

94. Kirillova, K.; Lehto, X.; Cai, L. What triggers transformative tourism experiences? *Tour. Recreat. Res.* **2017**, *42*, 498–511. [CrossRef]

95. Zatori, A.; Smith, M.K.; Puczko, L. Experience-involvement, memorability and authenticity: The service provider's effect on tourist experience. *Tour. Manag.* **2018**, *67*, 111–126. [CrossRef]

96. Oliveira, C.T.F.; Zouain, D.M.; Souza, L.A.V.; Duarte, A.L.F. Tourist destinations' competitiveness: Demand and performance factors. *Tour. Manag. Stud.* **2019**, *15*, 17–26. [CrossRef]

97. Iglesias-Sánchez, P.; Correia, M.P.; Jambrino-Maldonado, C. Challenges in linking destinations' online reputation with competitiveness. *Tour. Manag. Stud.* **2019**, *15*, 35–43. [CrossRef]

98. Perna, F.; Custódio, M.J.; Oliveira, V. Tourism Destination Competitiveness: An application model for the south of Portugal versus the Mediterranean region of Spain: Competitivtour. *Tour. Manag. Stud.* **2018**, *14*, 19–29. [CrossRef]

99. Goldstein, S.M.; Johnston, R.; Duffy, J.; Rao, J. The service concept: The missing link in service design research? *J. Oper. Manag.* **2002**, *20*, 121–134. [CrossRef]

100. Edvardsson, B. Quality in new service development: Key concepts and a frame of reference. *Int. J. Prod. Econ.* **1997**, *52*, 31–46. [CrossRef]

101. Cabeça, S.; Gonçalves, A.R.; Marques, J.F.; Tavares, M. Mapping intangibilies in creative tourism territories through tangible objects: A methodological approach for developing creative tourism offers. *Tour. Manag. Stud.* **2019**, *15*, 42–49. [CrossRef]

102. Cooper, R.G.; Kleinschmidt, E.J. Screening new products for potential winners. *Long-Range Plan.* **1993**, *26*, 74–81. [CrossRef]

103. Tax, S.S.; Stuart, I. Designing and implementing new services: The challenges of integrating service systems. *J. Retail.* **1997**, *73*, 105–134. [CrossRef]

104. Shostack, G.L. Service positioning through structural change. *J. Mark.* **1987**, *51*, 34–43. [CrossRef]

105. Laws, E. Conceptualizing visitor satisfaction management in heritage settings: An exploratory blueprinting analysis of Leeds Castle, Kent. *Tour. Manag.* **1998**, *19*, 545–554. [CrossRef]

Article

Pinpointing the Barriers to Recycling at Destination

Gonzalo Díaz-Meneses [1,*] and Neringa Vilkaite-Vaitone [2,*]

[1] Department of Management, University of Las Palmas de Gran Canaria, 35017 Las Palmas de Gran Canaria, Spain
[2] Department of Management, Vilnius Gediminas Technical University, Sauletekio av. 11, LT-10223 Vilnius, Lithuania
* Correspondence: gonzalo.diazmeneses@ulpgc.es (G.D.-M.); neringa.vilkaite-vaitone@vgtu.lt (N.V.-V.)

Received: 27 February 2020; Accepted: 24 March 2020; Published: 26 March 2020

Abstract: This paper aims to gain further understanding of the barriers that prevent tourists at tourist destinations from recycling. Methodologically, a survey was carried out with a questionnaire, reaching 371 units through a convenience sampling procedure on the island of Gran Canaria. The measuring instruments consisted of a Likert 'beliefs' scale, comprising statements related to a wide range of recycling barriers, as well as both sociodemographic and situational information. Firstly, we performed an exploratory factor analysis on the barriers scale, and several obstacles to recycling were identified, such as a lack of knowledge and familiarity, blaming of the system of collection, assumed incompatibility with a relaxing holiday, erroneous beliefs about environmental usefulness, disregard towards the place being visited and a certain sense of detachment, the non-existence of incentives, and an unwillingness to comply with perceived demands. Secondly, by means of ANOVA tests, we measured the causal relationship between these barriers to recycling and the tourists' sociodemographic and situational profiles. The practical implications shed light on how to overcome the difficulties that occur for the tourist at the destination with regards to recycling, by considering the tourists' beliefs and their sociodemographic and situational background.

Keywords: tourist recycling behaviour; environmental barriers; sociodemographic; situational

1. Introduction

Deepening our understanding of the barriers that affect tourists' recycling behaviour at a destination is a key topic in need of research, for multiple reasons. Firstly, recycling at home and at holiday destinations are different. Nevertheless, while the former has received quite a lot of attention, further research needs to be done with regards to the latter [1–3]. Secondly, barriers play a role in affecting this environmentally friendly behaviour when one is away from home, insofar as there is a marked change in the situation, lifestyle and perceptions. No doubt, recycling on holiday requires an extra effort and it is more inconvenient [4–8]. Therefore, the ability of the social marketer to overcome the barriers by helping the tourist to come to grips with the new circumstances is crucial. Thirdly, as ecological awareness and climate change concerns are becoming more important for tourists, the destination's environmental quality must live up to the new tourists' ecological demands and, in turn, their recycling desires [7,9–13]. Destination sustainability has become a key competitive edge, mainly for mass-tourism destinations [14–18]. Fourthly, with these research gaps in mind, this work raises the issue of recycling at particular destinations, like Gran Canaria, where the predominant type of accommodation is apartment-based and, hence, the need for tourist collaboration is more unavoidable than in hotel-based accommodation. What is more, not only is there a lack of research on the issue of tourist recycling behaviour, but also where the collaboration matters most, and the circumstances show a high degree of vulnerability, that is, mass-tourism, in apartment-based holidays in a small, insular and, thus, fragile oversea European territory.

In this context, this paper aims to gain a further understanding of the barriers affecting tourist recycling behaviour. We agree with Mee and Clewes [19], in acknowledging that most tourists are open to recycling, and the gap between attitudes and behaviour mainly stems from perceived barriers, as well as with their assertion that this topic requires further research.

Besides, this research work explores the sociodemographic profile of destination tourists to overcome the existing contradictory empirical evidence that the recycling literature faces, with regards to how gender [20], age [21] and education [22] affect environmentally friendly behaviours. While there are research works demonstrating the relationship between recycling behaviour and gender [23–25], age [23–25] and education [26], there are also those who do not verify this in the field of tourism [1,7,27]. Similarly, McKenzie-Mohr [28] recommends that researchers pay attention to cultural diversity to enhance recycling. Hence, nationality is a key variable to consider if recycling at tourism destinations matters [10,11]. Furthermore, the situational variables related to location and time are critical in tourism, insofar as tourists, by definition, are those who arrive for a limited period at a sustainable destination [29]. While the most influential variable to incite recycling behaviour is situational, that is, facilities and convenience, it is under-researched, seeing that we need to further understand how barriers exert a negative influence on recycling [30].

What is more, from a practical point of view, the sociodemographic and situational differences of tourists are accredited as the most visible, accessible and manageable characteristics, when one deals with such a volatile population for any destination. The vast majority of people only spend a limited amount of time and, hence, any social marketing plan should focus on profiling these quickly approachable variables, for example, sociodemographic and situational, rather than delving into other types of more time-consuming study object characteristics, for instance, psychographics.

With this research and practical aims in mind, this work is divided into four sections. First, the review of the literature in which the theoretical framework is developed. Second, the methodology, giving an account of the survey and measuring instruments. Third, the analysis of the results, which presents the obtained empirical evidence. Fourth, the conclusions, where we discuss the theoretical and practical outcomes of the paper, by acknowledging limitations and proposing future lines of research.

2. Review of the Literature

Schultz [31] defines a barrier as any factor that reduces the probability of the target engaging in a behaviour, for example, structural difficulties to access and costs associated with the campaign. It makes sense that any social marketing programme seeks to decrease barriers and increase the benefits and, hence, the analysis of recycling restraints and constraints becomes crucial.

As far as environmentally-friendly behaviour is concerned, there are two types of barrier. On the one hand, there are subjective restraints, such as perceived behavioural barriers and responsibility. These stem from learning and socialisation processes, and we say barrier when we mean perception, beliefs and motivation. On the other hand, there are objective constraints, such as place of residence, time limitations and infrastructure factors.

Of the two barriers, Tanner [32] demonstrates that perceived behavioural barriers represent the most significant restraint. In this vein, to gain insight into this absence of the recycling response, we can resort to the Ipsative theory to refer to circumstances in which individuals are forced to make up their minds between two desirable options. For example, recycling or desirable reasons for not recycling such as relaxing, saving time and space, and avoiding certain nuisances derived from producing insufficient waste and other miscellanea of minor motives. Some tourists overlook recycling even though they recycle at home, are favourable towards recycling and manifest ecological awareness. Following this, the reason for neglecting to recycle is a low degree of motivation, rather than a particular motive [32]. People do not recycle seeing that it demands an effort, and they choose another battle to fight. What is more, provided that curbside recycling facilities are continuously available in the neighbourhood, it denotes a sort of laziness, a lack of interest and a low degree of commitment to recycling [33]. It does not mean that they do not believe in recycling, it just means that they do not have enough information, interest and volitive resources to bridge the gap between what they think and what they do [34]. In this case, there is an attitude behaviour gap, undermining the possibility of shaping into action people's beliefs. This inconsistency might be due to several factors. First, the lack of information and skills [35–37]. Second, external locus of control, low level of self-efficacy and weak social support [3–43]. Third, an underdeveloped recycling habit, caused by a weak environmental concern [44]. Fourth, methodological shortcomings related to an incorrect interpretation of the 'no response' and 'bad measures' dimensions [37,45].

Juvan and Dolnicar [46] gained an understanding of why people engage in environmentally-friendly behaviour at home, yet decline to recycle on holiday, by resorting to cognitive dissonance theory, attribution theory, and the value-belief norm theory. To be precise, these authors explain that people want to recycle, but they cannot, and it makes feel them bad and under pressure, due to a heartfelt inconsistency. To avoid these feelings, they develop cognitive schemes, such as underestimating the supposed harm, considering vacation as being exceptional, and taking lightly the actual damage in comparison to the potential response. All of these represent a set of beliefs used to re-establish cognitive consonance and account for a low level of involvement and motivation. As it is easy to fault this personal incoherency and unethical response, people point to how others engage in recycling, argue a lack of time, and express defeatist sentiments. No doubt, it leads to a sort of tragedy of the commons, in which contradictory beliefs and sentiments might attack one's self-efficacy, and even produce feelings of hopelessness [47].

Nevertheless, the problem does not always lay in a mere lack of involvement seeing that reluctance exists. In fact, not wishing to recycle, people make excuses by neglecting their responsibilities, adducing external constraints and even blaming others. Thus, it may be the case that not only might there be a contradiction in beliefs that diminishes the will and causes recycling to be overlooked, but there may also be tourists who are opposed to recycling. Those who oppose recycling are infused with reluctant beliefs and an unfavourable attitude towards contributing. For instance, there could be those who base their stance on a belief that climate change does not exist and therefore show a general mistrust towards the presumed benefits of recycling [48]. Besides, some deny awareness of the environmental consequences related to their inaction and, arguably, they defer responsibility to technological solutions and even argue for the benefits associated with employment and carbonisation [46]. In any case, it is the type of motivation that causes people to reject recycling; there is a particular negative motive to be opposed to contributing and a sort of opinion against performing the desired conduct [49]. Be that as it may, people opposed to recycling are those who adduce more inhibitors, hindrances and barriers [50].

To deepen our understanding of this posture, the classic theory of attitude points out the existence of four dysfunctional arguments [51]. First, there could be the failure of a knowledge function, since recycling could be meaningless and does not provide enough certainty about its presumed sustainable quality, because either there exists a lack of evidence, or logical arguments to uphold its beneficial effects. Second, recycling could be associated with a negative image and its expression of value and purpose could be wrongly communicated. Third, people could decline to recycle, because they believe it hurts their own lives. For example, people could feel exploited and unfairly treated by private companies making money at the expense of those, like themselves, who volunteer their own time and get nothing tangible in return. Four, people could refuse to recycle, due to its inconveniences and nuisances. In this case, the community and the system of the waste collection would be maladaptive, insofar as it might produce discomfort and not meet people's needs [52].

On this basis, and considering that barriers to recycling are subjectively perceived by the tourists to a destination, we put forward hypothesis 1.

Hypothesis 1 (H1). *There is a wide variety of subjective restraints and barriers to recycling at the destination.*

Barriers for recycling are personal because, even though this desired conduct is carried out within a household, whether or not the individual collaborates, it is subject to their will and liberty, and their decision-making processes. Individuals cope with recycling barriers differently depending on their gender, age, education and nationality. The literature on recycling points out that females [37, 53–59], youngsters [53,60–63] and the highly educated [36,53,58–60,64–71] are more likely to recycle. Nevertheless, notwithstanding that sociodemographics matter less because the desired conduct is widely shared in society [72], it might make a difference by recovering its explanatory strength, only when the most favourable profiles can develop the desired response in such an adverse circumstance as being abroad on holiday [23–26].

The literature on recycling asserts different theoretical explanations related to why sociodemographics influence recycling. Concerning gender, McStay and Dunlap [73] claim that women are more prone to recycling and any other environmentally friendly responses due to cultural factors. To be specific, the male stereotype is one that is seen as being closer to instrumental values and the exploitation of resources, while women are more related to nature and care. Moreover, women tend to play a more significant role in the household in which recycling is performed.

Regarding age, one might argue that when the ecological paradigm was born in the seventies and during its early development in eighties, youngsters looked to be more inclined towards recycling than older people [62,74,75]. Nevertheless, once recycling became a widely shared value in society and no longer a novelty, it started to be performed predominantly by older people, owing to the natural process of ageing of those who used to be young and now have become more mature. Likewise, it seems that recycling is suitable for fully responsible and integrated citizens, as older people tend to be [59]. Finally, Dietz et al. [71] adduce that the elderly got used to being frugal and following the more simplistic lifestyle that recycling implies.

To find ground about the relationship between education and recycling, we might resort to a couple of arguments. First, the existing positive correlation between education and income and, in turn, the better facilities for recycling associated with holiday accommodation when tourists belong to a higher class. Second, the richer cognitive resources in terms of information about how, where and what to recycle when one shows a higher level of education. In this sense, we assume that highly educated tourists are more inclined to immediate environmental responses than those who are lowly educated and less knowledgeable.

What is more, nationality might play a role in explaining recycling at the destination. The reasons for not recycling are diverse and vary in function of the kind of system. Tourists come from different countries and in their respective countries, the recycling collection system is dissimilar [34]. From a kerbside scheme to a wide range of sites reached on foot, by car or located at supermarkets, tourists show quite a diverse background of experiences that condition how familiar they are with the recycling collection systems that they find at the destination. In this sense, it seems that northern European citizens are more prone to recycling [76], since environmental concern and recycling rates are higher in these countries.

In addition to arguing mobility from the accustomed recovery system, another explanation for the recycling barriers on holiday might refer to a sort of alienation. In other words, recycling at home but not at a destination generates an asymmetry that the 'tragedy of the commons' might give account for. This theory refers to communities in which people do not care about shared resources and express a sense of lack of belonging. In this context, there is a tendency to feel a lack of accountability because it is hard to see a tangible benefit related to the advocated environmental action and, in turn, this leads to being convinced that inaction does not cause damage. When this irresponsibility is questioned, it gives rise to quite paradoxical beliefs, such as that others do not do their part or that others will solve the problem. What is more, the tragedy of the commons instigates a sort of free-riding effect, whose consequences are to diminish one's contribution, because individuals can feel as though they are obtaining less than they are giving. Therefore, doing nothing turns out to be beneficial, since one gains without contributing, and this passive response maximises one's utility [47].

Finally, nationality might exert a significant influence through social norms, since not only is what others are doing important, but what they consider acceptable is also important (Cialdini et al.,

1990). Moreover, the principles of imitation [77] and reciprocity [78] are always underlying collective responses with regards to recycling [79].

Therefore, it is evident that there are personal restraints derived from the tourist's sociodemographic profile that might explain the probability of adopting the recycling behaviour at the destination. On this basis, we put forward hypotheses 2 as follows:

Hypothesis 2 (H2). *The recycling barriers are different depending on the tourist's sociodemographic profile.*

Hypothesis 2a (H2a). *The recycling barriers are different depending on the tourist's gender.*

Hypothesis 2b (H2b). *The recycling barriers are different depending on the tourist's age.*

Hypothesis 2c (H2c). *The recycling barriers are different depending on the tourist's education.*

Hypothesis 2d (H2d). *The recycling barriers are different depending on the tourist's nationality.*

In psychology, situationism emphasizes the existence of external variables that determine more the conduct than personality traits [30]. For this reason, a key line of research in environmental psychology focuses on analysing the gap between ecological values and environmental action, by ascribing to external factors the inexistence of realisation [33]. Therefore, the situational variables are highly relevant to understanding the barriers to recycling [80–82]. Of the barriers to recycling, the most significant is convenience [83], in which there are multiple facets [69,84,85].

First, the distance to the recycling kerb site plays a role in inhibiting the desired conduct. No doubt, the perception of convenience is chiefly determined by the distance to where people recycle and represents the most important factor to discourage recycling [22,65,86–88]. It stands to reason that distance and the number of recycling kerb sites are strongly associated [36,89]. Miafodzyeva and Brandt [90], after carrying out a meta-analysis, point out that lack of convenience is the most influential inhibitor to recycling. The cost of participation soars, especially when the distance to the recycling facility is not adequate.

Second, the availability of domestic space turns out to be relevant insofar as the recycling bin might affect the kitchen and the utility room. Robinson and Read [34] and Oskamp et al. [40] point out that space constraint is a key barrier. Similarly, Berger [91] demonstrates that recycling is more likely in spacious detached houses than in cramped apartments. Likewise, Miafodzyeva and Brandt [90]) stress that space constraints are more of a determining factor if there are multiple types of materials and the storage conditions are short of space. Furthermore, the lack of private and public space availability plays a role in inhibiting the desired conduct [92]. For this reason, recycling is more likely in uni-family houses than in little flats [40,89,91,93], and in big rooms than in small [94].

Third, the service quality of the recycling recovery systems might influence how convenient recycling is. Vining and Ebreo [84], Oskamp et al. [40] and Dahle and Neumayer [92] point out that recyclers and non-recyclers differ in the degree of relevance the latter ascribes to the absence of facilities and convenience. The reasons for not recycling are always related to poor service [34] and the lack of facilities [95].

On the one hand, people tend to attribute all the responsibility to others, mostly by blaming the authorities for their negligence [46]. On the other hand, the lack of facilities weakens the relationship between intention and self-efficacy and strengthens the importance of social norms that give rise to environmentally friendly conduct [96]. Similarly, another situational dimension is the frequency of selective recovery [22] and the moment the rubbish is gathered, since if it takes place when the recycling practice is visible, people can learn how and where they can recycle [88]. Finally, the better the conditions of the recycling points, the higher the probability of encouraging recycling [36,97,98].

It is worth saying that urban neighbourhoods recycle more than rural [60,69,91,99], due to the fact cities offer more facilities (Berger, 1997) and give more exposure to environmental problems [62]. The recycling campaigns carried out in cities are more successful than those in the countryside [100].

In summary, while the most significant determining factors in recycling are attitudinal, the most important barriers are situational—that is, distance and lack of time, insufficient space, and complications stemming from the programme, for example, an underdeveloped kerbside scheme [101]. Therefore, we put forward hypotheses 3 as follows:

Hypothesis 3 (H3). *The recycling barriers are different depending on the tourist's accommodation situation.*

Hypothesis 3a (H3a). *The recycling barriers are different depending on the tourist's accommodation category.*

Hypothesis 3b (H3b). *The recycling barriers are different depending on the tourist's accommodation location.*

Hypothesis 3c (H3c). *The recycling barriers are different depending on the tourist's accommodation brand type.*

Similarly, time as a barrier to recycling is also multidimensional. First, the most frequent excuse for neglecting to recycle is being too busy [83]. The reasons for not recycling are always related to lack of time [34]. Therefore, some have not thought of recycling, insofar as no time is mentioned as the main obstacle to recycling [102]. For this reason, Nixon and Saphores [33] acknowledge removing the barriers related to how time-consuming it is to recycle as a priority. In this sense, in addition to distance, space and convenience, time is the main deterrent to recycling [103]. Equally, Timlett and Williams [104] demonstrated that a transient population is less likely to recycle than a settled population, due to specific situational obstacles related to convenience, time and information. As a consequence, they adduce how busy they are, they uphold their right to have a break, and promise to offset the minimal output when they come back home [46]. Therefore, barriers to recycling are shaped by time availability [93].

From a theoretical perspective, it may be the case that when tourists arrive at a destination for the first time, they are in the contemplation stage: believing in recycling, but not necessarily being prepared to take action. Similarly, when tourists have been at a destination previously, they must logically have overcome the preliminary stages and might be placed somewhere in between the action and maintenance stages, depending on their experience and destination loyalty. Therefore, the Transtheoretical model of Prochaska and Marcus [105] might be used to explain how tourists adopt the desired conduct at a destination and move forward, since they acquire familiarity and overcome difficulties.

The second time dimension is the short length logic of holidays and, hence, the difficulty associated with a period whose fleeting nature can neither cause a habit to form, nor gain the subject a great deal of experience. According to Crosby et al. [44], people recycle by following a habit loosely based on ecological concern. In this vein, Pieters [106] and Pieters et al. [79] point out that any environmentally-friendly conduct is performed because people acquire the necessary knowledge and skills from which the habit stems, once they become accustomed to doing it. In this vein, the lack of knowledge and the absence of experience impede recycling [103]. Hence, the absence of experience is a significant inhibitor to recycling [101].

From a theoretical point of view, the discrepancy between home and holiday might come down to a mere temporal circumstance, whose difference might be overcome once the tourist finds their feet at the destination. Going by Kollmuss and Agyeman [107], the provisional gaps between attitude and behaviour are due to practical barriers, such as lack of time and information. Recycling is more behavioural than knowledge-based, since it is a simple task and only requires learning by doing. For this reason, while recycling might be explained by the models of responsible environmental behaviour and prosocial behaviour, non-recycling responses should be regarded as a practicality barrier. Without any doubt, many factors are competing in the daily decision-making process when one has just arrived, irrespective of one's constellation of environmental knowledge, values and attitudes. There are still those who state that recycling has not crossed their minds [102]. Therefore, it is not a responsibility that matters most, but rather other priorities in a system that is too complex.

Third, the absence of any sense of community and thus the ineffectiveness of the social influence and the collectivist spirit in the neighbourhood might shed light on why there is a low level of recycling at the destination. In this sense, it is worth noting that the sense of community correlates positively with recycling [90] and it stands to reason that, at a tourist destination, every so often there is not enough time to build it.

For a theoretical approach, the sense of community plays a role in bringing about recycling by considering self-utility. For example, McCarty and Shrum [95] claim that, while most environmentally friendly behaviours may not seem rewarding in the short term, they gain benefit in the long term. Thogersen [108] explains that the consumer appraisals about recycling are processed from a subjective utility perspective, by considering how to maximise value for their household. Therefore, the sense of neighbourhood matters if people are future-oriented [95], and thus neighbourhood sustainability affects one own life and wellness.

On this basis, we acknowledge that the importance of time is multifold and put forward hypotheses 4 as follows:

Hypothesis 4 (H4). *The recycling barriers are different depending on the tourist's time situation.*

Hypothesis 4a (H4a). *The recycling barriers are different depending on the visit frequency.*

Hypothesis 4b (H4b). *The recycling barriers are different depending on the duration of stay.*

3. Materials and Methods

A survey was conducted with a structured questionnaire following a non-probabilistic sampling procedure. To be specific, we followed a snowball method by meeting tourists that were spending their holiday in apartments during May 2019. The survey took place in the south of Gran Canaria. This more urban than rural destination attracted 4.19 million tourists, with an average trip length of 9 days and average spending of 1174 euros per tourist and per trip in 2019 [109–111]. During the last decade, the number of tourists in the year-round destination has increased by 44.50 %. 85.01 % of tourists in 2019 were international tourists, with a majority of tourists residing in Germany (20.36%), United Kingdom (18.13%), and Nordic countries (22.46%) [109]. In 2019, apartments were the prevailing type of accommodation at the destination. It is worth noting that 6491 apartments had a capacity of 97,375 bed spaces, while 208 hotels on the island were able to accommodate 63,795 tourists per day [110]. The most important factors determining the choice of destination are climate, safety, sea, tranquility, and beaches [112]. The most favourable activities of tourists in Gran Canaria include beaches, walks, wanders, swimming pools, facilities of hotels, exploration of the island on their own, and tasting local gastronomy [112]. Gran Canaria is a mature destination with an advanced system of waste collection, loosely based on kerbside bins, in which people are supposed to volunteer their recycling. Participation in the survey was voluntary. We ensured the anonymity of the research participants, as well. The survey takers were 100 students of the market research course, most of whom received exhaustive instructions about how to effectively administer the questionnaire. Not only did these students work in teams so that the burden was relatively small, but this interactive atmosphere also guaranteed social control.

The measuring instruments consisted of 35 items with a seven-point Likert 'beliefs' scale, comprising statements related to a wide range of recycling barriers, inhibitions, hindrances and reluctances, as well as both sociodemographic and situational information. While the barriers scale was inspired by a wide range of research works [47,90,107,113,114], the sociodemographic and situational scales followed an undetermined source.

The final sample reached 371 sampling units. Out of 371 responses, 308 were valid. Therefore, the subsequent analysis included only these cases. Of 308 survey respondents, a total of 152 participants were male (49.4%) and 156 participants were female (50.6%). When asked about education, 41.23% indicated graduate education, and 38.64% reported secondary education. The most substantial proportion of respondents were Spanish (47.79%), followed by British (15.58%), Germans (12.34%) and Italians (5.19%). A full description of the sample can be seen in Table 1.

Table 1. The description of the sample.

Gender	F	%	Age	F	%	Education	F	%
Male	152	49.4	18–24	52	16.9	None	3	1.0
Female	156	50.6	25–34	74	24.0	Primary	25	8.1
			35–49	92	29.9	Secondary	119	38.6
			50–64	76	24.7	Graduate	127	41.2
			>65	14	4.5	Postgraduate	23	7.5
						No answer	11	3.6
Place of residence	F	%	**Place of residence**	F	%	**Place of residence**	F	%
Spanish from GC	36	11.7	Norwegian	14	4.5	Italian	16	5.2
Spanish	111	36.0	Finish	3	1.0	French	8	2.6
German	38	12.3	Danish	2	0.6	Polish	9	2.9
British	48	15.6	Dutch	5	1.6	Other	8	2.6
Swedish	6	1.9	Belgium	4	1.3			
Visits	F	%	**Length of stay**	F	%	**Category**	F	%
Once	83	26.9	Less than a week	65	21.1	1	22	7.1
Twice	86	27.9	One week	141	45.8	2	91	29.5
Three times	69	22.4	Two weeks	64	20.8	3	148	48.1
Four times	24	7.8	Three weeks	15	4.9	4	26	8.4
Five times	46	14.9	More than three weeks	23	7.5	5	307	99.7
						No answer	21	6.8
Location	F	%	**Brand**	F	%			
Beach	253	82.1	Independent	234	76.0			
Urban	30	9.7	Chain	74	24.0			
Rural	14	4.5						
Airport	1	0.3						
Others	10	3.2						

IBM SPSS Statistics 20 software was used for the data analysis. Once the database was built, statistical tests were performed to maximise the quality control of the information gathered.

4. Results

To test the first hypothesis, an exploratory factor analysis was carried out. The reliability of the barriers scale was tested through an Alpha Cronbach test. As shown in Table 2, the exploratory factor analysis with Varimax rotation identified five different components and explained over 60% of the variance. The first factor is labelled as "demands of relaxing and rest as excuses for not recycling" since not only does it refer to the motives of being on holiday and having a break, but it also expresses mistrust and misbelief about recycling (F1). The second factor is named "reluctances and oppositions", because there are climate change denials and some assertions about the futility of recycling. For example, according to some tourists, climate change does not exist and recycling is not as environmentally friendly as it is assumed (F2). The third factor is called "lack of information about how to do it" and refers to those who claimed a lack of information or felt misguided (F3). The fourth factor is termed "extrinsically driven", insofar as it gathers a set of demands related to those who argue that they do not have enough rewards and do not receive anything in return for recycling (F4). The fifth factor is designated "inconvenience and nuisance", given that the distance between the apartment and the kerbside system, as well as not having enough space, are indicated as the hindrances to recycling (F5).

On this basis, as five distinctive kinds of inhibitors to recycling have been identified, Hypothesis 1 is confirmed.

Table 2. Exploratory factor analysis on motivational barriers to recycling.

	Rotated Component Matrix					
		Components				
Communality	Items	1	2	3	4	5
0.780	I am on holiday here and thinking about recycling makes me feel unrelaxed	**0.833**	0.149	0.190	0.131	0.100
0.770	Recycling interferes with the lifestyle of my holiday	**0.801**	0.288	0.161	0.092	0.105
0.725	I am not on duty here	**0.793**	0.202	0.144	0.154	0.107
0.683	Recycling here makes me feel stressed	**0.768**	0.176	0.131	0.191	0.093
0.721	Please, give me a break from being too strict on my recycling behaviours	**0.762**	0.255	0.199	0.149	0.114
0.745	I do not like recycling	**0.739**	0.387	0.176	0.118	0.066
0.494	I do not have any support from those who share the apartment	**0.670**	0.067	0.046	0.151	0.126
0.576	As nobody controls me here, I do not recycle	**0.669**	0.325	0.127	0.082	0.021
0.599	It is because recycling is messy and dirty that I do not recycle	**0.640**	0.398	0.069	0.126	0.099
0.564	I do not believe in recycling	**0.555**	0.426	0.134	0.224	0.074
0.697	Climate Change does not exist	0.254	**0.786**	0.072	0.080	0.047
0.646	Recycling might damage the environment	0.166	**0.779**	0.066	0.085	−0.026
0.663	Recycling is not environmentally friendly	0.362	**0.714**	0.132	0.072	0.024
0.684	I do not recycle given that it does not make any difference to environmental protection	0.466	**0.652**	0.063	0.186	0.057
0.704	Recycling does not make any sense to me	0.507	**0.648**	0.068	0.149	0.023
0.563	I do not recycle because I am a foreigner and hence I do not belong to Gran Canaria	0.465	**0.570**	0.122	−0.019	0.081
0.774	I need more information to recycle here	0.046	−0.059	**0.858**	0.161	0.073
0.738	I have no idea about what material I can recycle here	0.169	0.073	**0.825**	0.079	0.129
0.697	I have no information about it	0.130	0.113	**0.780**	0.023	0.242
0.687	I do not know how to do it here	0.155	0.130	**0.764**	0.111	0.225
0.423	I do not understand the colours associated with the recycling bins	0.219	0.156	**0.585**	−0.028	0.093
0.718	Recycling companies should pay people to recycle	0.182	0.202	0.097	**0.795**	0.050
0.553	There is not any monetary incentive to recycle	0.123	−0.114	0.061	**0.702**	0.167
0.603	Recycling companies take advantage of people	0.315	0.259	0.031	**0.659**	0.035
0.524	This task should be performed by the authorities rather by the citizens	0.289	0.306	0.333	**0.485**	0.033
0.689	The Green points are far away from my apartment	0.222	−0.102	0.101	−0.056	**0.785**
0.625	I do not have any facility at my accommodation to perform it	0.071	−0.073	0.274	0.045	**0.733**
0.519	The recycling system here is inconvenient	0.014	0.254	0.119	0.154	**0.646**
0.431	I do not have enough space at my apartment to recycle	0.173	0.082	0.272	0.232	**0.517**
	KMO: 0.932; Bartlett: 5409.689, df:406, sig:0.000; Explained variance:64.122%					

In order to contrast the second hypotheses, a student test and several ANOVA tests were carried out. As shown in Table 3, recycling barriers are different depending on the tourist's sociodemographic profile. To be specific, the mean difference test on barriers indicated that gender has a significant influence on the first and second factors. In this sense, it is clear that the motives of "demands to relax and rest as excuses for not recycling" and "reluctances and oppositions" lead male tourists to avoid recycling. Therefore, Hypothesis 2a is verified.

Conversely, the ANOVA Test demonstrates that the relationship between age and recycling does not exist at the tourist destination. Therefore, hypothesis 2b, which states that the recycling barriers are different depending on the tourists' age, is rejected.

An ANOVA Test considering education levels was performed. As reported in Table 4, there exists a relationship between this sociodemographic variable and the first and third factors. Consequently, this empirical evidence shows that the reason labelled "demands of relaxing and rest as excuses for not recycling" is not argued by tourists without formal education and with graduate-level, but is argued by those who hold primary, secondary and postgraduate education. What is more, if post-hoc results are examined, one can state that there is a glaring difference between those with graduate and primary education. Similarly, a "lack of information about how to do it" is mainly perceived by tourists with primary and secondary education, rather than those with none or with a university education. Moreover, the post-hoc analysis points out that there is a significant difference between those who hold primary and postgraduate education. Consequently, Hypothesis 2c is confirmed, insofar as the recycling barriers are different depending on the tourist's level of education.

Table 3. Mean difference test on barriers by distinguishing gender groups.

			Descriptives		
	Sex	**N**	**Mean**	**Standard Deviation**	**Standard Error Mean**
F1	Male	152	0.135	1.0744	0.087
	Female	156	−0.132	0.9059	0.073
F2	Male	152	0.110	1.0904	0.088
	Female	156	−0.107	0.8940	0.072
			Levene's Test for Equality of Variances		
		F	**Sig.**	**t**	**df**
F1	Equal variances	9.455	0.002	2.360	306
	Not Equal			2.355	294.829
F2	Equal variances	6.162	0.014	1.905	306
	Not Equal			1.901	291.683

Table 4. ANOVA analysis of barriers by distinguishing education groups.

		N	**Mean**	**Standard Deviation**	**Standard Error**
	Non Response	11	−0.668	0.7465	0.225
	None	3	−0.141	0.3863	0.223
	Primary	25	0.459	1.1252	0.225
F1	Secondary	119	0.131	1.0468	0.096
	Graduate	127	−0.166	0.9242	0.082
	Postgraduate	23	0.081	0.9025	0.188
	Total	308	0.000	1.0000	0.057
	Non Response	11	0.357	1.2439	0.375
	None	3	−0.265	0.9453	0.546
	Primary	25	0.446	1.1099	0.222
F3	Secondary	119	0.045	0.9656	0.089
	Graduate	127	−0.083	1.0037	0.089
	Postgraduate	23	−0.396	0.7361	0.153
	Total	308	0.000	1.0000	0.057
	Postgraduate	23	0.206	0.8700	0.181
	Total	308	0.000	1.0000	0.0570
			ANOVA				
		Sum of Squares	**df**	**Mean Square**	**F**	**Sig.**
	Between Groups	15.902	5	3.180	3.299	0.006
F1	Within Groups	291.098	302	0.964		
	Total	307.000	307			
	Between Groups	11.306	5	2.261	2.309	0.044
F3	Within Groups	295.694	302	0.979		
	Total	307.000	307			
			POSTHOC			
Tukey HSD		**I**	**J**	**M. Difference**	**SD**	**Sig.**
F1		Primary	Graduate	0.624	0.214	0.045
F3		Primary	Postgraduate	0.841	0.285	0.040

The proposed impact of nationality on recycling barriers was tested. The respondents were split into 14 groups according to their nationality. As can be seen in Table 5, the ANOVA Test confirms that the recycling barriers are different depending on the tourist's nationality and, hence, Hypothesis 2d is accepted. To be precise, the first two barriers, namely, "demands of relaxing and rest as excuses for not recycling" and "reluctances and oppositions" are refuted by Spaniards from Gran Canaria and German tourists, as well as Scandinavian tourists, but contended by the rest of nationalities, including mainland Spanish. Be that as it may, examining the post-hoc results one can state that the most glaring difference exists between those who live in France and Belgium and the main other nationalities.

Table 5. ANOVA analysis of barriers by distinguishing nationality groups.

	Place of Residence	N	Mean	Standard Deviation	Standard Error
	Spanish from Gran Canaria	36	−0.435	0.6785	0.113
	Spanish	111	0.029	1.0107	0.096
	German	38	−0.422	0.6980	0.113
	British	48	0.143	0.9092	0.131
	Swedish	6	0.216	1.2612	0.515
	Norwegian	14	−0.017	1.1086	0.296
	Finish	3	−0.231	0.6942	0.401
F1	Danish	2	−1.225	0.4731	0.335
	Dutch	5	0.145	0.7021	0.314
	Belgium	4	0.718	1.3195	0.660
	Italian	16	0.347	1.0853	0.271
	French	8	1.414	1.4345	0.507
	Polish	9	0.225	1.0754	0.358
	Other	8	0.149	1.1451	0.405
	Total	308	0.000	1.0000	0.057
	Spanish from Gran Canaria	36	−0.141	0.8614	0.144
	Spanish	111	−0.100	0.8431	0.080
	German	38	0.113	0.9174	0.149
	British	48	0.039	1.1979	0.173
	Swedish	6	−0.465	0.9745	0.398
	Norwegian	14	0.105	1.0115	0.270
	Finish	3	0.155	0.2924	0.169
F2	Danish	2	−0.199	0.1374	0.097
	Dutch	5	0.098	0.8588	0.384
	Belgium	4	1.568	1.2799	0.640
	Italian	16	−0.020	0.8731	0.218
	French	8	−0.476	1.4756	0.522
	Polish	9	0.999	1.6734	0.558
	Other	8	−0.050	0.7909	0.280
	Total	308	0.000	1.0000	0.057

		ANOVA				
		Sum of Squares	df	Mean Square	F	Sig.
	Between Groups	38.831	13	2.987	3.275	0.000
F1	Within Groups	268.169	294	0.912		
	Total	307.000	307			
	Between Groups	24.685	13	1.899	1.977	0.022
F2	Within Groups	282.315	294	0.960		
	Total	307.000	307			

		POST-HOC				
	Tukey HSD	I	J	M. Difference	Sd	Sig
F1		GC	France	−1.849	0.373	0.000
		Spain	France	−1.385	0.349	0.007
		German	France	−1.386	0.371	0.000
		British	France	−1.271	0.364	0.036
		Norwegian	France	−1.431	0.423	0.050
		Danish	France	−2.639	0.755	0.035
F2		Spain	Belgium	−1.677	0.498	0.056
		Belgium	France	2.044	0.600	0.046

Following the results obtained from the ANOVA, it can be said that the barriers differ depending on the apartment category (Table 6). If the apartment has one, two or four keys, tourists claim a lack of information, while if it holds three, they do not. Consequently, we can accept hypothesis3a and state that the recycling barriers are different depending on the tourist's accommodation category. Nevertheless, the post-hoc analysis does not prove any significant difference at the group levels.

Table 6. ANOVA analysis on barriers by distinguishing apartment category.

		N	Mean	Standard Deviation	Standard Error
	I do not know	20	−0.395	1.0108	0.226
	1 key	22	0.220	1.0465	0.223
F3	2 keys	91	0.152	1.0971	0.115
	3 keys	148	−0.129	0.9145	0.075
	4 keys	26	0.289	0.9276	0.182
	Total	307	−0.003	1.0002	0.057
			ANOVA		
		Sum of Squares	df	Mean Square	F	Sig.
	Between Groups	10.925	4	2.731	2.794	0.026
F3	Within Groups	295.205	302	0.977		
	Total	306.130	306			

In contrast, as the ANOVA test does not show statistically significant differences in terms of the apartment location, we reject Hypothesis 3b and state that the recycling barriers are not different depending on the tourist's accommodation location.

Similarly, Hypothesis 3c is rejected, because the recycling barriers are not different depending on the tourists' accommodation brand type.

In addition, an ANOVA analysis was established to test whether the frequency of visits matters and the obtained results lead us to state that there are two types of barriers, namely, "demands of relaxing and rest as excuses for not recycling" and "reluctances and oppositions" with statistically significant differences (Table 7). To be precise, when tourists come twice and four times, they are prone to arguing the former and when they come once, twice and four times, they are likely to claim the latter. On this basis, Hypothesis 4a is verified. To confirm this, the post-hoc analysis indicates significant differences between those who visit once and five times of more, with regards to the first factor, that is, "demands of relaxing and rest as excuses for not recycling".

Table 7. ANOVA analysis on barriers by considering the frequency of visits.

		Frequency	N	Mean	Standard Deviation	Standard Error
		Once	83	0.222	1.0190	0.112
		Twice	86	0.054	0.9599	0.104
	F1	Three times	69	−0.133	1.0030	0.121
		Four times	24	0.195	1.0457	0.213
		Five times	46	−0.405	0.8938	0.132
		Total	308	0.000	1.0000	0.057
		Once	83	−0.188	0.9756	0.107
		Twice	86	0.159	1.1097	0.120
	F2	Three times	69	0.138	1.0234	0.123
		Four times	24	−0.341	0.7657	0.156
		Five times	46	0.013	0.8210	0.121
		Total	308	0.000	1.0000	0.057
			ANOVA			
		Sum of Squares	df	Mean Square	F	Sig.
	Between Groups	14.027	4	3.507	3.627	0.007
F1	Within Groups	292.973	303	0.967		
	Total	307.000	307			
	Between Groups	9.234	4	2.309	2.349	0.054
F2	Within Groups	297.766	303	0.983		
	Total	307.000	307			
	Total	307.000	307			
			POSTHOC			
	Tukey HSD	I	J	M Difference	SD	Sig
F1		Once	Five times	0.627	0.180	0.005

In contrast, in the absence of evidence to the contrary, the length of the stay is not associated with any particular barrier and, therefore, Hypothesis 4b is rejected, by stating that the recycling barriers are not different depending on the duration of stay.

5. Discussion

The results of the present research confirmed that there is a broad range of barriers to recycling at the destination. On the one hand, subjective restraints stemming from a low level of motivation that might be explained by placing the tourists in a dilemma between two favourable choices—that is, recycling or having a relaxed holiday. In addition to this Ipsative sentiment, tourists might neglect recycling when there is a lack of information about how to do it and, in this case, they might suffer from cognitive dissonance [46]. Moreover, tourists might feel unmotivated by perceiving a lack of reward for making the effort. Therefore, some are extrinsically motivated [50]. Finally, perceived inconvenience and nuisances derived from the distance and time-consuming nature of recycling may discourage the desirable conduct. Following the literature, those subjects exhibit a low level of motivation, and this is the reason they demand some form of compensation [92]. On the other hand, some do not recycle because they are reluctant, or even opposed; they believe in neither climate change, nor the presumed benefits associated with recycling and, hence, they reject recycling without regret. In rejecting recycling, paraphrasing the Katz's theory of attitudes, there might be the failure to acquire knowledge and harness the benefits of taking part in the common effort, along with an attempt to self-protect against a feeling of exploitation and, all in all, some dysfunctional arguments [49,115]. In summary, this evidence is consistent with the literature on recycling, in that the inhibitors to recycling are always diverse and subjective by nature [30,89,93,96].

What is more, this diversity is also personal and, in turn, greater, insofar as all the hindrances and deterrents depend on the tourist's sociodemographic profile in terms of gender, education and nationality. It is worth noting that age does not show any significant relationship with recycling and the connection between education and recycling is not linear. However, women, locals, and German and Scandinavian tourists are prone to making an effort for recycling's sake at the destination. These findings might imply that being on holiday challenges the probability of recycling and only the most likely sociodemographic profiles show a significant resilience against the adverse circumstances that represent the maintenance of recycling away from home. The literature on recycling points out that those who perceive more barriers to recycling are also more demanding about external compensations, as well as being more sensitive about any potential deterrent [92,115].

Finally, of the situational factors affecting the variety of recycling barriers at the destination, the most important is the apartment category and the frequency of visits, in that the lower the former and the higher the latter, the stronger the barrier is perceived by the tourist. In this respect, it stands to reason that familiarity with the destination, insofar as it might enhance the sense of community and lead to the acquisition of the practical knowledge needed to recycle [90,107], as well as the much better conditions of the mid-class neighbourhood [89], might explain the greater success of recycling initiatives and how tourists overcome the tragedy of the commons [47]. These important findings are in line with the previous research works in the extant recycling behaviour literature, which points out the critical role of space and time situations as barriers [34].

6. Conclusions

Encouraging tourists to recycle is arguably as important a task as encouraging people to recycle at home. Nevertheless, researchers have paid little attention to the former topic when the much greater extent of literature stemming from the latter is considered. For this reason, this study has raised important issues regarding the barriers to recycling at destination in Maspalomas, Gran Canaria. Most significantly, the research has questioned the excuses and barriers to recycling and how they differ between specific groups that differ in sociodemographic and situational characteristics. The survey concluded that the main obstacles to recycling fall into five categories: demands of relaxing (1), reluctances and oppositions (2), lack of information (3), lack of external benefits (4), inconvenience and nuisance (5). The findings indicate that gender, education, nationality, apartment category and frequency of visits play a significant role in recycling intentions. The results of this research have contributed to a more comprehensive understanding of what should be considered to achieve a greater rate of recycling among tourists; to make recycling a tourist's personal lifestyle choice.

Nevertheless, of the five barriers, the most relevant are *"relaxation"*, *"reluctance"* and *"lack of information"*. Therefore, in order to ensure that there is a sufficient level of information about recycling at tourist destinations, it is advisable for the institutions that are responsible for the control of recycling to create a mobile application, pinpointing the benefits of recycling and providing useful tips on how to do it at a specific tourist destination. A negotiable alternative would be the accession to the scope of WasteApp, which already functions in 11 European cities [116,117]. Providing information about recycling to current and potential tourists through a convenient channel can be a meaningful solution for the increase of concern for recycling.

In addition, our results revealed that gender is a significant factor in explaining recycling behaviour at a tourist destination. Male tourists were found to refrain from recycling, due to "demands of relaxing" and "rest as excuses for not recycling", and "reluctances and oppositions". Therefore, tourism researchers and practitioners need to recognise the crucial role of gender in understanding the barriers to recycling at a tourist destination. In order to stimulate male tourists into exhibiting a pro-recycling behaviour, it is essential to pose recycling as an ease task fully compatible with relaxation, as well as implement special social marketing techniques suitable for reluctant target audiences, for example, the foot in the door, the face in the door and even the retirement of positive reinforcements. Similarly, it seems logical to provide the lower educated with more information about how to recycle, insofar as this represents the key inhibitor for this group.

Likewise, as locals, Germans and Scandinavians show a strong drive to recycle; one might suggest that social marketers think of recruiting them as volunteers and block leaders to set an example, and thus encourage the other national groups to contribute. Needless to say, there is no point in arguing that recycling at the destination is only a top-down concern for the tourist's sake since the tourists strongly demand sustainable destinations.

Equally, while tourists argue a certain lack of information when their loyalty to the destination is low, they adduce a demand to relax and an expression of reluctance if their apartment category is either low or high but not mid-level. On this basis, the authorities should be aware that more effort is needed to facilitate recycling behaviour for less loyal tourists and those who spend their holidays in premium and low rate apartments.

In summary, the results of the research confirmed that there exist differences in recycling barriers depending on the sociodemographic and situational background of tourists. Given that the kerbside system is fully developed and well equipped in Gran Canaria, all the tourists' arguments are grounded in their beliefs and perceptions.

Finally, let us acknowledge the existence of a few limitations. First of all, this research was conducted among tourists in Maspalomas, Gran Canaria. Therefore, the sample does not perfectly represent all tourists to Gran Canaria, Canary Islands, or Spain as a whole. It means that there exists a concern related to the generalisation of the results. Therefore, future research should cover samples from more destinations. Secondly, despite there being a high level of homogeneity in terms of the recycling recovery infrastructure at this destination, there must be a wide range of different circumstances affecting how easy it is to recycle for those who form the target audience. Therefore, we are far from a quasi-experiment setting in which the researcher can be aware of the external variables that potentially might be causing some biases in the questionnaire respondents. Thirdly, preliminary analyses consisting of normal tests; let us assume that the ANOVA groups do not follow a normal distribution, not even show a similar number of cases, and hence the obtained results are more representative of this particular destination than if they were potentially extrapolated to other places.

Author Contributions: While G.D.-M. has been engaged in all the tasks, N.V.-V. has made a significant contribution to the review of the literature, the conclusions and a wide range of formal tasks. All authors have read and agreed to the published version of the manuscript.

Sustainability **2020**, *12*, 2635

Funding: This research received no external funding, but the principal author is involved in the Soclimpact project. This project subject matter consists of fighting against Climate Change in the Islands and has received funding from the European Union's Horizon 2020 research and innovation programme under grant agreement No 776661.

Acknowledgments: We feel grateful for the support and help in performing the survey by a team of over 100 devoted students of the University of Las Palmas de Gran Canaria.

Conflicts of Interest: The authors declare no conflict of interest.

References

1. Heesup, H.; Hyun, S.S. College youth travellers' eco-purchase behaviour and recycling activity while traveling: An examination of gender difference. *J. Travel Tour. Mark.* **2018**, *35*, 740–754.
2. Whitmarsh, L.E.; Haggar, P.; Thomas, M. Waste reduction behaviors at home, at work, and on holiday: What influences behavioural consistency across contexts? *Front. Psychol.* **2018**, *9*, 1–13. [CrossRef] [PubMed]
3. Wang, S.; Wang, J.; Li, J.; Yang, F. Do motivations contribute to local residents' engagement in pro-environmental behaviors? Resident-destination relationship and pro-environmental climate perspective. *J. Sustain. Tour.* **2020**, *28*, 834–852. [CrossRef]
4. Dolnicar, S.; Grün, B. Environmentally friendly behaviour: Can heterogeneity among individuals and context/environments be harvested for improved sustainable management. *Environ. Behav.* **2009**, *41*, 693–714. [CrossRef]
5. Barr, S.; Shaw, G.; Coles, T.; Prillwitz, J. 'A holiday is a holiday': Practicing sustainability, home and away. *J. Transp. Geogr.* **2010**, *18*, 474–481. [CrossRef]
6. Miao, L.; Wei, W. Consumers' pro-environmental behaviour and the underlying motivations: A comparison between household and hotel settings. *Int. J. Hosp. Manag.* **2013**, *32*, 102–112. [CrossRef]
7. Han, J.; Nelson, C.M.; Kim, C. Pro-environmental behaviour in sport event tourism: Roles of event attendees and destinations. *Int. J. Tour. Spaceplace Environ.* **2015**, *5*, 719–737.
8. Oliver, J.; Benjamin, S.; Leonard, H. Recycling on vacation: Does pro-environmental behaviour change when consumers travel? *J. Gobal Sch. Mark. Sci.* **2019**, *29*, 266–280. [CrossRef]
9. Zeppel, H. Climate change and tourism in the Great Barrier Reef Marine Park. *Curr. Issues Tour.* **2012**, *15*, 287–292. [CrossRef]
10. Leonidou, L.C.; Coudounaris, D.N.; Christodoulides, P. Drivers and outcomes of green tourist attitudes and behaviour: Sociodemographic moderating effects. *Psychol. Mark.* **2015**, *6*, 635–650. [CrossRef]
11. Ramchurjee, N.A.; Suresha, S. Are tourists' environmental behaviour affected by their environmental perceptions and beliefs? *J. Environ. Tour. Anal.* **2015**, *3*, 26–44.
12. Lee, S.H.; Wu, S.C.; Li, A. Low-carbon tourism of small islands responding to climate change. *World Leis. J.* **2018**, *60*, 235–245. [CrossRef]
13. Shen, J.; Zhang, J. Design and research of resource recycling service system in tourist attractions: Taking international cruises as an example. In *Designing Sustainability for All, Proceedings of the 3rd LeNS World Distributed Conference, Milano, Italy, Mexico City, Mexico, Beijing, China, Bangalore, India, Curitiba, Brazil, Cape Town, South Africa, 3–5 April 2019*; Edizioni POLI.design: Milano, Italy, 2019; Volume 1, pp. 85–89.
14. Iaquinto, B.L. "I recycle, I turn out the lights": Understanding the everyday sustainability practices of backpackers. *J. Sustain. Tour.* **2015**, *23*, 577–599. [CrossRef]
15. Mathew, P.V.; Sreejesh, S. Impact of responsible tourism on destination sustainability and quality of life of community in tourism destinations. *J. Hosp. Tour. Manag.* **2017**, *31*, 83–89. [CrossRef]
16. Grazzini, L.; Padmali, R.; Aiello, G.; Viglia, G. Loss or gain? The role of message framing in hotel guests' recycling behaviour. *J. Sustain. Tour.* **2018**, *26*, 1944–1966. [CrossRef]
17. Butler, R. Contributions of tourism to destination sustainability: Golf tourism in St. Andrews, Scotland. *Tour. Rev.* **2019**, *74*, 235–245. [CrossRef]
18. Yang, X.; Li, H.; Chen, W.M.; Fu, H. Corporate community involvement and Chinese rural tourist destination sustainability. *Sustainability* **2019**, *11*, 1574. [CrossRef]
19. Mee, N.; Clewes, D. The influence of corporate communications on recycling behaviour. *Corp. Commun. Int. J.* **2004**, *9*, 1356–3289. [CrossRef]
20. Straughan, R.; Roberts, J. Environmental segmentation alternatives: A look at green consumer behavior in the new millenium. *J. Consum. Mark.* **1999**, *16*, 558–575. [CrossRef]

21. Shrum, L.; Lowrey, T.; McCarty, J. Recycling as a marketing problem: A framework for strategy development. *Psychol. Mark.* **1994**, *11*, 393–416. [CrossRef]

22. Wesley, P.; Oskamp, S.; Mainieri, T. Who recycles and when? A review of personal and situational factors. *J. Environ. Psychol.* **1995**, *15*, 105–121.

23. Heesup, H.; Jongsik, Y.; Hyeon–Cheol, K.; Wansoo, K. Impact of social/personal norms and willingness to sacrifice on young vacationers' pro-environmental intentions for waste reduction and recycling. *J. Sustain. Tour.* **2018**, *26*, 2117–2133.

24. Heesup, H.; Kiattipoom, K.; Bobby, R.H.; Heekyoung, J.; Wansoo, K. Determinants of young vacationers' recycling and conservation behaviour when traveling. *Soc. Behav. Personal. Int. J.* **2019**, *47*, 1–11.

25. Hu, H.; Zhang, J.; Wang, P.; Yu, P.; Chu, G. What influences tourists' intention to participate in the Zero Litter Initiative in mountainous tourism areas: A case study of Huangshan National Park, China. *Sci. Total Environ.* **2020**, *657*, 1127–1137. [CrossRef]

26. Little, M.E. Innovative recycling solutions to waste management challenges in Costa Rican tourism communities. *J. Environ. Tour. Anal.* **2017**, *5*, 33–52.

27. Briguglio, M.; Delaney, L.; Wood, A. Voluntary recycling despite disincentives. *J. Environ. Plan. Manag.* **2016**, *59*, 1751–1774. [CrossRef]

28. Mckenzie-Mohr, D. *Fostering Sustainable Bahavior*; New Society Publisher: Gabriola, BC, Canada, 1999.

29. Lee, W.H.; Moscardo, G. Understanding the impact of ecotourism resort experiences on tourists' environmental attitudes and behavioural intentions. *J. Sustain. Tour.* **2005**, *13*, 546–565. [CrossRef]

30. Latif, S.; Omar, M.; Bidin, Y.; Awang, Z. Environmental problems and quality of life: Situational factor as a predictor of recycling behaviour. *Procedia Soc. behav. Sci.* **2012**, *35*, 682–688. [CrossRef]

31. Schultz, W. Strategies for promoting proenvironmental behaviour. Lots of tools but few instructions. *Eur. Psychol.* **2014**, *19*, 107–117.

32. Tanner, C. Constraints on environmental behaviour. *J. Environ. Psychol.* **1999**, *19*, 145–157. [CrossRef]

33. Nixon, H.; Saphores, J. Information and the decision to recycle: Results from a survey of US households. *J. Environ. Plan. Manag.* **2009**, *52*, 257–277. [CrossRef]

34. Robinson, G.; Read, A. Recycling behaviour in London Borough: Results from large-scale household surveys. *Resour. Conserv. Recycl.* **2005**, *45*, 70–83. [CrossRef]

35. Newhouse, N. Implications of attitude and behavior research for environmental conservation. *J. Environ. Educ.* **1990**, *22*, 26–32. [CrossRef]

36. Katzev, R.; Blake, G.; Messer, B. Determinants of participation in multifamily recycling programs. *J. Appl. Soc. Psychol.* **1993**, *23*, 374–385. [CrossRef]

37. Mainieri, T.; Barnett, E.; Trisha, V.; Unipan, J.; Oskamp, S. Green buying: The influence of environmental concern on consumer behavior. *J. Soc. Psychol.* **1997**, *137*, 189–205. [CrossRef]

38. McGuiness, J.; Jones, P.; Cole, G. Attitudinal correlates of recycling behavior. *J. Appl. Psychol.* **1977**, *62*, 376–384. [CrossRef]

39. Gill, J.; Crosby, L.; Taylor, J. Ecological concern, attitudes and social norms in voting behavior. *Public Opin. Q.* **1986**, *50*, 537–554. [CrossRef]

40. Oskamp, S.; Harrington, M.; Edwards, T.; Sherwood, D.; Okuda, S.; Swanson, D. Factors influencing household recycling behavior. *Environ. Behav.* **1991**, *23*, 494–519. [CrossRef]

41. Biswas, A.; Licata, J.; McKee, D.; Pullig, C.; Daughtridge, C. The recycling cycle: An empirical examination of consumer waste recycling and recycling shopping behaviors. *J. Public Policy Mark.* **2000**, *19*, 93–105. [CrossRef]

42. Tucker, P. Normative influences in household waste recycling. *J. Environ. Plan. Manag.* **1999**, *42*, 63–82. [CrossRef]

43. Kornilaki, M.; Thomas, R.; Font, X. The sustainability behaviour of small firms in tourism: The role of self-efficacy and contextual constraints. *J. Sustain. Tour.* **2019**, *27*, 97–117. [CrossRef]

44. Crosby, A.; Gill, D.; Taylor, R. Consumer voter behaviour in the passage of michigan container law. *J. Mark.* **1981**, *45*, 19–32. [CrossRef]

45. Thogersen, J. A model of recycling behavior, with evidence from danish source separation pregrammes. *Int. J. Res. Mark.* **1994**, *11*, 145–163. [CrossRef]

46. Juvan, E.; Dolnicar, S. The attitude-behaviour gap in sustainable tourism. *Ann. Tour. Res.* **2014**, *48*, 76–95. [CrossRef]

47. Quimby, C.; Angelique, H. Identifying barriers and catalysts to fostering proenvironmental behaviour: Opportunities and challenges for community psychology. *Am. J. Community Psychol.* **2011**, *47*, 388–396. [CrossRef]

48. Hall, C.M.; Amelung, B.; Cohen, S.; Eijgelaar, E.; Gössling, S.; Higham, J.; Leemans, R.; Peeters, P.; Ram, Y.; Scott, D. On climate change skepticism and denial in tourism. *J. Sustain. Tour.* **2015**, *23*, 4–25. [CrossRef]

49. McCarty, J. A structural equation analysis of the relationships of personal values, attitudes and beliefs about recycling, and the recycling of the solid waste product. *J. Bus. Res.* **2000**, *36*, 41–52.

50. Young, R. Exploring the difference between recyclers and non recyclers: The role of information. *J. Environ. Syst.* **1988**, *18*, 341–351. [CrossRef]

51. Katz, D. The functional approach to the study of attitudes. *Public Opin. Q.* **1960**, *24*, 163–204. [CrossRef]

52. Grebosz-Krawczyk, M.; Siuda, D. Attitudes of young European consumers toward recycling campaigns of textile companies. *Autex Res. J.* **2019**, *19*, 394–399. [CrossRef]

53. Hines, J.; Hungerford, H.; Tamera, A. Analysis and synthesis of research on environmental behavior: A meta analysis. *J. Environ. Educ.* **1986**, *18*, 1–8. [CrossRef]

54. Steger, M.; Witt, S. Gender differences in environmental orientations: A comparison of publics and activists in Canada and the U.S. *West. Political Q.* **1988**, *42*, 627–649. [CrossRef]

55. Blocker, T.; Eckberg, D. Environmental issues as women's issues: General concerns and local hazards. *Soc. Sci. Q.* **1989**, *70*, 586–593.

56. Byrd, J.; Fulton, R.; Schutten, T.; Walsh, J. Recycling policy and implementation strategies for recycling. *Resour. Recycl.* **1989**, *8*, 34–36.

57. Baldassare, M.; Katz, C. The personal threat of environmental problems as predictor of environmental practices. *Environ. Behav.* **1992**, *24*, 602–616. [CrossRef]

58. Garcés, C.; Pedraja, M.; Rivera, P. Variables sociodemográficas determinantes del comportamiento ecológico de los españoles. In Proceedings of the VII Encuentro de Profesores Universitarios de Marketing, Barcelona, Spain, 1 September 1995.

59. Roberts, J. Green consumers in the 1990: Profile and implications for advertising. *J. Macromarketing* **1996**, *12*, 5–15. [CrossRef]

60. Arbuthnot, J. The roles of attitudinal and personality variables in prediction of environmental behavior and knowledge. *Environ. Behav.* **1977**, *9*, 217–232. [CrossRef]

61. Buttel, F. Age and environmental concern: A multivariate analysis. *Youth Soc.* **1979**, *10*, 237–256. [CrossRef]

62. Van Liere, K.; Dunlap, R. The social bases of environmental concern: A review of hypotheses, explanations and empirical evidence. *Public Opin. Q.* **1980**, *27*, 181–197. [CrossRef]

63. Leonard-Barton, D. Voluntary simplicity life styles and energy conservation. *J. Consum. Res.* **1981**, *8*, 246–252. [CrossRef]

64. Arbuthnot, J. Environmental knowledge and recycling behavior as a function of attitudes and personality characteristics. *Personal. Soc. Psychol. Bull.* **1974**, *1*, 119–121. [CrossRef]

65. Cummings, D. Voluntary strategies in the environmental movement: Recycling as cooptation. *J. Volunt. Action Res.* **1975**, *10*, 153–160.

66. McGuire, H. Recycling: Great expectations and garbage outcomes. *Am. Behav. Sci.* **1984**, *28*, 93–114. [CrossRef]

67. Sundeen, R. Explaining participation in the coproduction: A study of volunteers. *Soc. Sci. Q.* **1988**, *69*, 547–568.

68. Lansana, F. Distinguishsing potential recyclers from non recyclers: A basis for developing recycling strategies. *J. Environ. Educ.* **1992**, *23*, 16–23. [CrossRef]

69. Derksen, L.; Gartrell, J. The social context of recycling. *Am. Sociol. Rev.* **1993**, *58*, 434–442. [CrossRef]

70. Scholder, P. Do we know what we need to know? Objective and subjective knowledge effects on pro-ecological behaviors. *J. Bus. Res.* **1994**, *30*, 43–52.

71. Dietz, T.; Stern, P.; Guagnamo, G. Social structural and social psychological bases of environmental concern. *Environ. Behav.* **1998**, *30*, 450–471. [CrossRef]

72. Carrus, G.; Pasafaro, P.; Bonnes, M. Emotions, habits and rational choices in ecological behaviours: The case of recycling and use of public transportation. *J. Environ. Psychol.* **2008**, *28*, 51–62. [CrossRef]

73. McStay, J.; Dunlap, R. Male-female differences in concern for environmental quality. *Int. J. Women's Stud.* **1983**, *6*, 291–301.

74. Mohai, P. Public concern and elite involvement in environmental conservation issues. *Soc. Sci. Q.* **1984**, *66*, 820–838.

75. Mohai, P.; Twight, B. Age and environmentalism: An elaboration of Buttel model using national survey evidence. *Soc. Sci. Q.* **1987**, *68*, 798–815.

76. European Environment Agency. Waste Recycling. Available online: https://www.eea.europa.eu/data-and-maps/indicators/waste-recycling-1/assessment-1 (accessed on 22 November 2019).

77. Marsden, P. Memetics: A new paradigm for understanding customer behaviour and influence. *Mark. Intell. Plan.* **1998**, *16*, 363–368. [CrossRef]

78. Wiener, J.; Tabitha, A. Cooperation and expectations of cooperation. *J. Public Policy Mark.* **1994**, *13*, 259–270. [CrossRef]

79. Pieters, R.; Bijmolt, T.; Raaij, F.; Kruijk, M. Consumer's attibutions of proenvironmental behavior, motivation, and ability to self and others. *J. Public Policy Mark.* **1998**, *17*, 215–225. [CrossRef]

80. Hanson, J. A proposed paradigm for consumer product disposition processes. *J. Consum. Aff.* **1980**, *14*, 49–67. [CrossRef]

81. Durdan, C.; Reeder, G.; Hecht, P. Litter in a university cafeteria: Demographic data and the use of prompts as an intervention strategy. *Environ. Behav.* **1985**, *17*, 387–404. [CrossRef]

82. Pearce, D.; Turner, R. Market-based approaches to solid waste management. *Resour. Conserv. Recycl.* **1993**, *8*, 63–90. [CrossRef]

83. Read, A. A weekly doorstep recycling collection. I had no idea we could. Overcoming the local barriers to participation. *Resour. Conserv. Recycl.* **1999**, *26*, 217–249. [CrossRef]

84. Vining, J.; Ebreo, A. Whats makes a recycler? A comparison of recyclers and non recyclers. *Environ. Behav.* **1990**, *22*, 55–73. [CrossRef]

85. Folz, D. Recycling program design, management and participation: A national survey of municipal experience. *Public Adm. Rev.* **1991**, *51*, 222–231. [CrossRef]

86. Reid, H.; Luyben, D.; Rawers, J.; Bailey, S. Newspaper recycling behavior: The effects of prompting and proximity of containers. *Environ. Behav.* **1976**, *8*, 471–482. [CrossRef]

87. Kok, G.; Siero, S. Tin recycling: Awareness, comprehension, attitude, intention and behavior. *J. Econ. Psychol.* **1985**, *16*, 157–173. [CrossRef]

88. Porter, B.; Leeming, F.; Dwyer, W. Solid waste recovery. A review of behavioral programs to increase recycling. *Environ. Behav.* **1995**, *27*, 122–152. [CrossRef]

89. Everett, J.; Peirce, J. Social networks, socioeconomic status, and environmental collective action: Residential curbside block leader recycling. *J. Environ. Syst.* **1992**, *21*, 65–84. [CrossRef]

90. Miafodzyeva, S.; Brandt, N. Recycling behaviour among householders: Synthesizing determinants via a meta-analysis. *Waste Biomass Valor* **2013**, *4*, 221–235. [CrossRef]

91. Berger, I. The demographics of recycling and the structure of environmental behavior. *Environ. Behav.* **1997**, *29*, 515–531. [CrossRef]

92. Dahle, M.; Neumayer, E. Overcaming barriers to campus greening: A survey among higher educational institutions in London, UK. *Int. J. Sustain. High. Educ.* **2001**, *2*, 139–159. [CrossRef]

93. Hornik, J.; Cherian, J.; Madansky, M.; Narayana, C. Determinants of recycling behavior: A synthesis of research results. *J. Socio-Econ.* **1995**, *24*, 105–127. [CrossRef]

94. Williams, E. College students and recycling: Their attitudes and behaviors. *J. Coll. Stud. Dev.* **1991**, *32*, 86–88.

95. McCarty, J.; Shrum, J. The influence of individualism, collectivism, and locus of control on environmental beliefs and behavior. *J. Public Policy Mark.* **2001**, *20*, 93–105. [CrossRef]

96. Chen, M.; Tung, P. The moderating effect of perceived lack of facilities on consumers' recycling intentions. *Environ. Behav.* **2010**, *42*, 824–844. [CrossRef]

97. Cote, J.; McCullough, R. Effects of unexpected situations on behavior intention differences: A garbology analysis. *J. Consum. Res.* **1991**, *12*, 188–194. [CrossRef]

98. Wood, J. The challenge of multifamily recycling. *Resour. Recycl.* **1991**, *6*, 33–40.

99. López, M. Ecología y marketing. In Proceedings of the IV Encuentro de Profesores Universitarios de Marketing, Madrid, Spain, 1 September 1992.

100. Folz, D.; Hazlett, J. Public participation and recycling performance: Explaining program success. *Public Adm. Rev.* **1991**, *51*, 526–532. [CrossRef]

101. Tonglet, M.; Phillips, P.; Read, A. Using the theory of planned behaviour to investigate the determinants of recycling behaviour: A case study from Brixworth, U.K. *Resour. Conserv. Recycl.* **2004**, *41*, 191–214. [CrossRef]

102. Perrin, D.; Barton, J. Issues associated with transforming household attitudes and opinions into materials recovery: A review of two kerbside recycling schemes. *Resour. Conserv. Recycl.* **2001**, *33*, 61–74. [CrossRef]

103. Tonglet, M.; Phillips, P.; Bates, M. Determining the drivers for householder pro-environmental behaviour: Waste minimisation compared to recycling. *Resour. Conserv. Recycl.* **2004**, *42*, 27–48. [CrossRef]

104. Timlett, R.; Williams, I. The impact of transient populations on recycling behaviour in a densely populated urban environment. *Resour. Conserv. Recycl.* **2009**, *53*, 498–506. [CrossRef]

105. Prochaska, J.O.; Marcus, B.H. The transtheoretical model: Applications to exercise. In *Advances in Exercise Adherence*; Dishman, R.K., Ed.; Human Kinetics Publishers: Windsor, ON, Canada, 1994; pp. 161–180.

106. Pieters, R. Changing garbage disposal patterns of consumers: Motivation, ability and performance. *J. Public Policy Mark.* **1991**, *10*, 59–77. [CrossRef]

107. Kollmuss, A.; Agyeman, J. Mind the gap: Why do people act environmentally and what are the barriers to proenvironmental behaviour? *Environ. Educ. Res.* **2002**, *8*, 239–260. [CrossRef]

108. Thogersen, J. Recycling and morality: A critical review of the literature. *Environ. Behav.* **1996**, *28*, 536–558. [CrossRef]

109. Gobierno de Canarias. Tourist Arrivals. Historical Data: 2010–2019. Available online: https://turismodeislascanarias.com/sites/default/files/promotur_serie_frontur_1997-2019_en.pdf (accessed on 3 February 2020).

110. Gobierno de Canarias. Gran Canaria Tourist Accommodation Capacity. Historical Data (2004–2019). Available online: https://turismodeislascanarias.com/sites/default/files/promotur_plazas_alojativas_gran_canaria_2004-2019_en.pdf (accessed on 5 March 2020).

111. Gobierno de Canarias. Tourist Expenditure Survey (2019) Main Indicators by Island of Stay. Available online: https://turismodeislascanarias.com/sites/default/files/promotur_indicadores_egt_2019_en.pdf (accessed on 4 March 2020).

112. Gobierno de Canarias. Tourist Profile by Source Markets (2018). Gran Canaria: Main Source Markets. Available online: https://turismodeislascanarias.com/sites/default/files/promotur_gran_canaria_mercados_principales_2018_en.pdf (accessed on 29 November 2019).

113. Semenza, J.; Hall, D.; Wilson, D.; Bontempo, B.; Sailor, D.; George, L. Public perception of climate change. Voluntary mitigation and barriers to behaviour change. *Am. J. Prev. Med.* **2008**, *35*, 479–487. [CrossRef] [PubMed]

114. Wall, G. Barriers to individual environmental action: The influence of attitudes and social experiences. *Can. Rev. Sociol. Anthropol.* **1995**, *31*, 465–491. [CrossRef]

115. Young, R. Motivationg people to recycle: The use of incentives. *Resour. Recycl.* **1984**, *42*, 14–15.

116. Aguiar-Castillo, L.; Clavijo-Rodriguez, A.; Saa-Perez, P.; Perez-Jimenez, R. Gamification as an approach to promote tourist recycling behaviour. *Sustainability* **2019**, *11*, 2201. [CrossRef]

117. Aguiar-Castillo, L.; Rufo-Torres, J.; Saa-Perez, P.; Perez-Jimenez, R. How to encourage recycling behaviour? The case of WasteApp: A gamified mobile application. *Sustainability* **2018**, *10*, 1–20.

Article

Evaluation of the Reception Capacity of a Certain Area Regarding Tourist Housing, Addressing Sustainable-Tourism Criteria

Jose Antonio Fernández Gallardo [1,*], Jose María Caridad y Ocerín [2] and María Genoveva Millán Vázquez de la Torre [3]

[1] Department Agricultural Economics, Sociology, and Policy, Faculty of Economics and Business Sciences, University of Cordoba, 14002 Cordoba, Spain
[2] Department of Statistics and Econometrics, Faculty of Economics and Business Sciences, University of Cordoba, 14002 Cordoba, Spain; ccjm@uco.es
[3] Department of Quantitative Methods, Faculty of Economics and Business Sciences, Universidad Loyola Andalucia, 14004 Cordoba, Spain; gmillan@uloyola.es
* Correspondence: jose.fernandez@uco.es

Received: 18 September 2019; Accepted: 11 November 2019; Published: 15 November 2019

Abstract: The emergence of new 2.0 net collaborative economies has brought an increase in the number of tourists, changing the paradigm of the tourist-housing sector in the main cities around the world. This has directly impacted inhabitants and land-use planning, and there is no general agreement yet between different public and private agents on how to deal with the problem. In this document, a model supported by scientific approaches is presented to assist in planning for sustainable land use through assessing its reception capacity to host tourist housing. The area of study is a medium-sized city in Spain with four UNESCO World Heritage Sites. The methodology is based on the application of the multicriteria decision paradigm in the geographical information systems' field to deal with complex problems with several alternatives and various criteria to be evaluated. As a result, we obtained a classification of every part of the study area, depending on the reception capacity of the considered uses. The main conclusion is that tourist housing must be regulated, although its effects cannot be generalized, since specific analysis for every neighborhood in a territory is needed.

Keywords: real-estate market; tourist housing; territorial sustainability; sustainable tourism; multicriteria assessment; geographical information systems

---

1. Introduction

Tourist activity is one of the main sources of wealth in many areas. However, it also affects the environment, cultural resources, and the hosting population. Due to this, the World Tourism Organization (UNWTO) is urging different governments to consider sustainability as a global goal.

The emergence of new 2.0 net collaborative economies has brought about an increase in the number of travelers and the intensification of mass tourism, induced by a change in paradigm on the tourist-housing sector in major cities around the world, due to the proliferation of tourist housing.

There does not seem to be consensus on the definition of the collaborative-economy concept [1]; neither the European legal system nor that of each of the member states seems to be able to solve the problems that could arise from these new forms of business [2]. Hence, the European Commission decided to publish the "European Agenda for the collaborative economy" in which recommendations were directed to national legislators to adapt the regulations of the member states to the new needs of the emerging market for a collaborative economy. The European Commission [3] defines a collaborative economy as "Business models in which activities are facilitated through collaborative platforms that create an open market for the temporary use of goods or services often offered by individuals. In general, collaborative-economy transactions do not imply a change in ownership and can be done with or without profit". Within a collaborative economy, the services that have experienced the fastest growth have been those related to transport and accommodation, both being closely related to tourism. Regarding the accommodation sector, one can find modalities in which there is no compensation, such as "couch-surfing" or "warm showers" [4]; in others, such as "home-swapping" or "night-swapping", there is reciprocity between participants [5]. On the other hand, we find modalities in which monetary consideration is paid, which is the case with our study. This sector has already accounted for more than 50% of the total number of operations carried out in Europe in 2015 within the scope of the collaborative economy [6].

According to information provided by DataHippo [7], over 238,000 adverts on Airbnb, one of the most globally important collaborative-economy sites, colonizes cities and tourist areas around Spain. Madrid and Barcelona are at the top of the list, followed by accommodation adverted on the Mediterranean coastline and the Canary and Balearic archipelagos. This is a specialized market, where only 5% of property owners are professionals, and individuals with more than one property represent one-third of tourist-housing offers.

However, not all tourist increase has been positive in its entirety; there are critical movements of the recent tourist development and growth, which shows that this is a globally shared phenomenon. Some of these negative effects can be seen in issues such as Touristification and gentrification processes in Berlin [8,9], tensions due to socio-spatial transformations and touristification processes in the slums in Rio de Janeiro [10]; social unrest because of housing dispossession and the urban revalorization and touristification processes in Palma de Mallorca historical center [11]; the rising unrest and annoyance regarding the overcrowding and socio-spatial transformations in the center of Amsterdam [12,13]; the emergent mobilization related to the impact of tourism on Paris, especially regarding the proliferation of tourism housing [14]; the so-called Airbnb syndrome in Reykjavik [15]; the riots against cruises because of the increase in cruise passengers [16] and the consultative referendum held in Venice; the protests carried out by Hong Kong citizens against Chinese tourists [17]; and the emergence of people resisting the use of the land and local resources in Goa, India [18].

In many tourist destinations, the debate has focused on wider analysis of urban and political processes, and existing forces favor a growing "politicization from the grassroots" [19]. It should be noted that, in the tourist landscape, it is not only a matter of draining resources but also the rupture of necessary conditions for tourist activity to be satisfactory for all involved agents. Thus, every destination, depending on its particularities, products, and services, has to be assessed considering their capacity to bear tourist pressure [20].

One of the most significant cases is how tourist housing is affecting the prices of the real-estate market. In Spain, the average housing-rent price has increased by 18.6% in the last five years, between 2013 and 2018, Barcelona being the city with the highest increase (47.5%), followed by Madrid (38%), according to real-estate agency Fotocasa [21]. Moreover, five provinces, Baleares, Las Palmas, Salamanca, Barcelona, and Madrid, have already reached their historical maximum in 2018, exceeding the figures in 2007. Henceforth, although there are barely surveys to confirm it, many sectors relate this increase in rent prices to the proliferation of tourist housing, which is also said to be accelerating urban-gentrification processes.

As can be observed, the tourist-housing phenomenon is not free from controversy. There is confrontation between social and economic agents in the cities, since there is no global legal regulation regarding this phenomenon; in the case of Spain, autonomous communities and city councils are the responsible institutions for launching various regulatory initiatives.

The lack of a model regulating the tourist-housing phenomenon might involve serious risks. Before such a situation, deciding agents need to be provided with a tool that enables them to diagnose the situation, so that they can suggest initiatives to move towards a sustainable tourist model. It is necessary for them to analyze the concept of reception capacity that theoretically refers to the optimal use of land pursuant to its sustainability. Gómez and Gómez [22] defines it as "an area's degree of adequacy or capacity for a certain activity, bearing in mind both how the environment meets its locational requirements and the effects of that activity on the environment," outlining the contribution by Canter [23–25], Clark and Bisset [26], Rau and Wooten [27], Hollick [28], and Lee [29,30], among others. To study reception capacity, different authors have offered a scientific basis to techniques and procedures: Voogd [31], Janssens [32], Eastman et al. [33], Jankowski [34], Triantaphyllou [35], Roy [36], and Munda [37], and, in Spain, Romero [38], Barredo [39], Barba and Pomerol [40], Santos [41], Moreno [42,43], and Galacho and Arrebola [44]. In this sense, the bibliography highlighting multicriteria assessment techniques, combined with geographical information systems to evaluate an area's reception capacity on various topics, is extensive: Barredo and Bosque [45], Ocaña and Galacho [46], Bosque and Moreno [47], Gómez y Barredo [48], Molero et al. [49], Moreno and Buzai [50], and Galacho and Arrebola [44].

To face the issue of the development of tourist housing, the present work's objective is to offer a methodology supported by multicriteria decision methods in the field of geographical information systems, that enables us to assess tourist-housing reception capacity in Cordoba (Spain) based on tourist-sustainability criteria. Cordoba is a city with four UNESCO World Heritage Sites, with a great tourist claim, and with important threats and weaknesses regarding tourist housing according to a study carried out by the Council of Cordoba [51].

According to Galacho and Ocaña [46], "the advantage of the combined use of multicriteria decision methods and geographical information systems is the possibility of rigorously solving the interrelation between the different variables of the area". As a result, we obtained an information layer about the city's central district that classifies every neighborhood based on an assigned rating according to value judgments. These judgments were defined following the guidelines set by the World Tourism Organization regarding issues that must be considered when planning a destination under sustainability goals.

2. Materials and Methodology

To analyze the tourist-housing reception capacity of Cordoba, we used the analytic hierarchical process (AHP), developed by Tomas L. Saaty [52]. This is a tool to address the discrete multicriteria decision problems, consisting of different criteria and a certain number of alternatives, considering the opinions of all the agents that intervene in the decision. The problem is displayed on a hierarchical structure that indicates the objective, criteria, subcriteria, and corresponding alternatives to then calculate the influence of every factor that is part of the problem. The resulting choice is then justified since it is based on the obtained numerical results, favoring the transparency and objectivity of the process.

The chart below represents the phases of the analytic hierarchical process (see Figure 1).

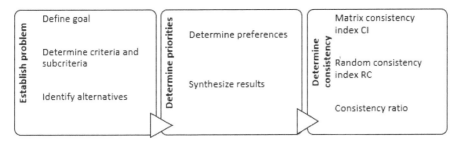

Figure 1. Phases of analytic hierarchical process. Source: Casañ [53].

2.1. Determining Criteria, Subcriteria, and Alternatives

According to the World Tourism Organization (UNTWO) [54], sustainable tourism is defined as the one that "meets the needs of present tourists and host regions while protecting and enhancing opportunities for the future. It is envisaged as leading to the management of all resources in such a way that economic, social, and aesthetic needs can be fulfilled while maintaining cultural integrity, essential ecological processes, biological diversity, and life-support systems". To measure the degree of sustainability, the OECD [55] distinguishes two approaches, the accounting and the analytical; in our study, we opted for the analytical since it provides adequate multidimensional evaluation as a local planning tool according to the objective of our research. This instrument, according to this approach, is given by "a set of indicators of sustainable tourism, understanding as such the measures that provide the necessary information to better understand the links and impact of tourism with respect to the cultural and natural environment in which it develops activity and on which it is widely dependent" [56]. Therefore, to obtain an analytical measure of sustainability, it is necessary to disaggregate the sustainable-tourism objective by identifying the aspects that constitute each dimension, and identifying the indicators that allow measuring each of the above aspects. To ensure that their values show progress towards a more sustainable state, indicators must meet the criteria of scientific validity, representativeness, relevance, reliability, sensitivity, predictive nature, understandability, comparability, quantification, cost efficiency, transparency, and geographical coverage [57]. Once the system was defined, we assigned the variables taking as reference specialized works that define sustainability indicators at the local level. Attending to the objective of our research and our area under study being the city of Cordoba (Spain), we took works as reference that defined a set of synthetic indicators of sustainable tourism for the tourist destinations of Andalusia (Spain): Blancas et al. [58]; Ávila et al. [59]; Dachary and Arnáiz [60]; Fullana and Ayuso [61]. For this, we developed a hierarchical structure with three levels (Figure 2). On the first level, the three main criteria (social, economic, and environmental dimension) are shown, each one defined based on new subcriteria corresponding to the second (13 subcriteria) and a third level (10 subcriteria), respectively. In the social dimension, issues related to the socio-cultural impact that tourist housing has on the environment, the resident population, and cultural heritage were collected; in the economic dimension, aspects related to tourism activity as economic activity and its viability are represented in the long term; finally, in the environmental-dimension criterion, aspects related to the protection and preservation of the environment, as well as the future viability of tourism, were considered.

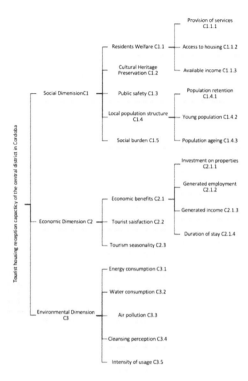

Figure 2. Chart of criteria, subcriteria, and alternative hierarchies. Source: Information compiled from Blancas et al. [58]; Gallego and Moniche [62]; Sancho and García [63]; Bowen and Valenzuela [64].

The criteria and subcriteria obtained from the three previously mentioned dimensions were used to value the alternatives in the different neighborhoods in the central district of Cordoba (Figure 2). These are the possible approaches to the problem, although the choice does not imply that the chosen alternative is optimal to solve it, but the best among all available possibilities to reach the goal [53].

2.2. Determining Preferences

To establish priorities, we needed to compare criteria, subcriteria, and alternatives in pairs. To do so, we made value judgments expressed numerically using Saaty's AHP fundamental scale [52]. This scale gives punctuations from 1 to 9, 1 being the same importance between two elements and 9 extreme importance of an element over the other. These value judgments were issued by a representation of different groups that are affected by the tourist-housing phenomenon, such as the public sector (public managers) and private sector (restaurant managers, taverns, souvenir shops, traditional commerce, resident residents, tourists, and neighborhood associations); through a total of 148 conducted interviews, nonprobabilistic sampling was carried out for convenience in the case of public officials, the private sector, and neighborhood associations, while for residents and tourists residents, simple random probabilistic sampling was followed. Subsequently, comparisons are represented through the paired-comparison matrix (Figure 3) that shows the dominant and dominated values. It is a square matrix $n \times n$, in which a_{ij}, numerically expresses the preference of an element in the i row when compared with an element of the j column, for $i= 1, 2, 3, \ldots n$ and $j= 1, 2, 3, \ldots n$; therefore, when $i = j$, the value of $a_{ij} = 1$, since the element is being compared to itself.

$$A = \begin{pmatrix} 1 & a_{12} & \cdots & a_{1n} \\ a_{21} & 1 & \cdots & a_{2n} \\ \vdots & \vdots & \vdots & \vdots \\ a_{n1} & a_{n2} & \vdots & 1 \end{pmatrix}$$

Figure 3. Paired-comparison matrix.

This matrix is based on four axioms [65]: reciprocity: $a_{ij} = 1/a_{ji}$; homogeneity, since all compared elements must belong to the same hierarchical level; dependence, which means that there must be hierarchical dependence between elements from two consecutive levels; and consistency, meaning that, when the paired-comparison matrix is perfectly consistent, the following is fulfilled: $a_{ij} = a_{ik}/a_{jk}$ for i, j and $k = 1, 2, 3 \ldots n$.

Hereafter, we used an approximation method to obtain priorities from judgments given in the comparison matrix $n \times n$. The first step was to procure the normalized matrix: we summed the values on every column and divided every box of the column by its summation:

$$C_j = \sum_{i=1}^{n} a_{ij} \; j = 1, 2, 3 \ldots n. \tag{1}$$

The normalized paired-comparison matrix is

$$N = \left\| n_{ij} = a_{ij}/c_j \right\| ij = 1, 2, 3 \ldots n. \tag{2}$$

Once we had the normalized matrix, we calculated the relative priority of each of the compared elements. We obtained an average value for every row in the normalized matrix, these values being

$$p_i = \frac{1}{n} \sum_{j=1}^{n} n_{ij}. \tag{3}$$

Since the hierarchy (Figure 2) is made of criteria and subcriteria, the three criteria's priorities were calculated according to the objective. Then, comparison matrices were made for each subcriterion, resulting in the relative priorities for each subcriterion on the second level. Those were multiplied by the corresponding criterion's priority to determine how it affects the objective. The process for the third-level subcriteria was the same. Afterward, to determine each alternative's priority, 20 relative comparisons matrices were made (corresponding to the 20 not-itemized subcriteria). Subsequently, aspects taken into account and data sources used for the pertinent survey are indicated (Table 1), and all of them properly georeferenced:

- Provision of services: sociocultural effects of the activity on the environment and the inhabitants of each neighborhood. This aspect was assessed, taking account of the provision of educational, sports, and health centers, financial and service-sector activity establishments, transport services, and pharmacies [58].
- Access to housing: evaluated according to the average price per square meter of the houses in each alternative [58].
- Available income: valued depending on the average net annual income per inhabitant in each area.
- Cultural-heritage preservation: assessed according to the number of protected sites appointed [58].
- Public safety: evaluated depending on crimes committed in each region.
- Population retention: valued according to the resident population in each area.
- Young population: assessed depending on population percentage aged less than or equal to 15 years old in the total of each region.
- Population aging: evaluation of population percentage aged more than or equal to 65 years old in the total of each area.
- Social burden: evaluates the imposition of a foreign culture on the inhabitants' culture, and it is valued according to the percentage of a foreign population over the total population in each region.

- Investment on properties: valued according to the average price per square meter of houses in each area.
- Generated employment: assessed depending on the percentage of the registered population in social security over the total population at working age (16–65 years old).
- Generated income: evaluated according to generated income by activity in the last year.
- Duration of stay: measurement of the effects that the activity has on the average duration of tourists stay in each region.
- Tourist satisfaction: measured according to the level of satisfaction declared by tourists in each area.
- Tourism seasonality: measured depending on the percentage of days that tourist housing is occupied in the last year.
- Energy consumption: measured according to the consumption of energy in each region.
- Water consumption: measured depending on the consumption of water in each area.
- Air pollution: evaluates acoustic contamination during the day, evening, and night, as well as polluting emissions sent to the atmosphere in each region.
- Cleansing perception: measured according to tourists' level of satisfaction regarding cleansing.
- Intensity of usage: measures the proportion of tourist housing over the total of built houses.

Table 1. Database used to evaluate each subcriterion.

Subcriterion	Data sources
Provision of services	Spatial reference data. Andalusia Statistics and Cartography Institute [66]
Access to housing	Database provided by the Idealista real-estate portal
Available income	Urban Audit indicators for submunicipal areas. Statistics National Institute [67]
Preservation of heritage	Spatial reference data. Andalusia Statistics and Cartography Institute [68]
Public safety	Personal interview with security officers from the Ministry of Internal Affairs
Population retention	250 × 250 m spatial data net from the Andalusian Statistics and Cartography Institute [69]
Young population	250 × 250 m spatial data net from the Andalusian Statistics and Cartography Institute [69]
Aging population	250 × 250 m spatial data net from the Andalusian Statistics and Cartography Institute [69]
Social burden	250 × 250 m spatial data net from the Andalusian Statistics and Cartography Institute [69]
Investment on properties	Database provided by the Idealista real estate portal
Generated employment	250 × 250 m spatial data net from the Andalusian Statistics and Cartography Institute [69]
Generated income	Database provided by www.airdna.co
Duration of stay	Database provided by www.airdna.co
Tourist satisfaction	Tourism and Sports Department from Andalusia Statistics [70]
Tourism seasonality	Database provided by www.airdna.co
Energy consumption	Personal interview with officers from ENDESA (National Electricity Company)
Water consumption	Personal interview with officers from EMACSA (Municipal Water Company)
Air pollution	Quality of air plan (Council of Cordoba) [71]
Noisy pollution	Noise strategic map (Council of Cordoba) [72]
Cleansing perception	Personal interview with officers from the SADECO company
Intensity of usage	Council of Cordoba [51]

Source: Own elaboration.

QGIS software was used for treating georeferenced information. It was necessary to apply a spatial-disaggregation technique for the following layers of information: population retention, young population, aging population, social burden, and generated employment. Those layers have a 250 × 250 m square polygon vector format, so when assigning data to the territory subject of study, some polygons were divided. To do so, the areal-interpolation technique was used: information about the distribution values of a variable from an origin layer for a certain territory (in this analysis, demographic spatial data in statistical enmeshes) was transferred to another layer of destiny information (territory subject of study) through their intersection. Then, the superficial proportion that each polygon on the origin layer had on the destiny layer was calculated to obtain the distribution of each variable in the new spatial units.

Afterward, we obtained each alternative's relative priority regarding the corresponding criterion or subcriterion; then, each alternative's general priority regarding the corresponding criterion or subcriterion was calculated by multiplying the relative priority by the compared criterion or subcriterion's general priority. Then, all priorities for each alternative were summed to obtain its priority regarding the objective [73]. Finally, the AHP allowed measuring the inconsistence of judgments through the consistency ratio, and they had to be revised and corrected. For 3 by 3 matrices, the value of the consistency ratio had to not be higher than 5%; in the case of 4 by 4 matrices, it would not exceed 9%; for all the other matrixes, it would be 10% or less [73]. The software used to carry out the analytic hierarchical process was Total Decision.

The result of the process is summarized in a layer of information that shows zoning of the studied area with a valuation assigned to every part of the territory depending on its capacity to accept the evaluated uses.

2.3. Implementation on Urban Area

The territory subject of study was Cordoba (Spain), a city whose four UNESCO World Heritage Sites have had increased mass tourism in the last few years, besides an unregulated increase in tourist accommodation. Out of the 10 total territorial districts that conform to the city of Cordoba, we chose the central district since it hosts the highest concentration of tourist housing, with 1456 tourist housing over a total of 24,457 built houses, that is, 5.95% [51]. Here (Figure 4), the distribution of tourist housing for each neighborhood in the central district is shown:

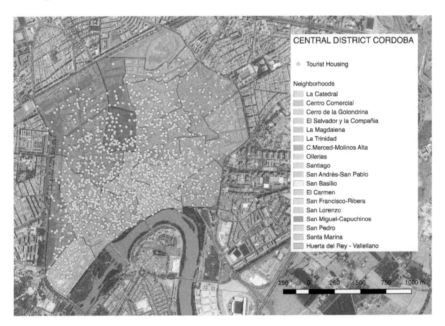

Figure 4. Tourist housing per neighborhood in the central-district map. Source: Own elaboration.

There are eight neighborhoods over the tourist-housing average (6.02%), such as the neighborhoods of La Catedral, San Francisco-Ribera, El Salvador y la Compañia, and San Pedro, which exceed 10% of tourist housing. There are also ten neighborhoods under the average, such as Cerro de la Golondrina, Ollerías, and El Carmen, which do not reach 1%.

According to a recent study carried out by the Council of Cordoba [51] on the effects that tourist housing has on the city of Córdoba, the city has the following threats and weaknesses: Regarding threats, there is a gradual loss of population and the substitution of residential use for other uses, weakening of traditional commerce, saturation of public spaces, and coexistence deterioration, detraction of housing from the rental market, and price increase, and deterioration of cultural tourism. With respect to weaknesses, there is a lack of knowledge about existing tourist homes and clandestinity in the activity of some caused due to the autonomous regulatory framework, the absence of municipal regulation of housing for tourism purposes, the existence of empty buildings, and dizzying growth in the supply of housing for tourism purposes.

3. Results

The obtained results regarding the criteria and subcriteria preferences are shown in Figure 5.

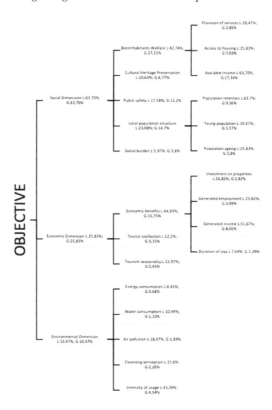

Figure 5. Criteria and subcriteria preferences. Source: Own elaboration.

Regarding the first-level criteria, the social dimension (with 63.7%) was the one with the highest weight in the model, followed by the economic dimension (25.83%) and the environmental dimension (10.47%). In the second level of subcriteria, the most important ones were residents' welfare (27.22%) and structure of the local population (14.7%), hierarchically dependent on the economic-dimension criterion. Regarding the third-level subcriteria, the most relevant were available income (17.03%), population retention (9.36%), and generated income (8.65%).

Regarding the areal-interpolation process (necessary for evaluating subcriteria through 250 × 250 m spatial-data enmeshes (Table 1)), the following results were obtained:

As can be seen in the image (Figure 6), many of the 250 × 250 m cells that contain information on several criteria were divided into one, two, and up to three neighborhoods. Then, it was necessary to calculate the portion corresponding to each one for its calculation. An example would be the evaluation of the population-maintenance subcriterion (Figure 7):

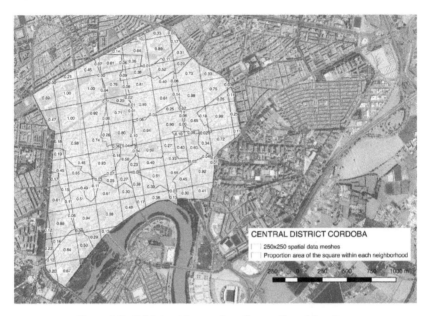

Figure 6. Spatial-data grid proportions. Source: Own elaboration.

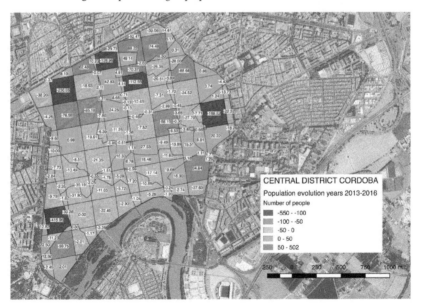

Figure 7. Variation of population in the central district of Cordoba. Source: Own elaboration.

In the central district, there has been a population decrease of 1679 people, with the highest decrease at the Centro Comercial (435 people) and the highest increase in the neighborhood of Santiago (73 people). In the figure, it can be seen that there was a decrease in population (in blue) of less than 50 people, with five areas exceeding 100 people in most enmeshes. Green colors correspond to areas where there has been a population increase (with values lower than 100 people).

The obtained results regarding the weight of the alternatives for each criterion and subcriterion are as follows (see Table 2):

Table 2. Relevant weights of alternatives for social-dimension subcriteria.

	Social Dimension	Residents' Welfare	Heritage Preservation	Public Safety	Population Structure	Population Retention	Social Burden
La Catedral	3.69%	4.25%	1.67%	5.26%	2.86%	2.38%	1.85%
San Francisco-Ribera	5.84%	5.68%	5.00%	5.26%	7.50%	7.14%	3.70%
El Salvador y La Compañía	5.05%	4.34%	5.00%	5.26%	6.56%	7.14%	3.70%
San Pedro	5.80%	5.40%	5.00%	3.51%	9.22%	9.52%	3.70%
La Trinidad	4.87%	5.11%	5.00%	5.26%	3.91%	4.76%	5.56%
San Basilio	5.14%	5.49%	3.33%	5.26%	4.64%	4.76%	7.41%
San Andrés-San Pablo	6.03%	6.07%	6.67%	7.02%	5.05%	4.76%	5.56%
San Miguel Capuchinos	5.21%	4.05%	6.67%	7.02%	5.22%	7.14%	5.56%
La Magdalena	5.87%	5.29%	5.00%	5.26%	7.90%	7.14%	5.56%
Santiago	6.46%	5.96%	3.33%	5.26%	10.94%	11.90%	1.85%
Santa Marina	4.74%	5.01%	5.00%	5.26%	3.53%	2.38%	5.56%
Huerta del Rey Vallellano	5.58%	5.88%	8.33%	7.02%	2.19%	2.38%	7.41%
Centro Comercial	4.74%	4.63%	5.00%	7.02%	2.86%	2.38%	5.56%
San Lorenzo	5.38%	5.87%	5.00%	5.26%	4.20%	2.38%	7.41%
C. Merced-Molinos Alta	6.00%	6.76%	8.33%	5.26%	3.70%	4.76%	7.41%
Cerro de la Golondrina	5.12%	5.01%	6.67%	5.26%	3.93%	2.38%	7.41%
Ollerías	6.47%	7.13%	8.33%	5.26%	5.05%	4.76%	7.41%
El Carmen	8.01%	8.09%	6.67%	5.26%	10.74%	11.90%	7.41%

Source: Own elaboration.

In the social-dimension criterion (Table 2), certain values exceeded 9%, the population-retention subcriterion having the highest value (11.90%), which corresponds to Santiago and El Carmen, respectively. On the other hand, the heritage-conservation subcriterion had the lowest score to the alternative La Catedral. Within the social dimension, the Santiago and El Carmen neighborhoods corresponded, respectively, to the highest scores, while La Catedral, San Miguel Capuchinos, Huerta del Rey Vallellano, and C. Merced-Molinos Alta had the lowest scores.

Regarding the economic-dimension criterion, alternatives La Catedral and Centro Comercial stood out as high values, while C. Merced-Molino Alta stood out as the alternative with the lowest scores (Table 3).

The environmental-dimension criterion (Table 4) includes the air-pollution subcriterion, which was over 9% in five values in alternatives El Salvador y La Compañía, San Pedro, San Andrés-San Pablo, La Magdalena, and Santa Marina.

Table 3. Relevant weights of alternatives for economic-dimension subcriteria.

	Economic Dimension	Economic Benefits	Generated Income	Tourist Satisfaction	Tourism Seasonality
La Catedral	8.99%	9.25%	10.64%	7.14%	9.26%
San Francisco-Ribera	4.61%	4.79%	6.38%	5.36%	3.70%
El Salvador y La Compañía	5.21%	5.71%	6.38%	5.36%	3.70%
San Pedro	7.56%	8.03%	10.64%	5.36%	7.41%
La Trinidad	6.49%	7.03%	6.38%	5.36%	5.56%
San Basilio	5.26%	5.45%	4.26%	7.14%	3.70%
San Andrés-San Pablo	6.98%	6.47%	8.51%	5.36%	9.26%
San Miguel Capuchinos	5.45%	6.09%	4.26%	5.36%	3.70%
La Magdalena	4.99%	4.71%	4.26%	5.36%	5.56%
Santiago	4.41%	3.82%	4.26%	5.36%	5.56%
Santa Marina	6.23%	5.98%	6.38%	5.36%	7.41%
Huerta del Rey Vallellano	5.71%	5.18%	4.26%	5.36%	7.41%
Centro Comercial	7.50%	9.25%	10.64%	5.36%	3.70%
San Lorenzo	4.47%	4.57%	4.26%	5.36%	3.70%
C. Merced-Molinos Alta	3.75%	4.12%	2.13%	5.36%	1.85%
Cerro de la Golondrina	3.76%	3.47%	2.13%	5.36%	3.70%
Ollerías	4.34%	3.06%	2.13%	5.36%	7.41%
El Carmen	4.30%	3.01%	2.13%	5.36%	7.41%

Source: Own elaboration.

Table 4. Relevant weights of alternatives for environmental-dimension subcriteria.

	Environmental Dimension	Energy Consumption	Water Consumption	Air Pollution	Cleansing Perception	Usage Intensity
La Catedral	3.73%	3.77%	3.77%	7.55%	5.08%	1.45%
San Francisco-Ribera	3.37%	5.66%	5.66%	3.77%	5.08%	1.45%
El Salvador y La Compañía	5.02%	5.66%	5.66%	9.43%	5.08%	2.90%
San Pedro	5.02%	5.66%	5.66%	9.43%	5.08%	2.90%
La Trinidad	4.63%	5.66%	5.66%	3.77%	5.08%	4.35%
San Basilio	5.62%	5.66%	5.66%	3.77%	6.78%	5.80%
San Andrés - San Pablo	6.64%	5.66%	5.66%	9.43%	6.78%	5.80%
San Miguel Capuchinos	5.96%	5.66%	5.66%	5.66%	6.78%	5.80%
La Magdalena	6.28%	5.66%	5.66%	9.43%	5.08%	5.80%
Santiago	5.25%	5.66%	5.66%	3.77%	5.08%	5.80%
Santa Marina	7.27%	5.66%	5.66%	9.43%	6.78%	7.25%
Huerta del Rey Vallellano	5.93%	3.77%	3.77%	3.77%	6.78%	7.25%
Centro Comercial	5.22%	3.77%	3.77%	1.89%	5.08%	7.25%
San Lorenzo	5.88%	5.66%	5.66%	3.77%	5.08%	7.25%
C. Merced-Molinos Alta	6.20%	7.55%	7.55%	3.77%	5.08%	7.25%
Cerro de la Golondrina	5.56%	3.77%	3.77%	3.77%	5.08%	7.25%
Ollerías	6.20%	7.55%	7.55%	3.77%	5.08%	7.25%
El Carmen	6.20%	7.55%	7.55%	3.77%	5.08%	7.25%

Source: Own elaboration.

The final results for each alternative are shown in Figure 8.

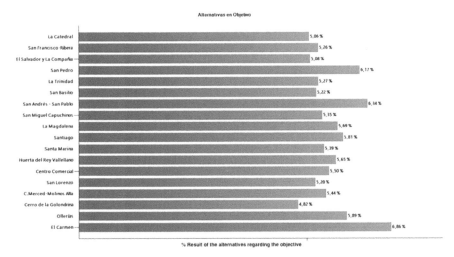

Figure 8. Results of alternative evaluation. Source: Own elaboration.

The global inconsistency of the model is 4.69%, with no paired-comparison matrices showing ratios higher than 10%. The highest value corresponds to the social-dimension matrix, with a ratio of 6.72%.

Here, the information layer of the global model for each alternative is shown (Figure 9). The neighborhoods are categorized by colors depending on their tourist-housing reception capacity.

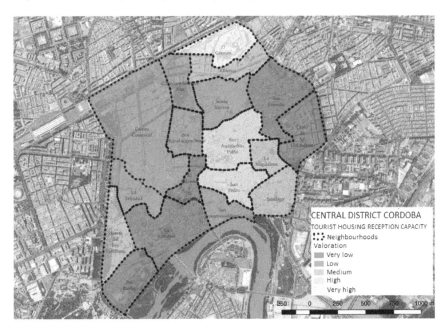

Figure 9. Information layer about the evaluation of tourist-housing reception capacity. Source: Own elaboration.

The El Carmen neighborhood was the only one with reception capacity classified as "very high", followed by San Andrés-San Pablo and San Pedro, which showed "high" reception capacity. On the other hand, San Lorenzo, Cerro de la Golondrina, El Salvador y La Compañía, San Basilio, and La Catedral had the worst reception capacity.

To reinforce the survey, a sensitivity analysis was carried out to determine the variation in the selection of alternatives when the relative importance of criteria and subcriteria changes. Here, obtained results from sensitivity analysis, applied to the three main criteria of alternatives Barrio del Carmen and La Catedral, are displayed:

As can be seen in the image (Figure 10), the vertical red line represents the starting point, and it can be moved towards the right or left depending on what we mean to simulate (right for an increase, left for a decrease) regarding the preference of the social dimension with respect to the objective. That can check the evaluation of alternatives for each case: If the red line moves towards the black (10%), alternative La Catedral (7.09%) would receive better evaluation than El Carmen (5.17%).

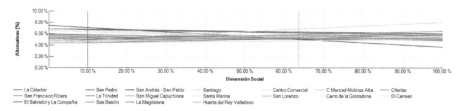

Figure 10. Sensitivity analysis of social dimension. Source: Own elaboration.

In the case of the economic dimension (Figure 11), the evaluation of the alternatives changes when moving from the red line's value (25.83%) to the black one's (80%), La Catedral being the best valued (7.93%), while El Carmen would obtain 5%.

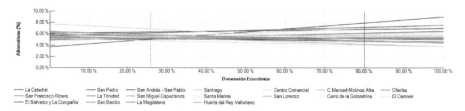

Figure 11. Sensitivity analysis of economic dimension. Source: Own elaboration.

Regarding the environmental-dimension criterion (Figure 12), when moving from the initial 10.56% to 80%, the best-valued alternative would be El Carmen (6.35%), while La Catedral would have 4.03%.

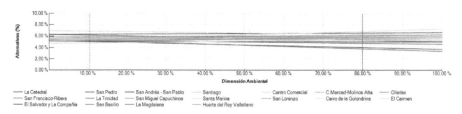

Figure 12. Sensitivity analysis of environmental dimension. Source: Own elaboration.

4. Discussion

The emergence of new 2.0 net collaborative economies has brought along a change in paradigm in the tourist-accommodation sector in the major cities of the world due to the proliferation of tourist housing. According to surveys by Guillen and Iñiguez [74], there is certain opacity in the market besides a phenomenon that is causing gentrification processes in the main cities of the world. It also has a strong impact on real-estate market prices, with subsequent implications on cities' territorial sustainability. Thus, tourist housing is a complex problem for administrations, since there are conflicting interests among the different economic and social agents in these cities. Multicriteria assessment techniques, applied with geographical information systems, are a good tool that helps in the decision-making process regarding problems where there are different agents and criteria to take into account intervening. Surveys, such as the one carried out by Dredge et al. [75], support this investigation.

The concept of "reception capacity", which theoretically refers to the optimal usage of territory for its sustainability, is adequate for evaluating the loading capacity that every territory has. This is done based on guidelines provided by the World Tourism Organization regarding issues to consider when planning a destination under sustainability objectives.

The city of Cordoba has an unequal tourist-housing occupation in each geographical area, similarly to the obtained results for Madrid [76]. The central district, having 5.85% tourist housing over the total of built houses, is the one with the highest percentage, and it is composed of neighborhoods with unequal data, ranging from 17.14% (La Catedral) to 0.11% (El Carmen). This is the reason why it is not possible to generalize when talking about positive or negative effects since analysis for every neighborhood is necessary.

The results of our model conclude that the alternative neighborhood of El Carmen was the one that had the highest score, mainly due to the greater relative weight that decision-makers gave to the social-dimension criterion over the two other main criteria, economic dimension and environmental dimension, respectively. There are up to a total of five neighborhoods (La Catedral, San Basilio, El Salvador and La Compañía, San Lorenzo, and Cerro de la Golondrina) that have a very low reception capacity caused by different reasons. The Barrio de la Catedral is greatly influenced by the very low score of the subcriteria that form the social dimension, mainly due to population loss. Instead, it has a very good valuation in the economic-dimension subcriteria since having a greater number of tourist homes increases the income of owners as well as that of adjoining businesses.

Sensitivity analysis (Figures 10–12) allowed the simulation of what the score of each neighborhood would be if the relative importance of the different criteria and subcriteria changes; it is a very valuable tool for political leaders when it comes to taking decisions since it allows the continuous monitoring of neighborhood classification according to their more or less relative importance to each criterion. An example is the case of the La Catedral neighborhood, whose valuation increased as the relative importance of the economic-dimension criterion with respect to the social-dimension criterion increased.

The results obtained about the variation of population indicate that there are neighborhoods where, even though there are high percentages of tourist housing, there is no population exodus, such as the San Pedro neighborhood (Table 2). Likewise, the neighborhoods with the greatest population decline, such as the Centro Comercial and Huerta del Rey Vallellano, do not have the highest percentages of tourist housing, but instead, they do have a higher percentage of the population over 65 years of age with 26.28% and 30%, respectively. Therefore, it can be concluded that the neighborhoods that tend to lose population are those with the highest percentages of population over 65 years. These results contradict the studies that state that tourist housing causes depopulation in a generalized manner, and, according to them, a diagnosis of the demographic situation of each territory under study should be established. These conclusions are very important for public administrations responsible for deciding on tourism management, due to the impact it can have on the territorial development of any city.

Tourist housing is a tourism modality in expansion that must be regulated and cohabit with traditional offers. To do so, specific legislation is necessary to analyze each district's burden capacity based on surveys, such as the one planned for the central district of Cordoba. Analyses such as these provide a better answer to tourist-accommodation offers and demand cohabitation, which would make tourist housing sustainable and integrate it into the local economy. Therefore, the present work

Sustainability **2019**, *11*, 6422

provides a valuable tool to public councilors of different cities with a tourist tradition to help them make decisions regarding the regulation of tourist housing. It is very useful for the political leaders and social agents of Córdoba since it allows decisions about permissiveness in areas where tourist housing can be beneficial for society as a whole or nonpermissiveness in areas where saturation exists and causes negative effects.

The tool presents some weaknesses, such as the need for large up-to-date information flows of a large number of georeferenced qualitative and quantitative variables.

Author Contributions: The authors are contributed each part of a paper by conceptualization. J.A.F.G.: introduction, theoretical framework, methodology, results, discussion, writing original draft preparation, writing review and editing; J.M.C.y.O.: methodology and supervision; M.G.M.V.d.l.T.: methodology, results, discussion and supervision.

Funding: This research received no external funding.

Conflicts of Interest: The authors declare no conflict of interest.

References

1. García, M.F.; del Moral-Espín, L. The hacker ethic vs netarchical capitalism free software and peer production within collaborative economic practices in Andalusia. *Teknokultura* **2016**, *13*, 141–168.

2. Montoro, L.G. *European Agenda for the Collaborative Economy*; Castilla la Mancha University: Ciudad Real, Spain, 2016.

3. European Comissión. Communication from the commission to the european parliament. To the council, the european economic and social committee and the committee of the regions. In *A European Agenda for the Collaborative Economy*; European Comissión: Brussels, Belgium, 2016.

4. Jarne, P. Collaborative consumption in Spain: Relevant experiences and future challenges. *Rev. CESCO Derecho Consum.* **2016**, *17*, 62–75.

5. Andriotis, K.; Agiomirgianakis, G. Market escape through exchange: Home swap as a form of non-commercial hospitality. *Curr. Issues Tour.* **2014**, *17*, 576–591. [CrossRef]

6. Vaughan, R.; Daverio, R. *Assessing the Size and Presence of the Collaborative Economy in Europe*; Publications Office of the European Union: Brussels, Belgium, 2016.

7. DataHippo. 2018. Available online: http://datahippo.org/es/ (accessed on 27 May 2019).

8. Füller, H.; Michel, B. Stop being a tourist! New dynamics of urban tourism in Berlin-Kreuzberg. *Int. J. Urban Reg. Res.* **2014**, *38*, 1304–1318. [CrossRef]

9. Novy, J. The selling (out) of Berlin and the de-and re-politicization of urban tourism in Europe´s 'Capital of Cool'. In *Protest and Resistance in the Tourist City*; Colomb, C., Novy, J., Eds.; Routledge: Abingdon, UK, 2016; pp. 52–72.

10. Broudehoux, A.M. Favela tourism: Negotiating visitors, socio-economic benefits, image and representation in pre-Olympics Rio de Janeiro. In *Protest and Resistance in the Tourist City*; Colomb, C., Novy, J., Eds.; Routledge: Abingdon, UK, 2016; pp. 191–209.

11. Vives-Miró, S.; Rullan, O. Housing dispossession due to tourism? Revaluation and travel in the historic center of Palma (Mallorca). *Rev. Geogr. Norte Gd.* **2017**, *71*, 53–71. [CrossRef]

12. Gerritsma, R.; Vork, J. Amsterdam residents and their attitude towards tourists and tourism. *Coactivity Philos. Commun.* **2017**, *25*, 85–98. [CrossRef]

13. Pinkster, F.M.; Boterman, W.R. When the spell is broken: Gentrification, urban tourism and privileged discontent in the Amsterdam canal district. *Cult. Geogr.* **2017**, *24*, 457–472. [CrossRef]

14. Gravari-Barbas, M.; Jacquot, S. No conflict? Discourses and management of tourism related tensions in Paris. In *Protest and Resistance in the Tourist City*; Colomb, C., Novy, J., Eds.; Routledge: Abingdon, UK, 2016; pp. 31–51.

15. Mermet, A.-C. Airbnb and tourism gentrification. In *Tourism and Gentrification in Contemporary Metropolises*; Routledge: Abingdon, UK, 2017; pp. 52–74.

16. Vianello, M. The No Grandi Navi campaign: Protests against cruise tourism in Venice. In *Protest and Resistance in the Tourist City*; Colomb, C., Novy, J., Eds.; Routledge: Abingdon, UK, 2016; pp. 171–190.

17. Garrett, D. Contesting China's tourism wave: Identity politics, protest and the rise of the Hongkonger city state movement. In *Protest and Resistance in the Tourist City*; Colomb, C., Novy, J., Eds.; Routledge: Abingdon, UK, 2016; pp. 107–128.

18. Sampat, P. The 'Goan Impasse': Land rights and resistance to SEZs in Goa, India. *J. Peasant Stud.* **2015**, *42*, 765–790. [CrossRef]

19. Novy, J.; Colomb, C. Urban tourism and its discontents: An introduction. In *Protest and Resistance in the Tourist City*; Colomb, C., Novy, J., Eds.; Routledge: Abingdon, UK, 2016; pp. 1–30.

20. Nogués-Pedregal, A.M.; Travé-Molero, R.; Carmona-Zubiri, D. Thinking against "empty shells" in tourism development projects. *Etnoloska Trib.* **2017**, *47*, 88–108. [CrossRef]

21. Lopez, S. Spain Speculates Again with Housing. Available online: https://elpais.com/economia/2018/08/30/actualidad/1535643025_269129.html (accessed on 2 September 2018).

22. Gomez Orea, D.; Gomez Villarino, M.T. *Environmental Impact Assessment*; Eds. Mundi-Prensa: Madrid, Spain, 2013.

23. Canter, L.W. *Environmental Impact Assessment*; McGraw-Hill: New York, NY, USA, 1977.

24. Canter, L.W.; Hill, L.G. *Handbook of Variables for Environmental Impact Assessment*; Ann Arbor Science Publishers, Inc.: Ann Arbor, MI, USA, 1979.

25. Canter, L.W. *Environmental Impact Assessment*; McGraw-Hill: New York, NY, USA, 1996.

26. Clark, B.D.; Chapman, K.; Bisset, R.; Wathern, P. Methods of environmental impact analysis. *Built Environ.* **1978**, *4*, 111–121.

27. Rau, J.G.; Wooten, D.C. *Environmental Impact Analysis Handbook*; MacGraw Hill: New York, NY, USA, 1980.

28. Hollick, M. The role of quantitative decision-making methods in environmental impact assessment. *J. Environ. Manag.* **1981**, *12*, 65–78.

29. Lee, N. The future development of environmental impact assessment. *J. Environ. Manag.* **1982**, *14*, 71–90.

30. Lee, N. Environmental impact assessment: A review. *Appl. Geogr.* **1983**, *3*, 5–27. [CrossRef]

31. Voogd, J.H. *Multicriteria Evaluation for Urban and Regional Planning*; Pion London: London, UK, 1982.

32. Janssen, R. *A Multiobjective Decision Support System for Environmental Problems*; Springer: Berlin, Germany, 1992; pp. 107–125.

33. Eastman, R.J. *Explorations in Geographic Information Systems Technology: GIS and Decision Making*; United Nations Institute for Training and Research: Geneva, Switzerland, 1993.

34. Jankowski, P. Integrating geographical information systems and multiple criteria decision-making methods. *Int. J. Geogr. Inf. Syst.* **1995**, *9*, 251–273. [CrossRef]

35. Triantaphyllou, E. *Multi-Criteria Decision Making Methods*; Springer: Berlin, Germany, 2000; pp. 5–21.

36. Roy, B.; Garcia, B.A. *Multicriteria Decision Support Methodology*; Torculo Editions: Santiago de Compostela, Spain, 2007.

37. Munda, G. *Social Multi-Criteria Evaluation for a Sustainable Economy*; Springer: Berlin, Germany, 2008.

38. Romero, C. *Multicriteria Decision Theory: Concepts, Techniques and Applications*; Editorial Alliance: Madrid, Spain, 1993.

39. Barredo Cano, J.I. *Geographic Information Systems and Multicriteria Evaluation in the Territory Order*; Ra-Ma: Madrid, Spain, 1996.

40. Romero, S.B.; Pomerol, J.-C. *Multicriteria Decisions: Theoretical Foundations and Practical Use*; Alcala de Henares University: Madrid, Spain, 1997.

41. Santos, J.M. The multiobjective/multicriteria theoretical approach and its application to the resolution of environmental and territorial problems, by means of GIS. *Sp. Time Form. Ser. VI Geogr.* **1997**, *10*, 129–155.

42. Moreno Jimenez, J.M.; Escobar Urmeneta, M.T. Regret in the hierarchical analytical process. *Appl. Econ. Stud.* **2000**, *14*, 95–115.

43. Moreno, J.M. The analytic hierarchy process (AHP). Fundamentals, methodology and applications. *ASEPUMA Electron. Commun. Work. Mag.* **2002**, *1*, 21–53.

44. Jimenez, F.B.G.; Castaño, J.A.A. Model for assessing the capacity to receive the territory with GIS and multicriteria decision techniques regarding the implementation of buildings in rural areas. *Geogr. Investig.* **2013**, *60*, 69–85.

45. Barrero, J.; Sendra, J.B. Integration of multicriteria evaluation and geographic information systems for the evaluation of the reception capacity of the territory and allocation of land uses. In *IV Spanish Congress of Geographic Information Systems*; AESIG: Madrid, Spain, 1995; pp. 191–200.

46. Galacho, F.B.; Ocaña, C. Treatment with GIS and Multicriteria Evaluation Techniques of the territory's reception capacity for urban uses. *Access Spat. Inf. New Geogr. Technol.* **2006**, *1*, 1509–1526.

47. Sendra, J.B.; Jimenez, A.M. *Geographic Information Systems and Optimal Location of Facilities and Equipment*; Ra-Ma: Madrid, Spain, 2004.

48. Gomez, M.; Barredo, J.I. *Geographic Information Systems and Multicriteria Evaluation in Land Management*; Ra-Ma Editorial: Madrid, Spain, 2005.

49. Molero, E.; Grindlay, A.; Asensio, J.A. Scenarios of aptitude and cartographic modeling of urban growth through multicriteria evaluation techniques. *Geofocus Int. J. Geogr. Inf. Sci. Technol.* **2007**, *7*, 120–147.

50. Moreno, A.; Buzai, G. *Analysis and Planning of Collective Services with Geographic Information Systems*; Autonomous University of Madrid: Madrid, Spain, 2008.

51. Council of Cordoba. *Study on the Dimensioning of the Offer of Housing with Existing Tourist Purposes in the City of Cordoba, Proposal for Management Measures and Situation Communication Strategy*; Council of Cordoba: Cordoba, Spain, 2019.

52. Saaty, T. *The Analytic Hierarchy Process*; Mc Gran Hill: New York, NY, USA, 1980.

53. Casañ, A. *The Multi-Criteria Decision, Application in the Selection of Competitive Offers in Building*; Valencia University: Valencia, Spain, 2013.

54. UNTWO. *Tourism the Year 2000 and Beyond Qualitative Aspects*; UNTWO: Madrid, Spain, 1993.

55. Organisation for Economic Co-operation and Development. *Frameworks to Measure Sustainable Development: An OECD Expert Workshop*; OECD Publishing: Paris, France, 2000.

56. Manning, E.; Clifford, G.; Dougherty, D.; Ernst, M. *What Every Tourist Manager Should Know. Practical Guide for the Development and Use of Sustainable Tourism Indicators*; OMT: Madrid, Spain, 1997.

57. Romero, E. *The Assessment of Sustainable Development. A Methodological Proposal*; Edn. Andalucía Ecológica Medio Ambiente: Sevilla, Spain, 2003; ISBN 84-607-8913-6.

58. Peral, F.J.B.; Lozano, M.G.; Casas, F.M.G.; Lozano-Oyola, M. Synthetic indicators of sustainable tourism: An application for tourist destinations in Andalusia. *Rect ASEPUMA Electron. Commun. Work. Mag.* **2010**, *11*, 85–118.

59. Avila, R.; Iniesta, A.; Herrero, D.; Aguierre, G.; Guereña, A.; Giraldo, A. Sustainable Tourism. In *International Problems Collection*; EIPALA: Madrid, Spain, 2002.

60. Dachary, A.; Arnáiz, S. *Globalization, Tourism and Sustainability*; University of Guadalajara: Puerto Vallarta, Mexico, 2002.

61. Fullana, P.; Ayuso, S. *Sustainable Tourism*; Rubes: Barcelona, Spain, 2002.

62. Gallego, I.; Moniche, A. System of territorial indicators for a tourist destination. *Enzo Paci. Pap. Meas. Econ. Significance Tour.* **2005**, *5*, 259–279.

63. Sancho, A.; Garcia, G. What does an indicator indicate? Comparative analysis in tourist destinations. *Tour. Anal. Mag.* **2006**, *2*, 69–85.

64. Bowen, S.; Valenzuela, A. Geographical indications, terroir, and socioeconomic and ecological sustainability: The case of tequila. *J. Rural Stud.* **2009**, *25*, 108–119. [CrossRef]

65. Toskano, G. *The Hierarchical Analytical Process (AHP) as a Tool in Decision Making in the Selection of Suppliers: Application in the Selection of the Supplier for the Graphic Company MYE S.R.L*; UNMSM: Lima, Peru, 2005.

66. Andalusia Statistics and Cartography Institute. Services. Spatial Reference Data. 2019. Available online: http://www.juntadeandalucia.es/institutodeestadisticaycartografia/DERA/g12.htm (accessed on 10 May 2019).

67. Statistics National Institute. Urban Audit Indicators for Submunicipal Áreas. 2019. Available online: https://www.ine.es/jaxiT3/Tabla.htm?t=30140 (accessed on 11 May 2019).

68. Andalusia Statistics and Cartography Institute. Heritage. Spatial Reference Data. 2019. Available online: http://www.juntadeandalucia.es/institutodeestadisticaycartografia/DERA/g11.htm (accessed on 10 May 2019).

69. Andalusia Statistics and Cartography Institute. Population. Spatial Reference Data. 2019. Available online: http://www.juntadeandalucia.es/institutodeestadisticaycartografia/distribucionpob/index.htm (accessed on 10 May 2019).

70. Tourism and Sports Department from Andalusia Statistics. Tourist satisfaction. 2019. Available online: http://www.juntadeandalucia.es/turismoydeporte/opencms/estadisticas-consejeria/estadisticas-de-turismo/index.html (accessed on 10 May 2019).

71. Council of Cordoba. *Local Improvement Plan of Air Quality of the Aglomeration Urban of Cordoba*; Council of Cordoba: Cordoba, Spain, 2017.

72. Council of Cordoba. *Strategic Map of Noise of Cordoba*; Council of Cordoba: Cordoba, Spain, 2016.

73. Saaty, T. *Toma de Decisiones Para Líderes: El Proceso Analítico Jerárquico: La Toma de Decisiones en un Mundo Complejo*; RWS Publications: Pittsburgh, Pennsylvania, 1997.

74. Navarro, N.A.G.; Berrozpe, T.I. Public action and collaborative consumption. Regulation of tourist dwellings in the p2p context. *Pasos* **2016**, *14*, 751–768.

75. Dredge, D.; Gyimóthy, S.; Birkbak, A.; Jensen, T.E.; Madsen, A. *The Impact of Regulatory Approaches Targeting Collaborative Economy in the Tourism Accommodation Sector: Barcelona, Berlin, Amsterdam and Paris*; Aalborg University: Copenhagen, Denmark, 2016.

76. Red2Red Consultores. *Analysis of the Impact of Tourist Dwellings in the Downtown District*; Red2Red Consultores: Madrid, Spain, 2017.

Article

Internet's User Perception of Corporate Social Responsibility in Hotel Services

Alejandro García-Pozo [1], José Mondéjar-Jiménez [2] and José Luis Sánchez-Ollero [1,*]

[1] Department of Applied Economics, University of Malaga, 29071 Malaga, Spain; alegarcia@uma.es
[2] Department of Applied Economics, University of Castile La Mancha, 16002 Cuenca, Spain; jose.mondejar@uclm.es
* Correspondence: jlsanchez@uma.es; Tel.: +34952137315

Received: 19 April 2019; Accepted: 20 May 2019; Published: 22 May 2019

Abstract: The objective of this study was to use the perceptions of internet users to analyse the effect of the social, economic and environmental dimensions of corporate social responsibility (CSR) implemented by hotel establishments in order to determine whether those dimensions are perceived by consumers. Our analysis was based on a sample, distributed by age, sex and province segments, obtained from the Andalusian population between 16 and 74 years of age who are users of travel websites (e.g., TripAdvisor, Booking) and hotels corporate websites. A questionnaire was used to investigate each latent factor related to the three main dimensions of CSR that may affect the perceptions of accommodation service consumers. The questionnaire was statistically validated and developed in previous economic studies in this field. The data were analysed using Partial Last Square (PLS) methodology. The results confirm the validity of the three dimensions analysed, although consumers appear to play more relevance upon economic and environmental factors than upon the social components of CSR.

Keywords: corporate social responsibility; economic; environmental and social responsibility; Internet; hotel services; Spain

---

1. Introduction

The starting point for the modern analysis of CSR in the scientific literature was the publication in 1953 of Howard Bowen's book Social Responsibilities of the Businessman [1]. Bowen provided a new paradigm for obtaining business results that took into account the benefits to the community in which the company was based, but he did not provide a definition of the concept. Since Bowen, several institutions and firms have tried to define it, but no uniform definition of CSR exists to date [2].

Among these public institutions, and in relation to the geographic and social environment in which our analysis is framed, the European Commission has indicated the way forward for companies by noting that they must fully assume their social responsibilities and, in line with their network of relationships, they must establish a process designed to integrate social, environmental and ethical concerns into their business operations. For the European Commission, this triple field of action (i.e. social, environmental, and ethical) forms the basis for companies and institutions to take action. Following the EC suggestions, some European countries (e.g., Italy) have introduced ethical dimensions in some sectors into their legal systems [3].

However, from the companies' point of view, the economical dimension is more important than the ethical one; the basis of the CSR used to be the social, environmental and economical dimension. In this sense, the Financial Times defines CSR as *"a business approach that contributes to sustainable development by delivering economic, social and environmental benefits for all stakeholders"*.

Traditionally, companies have been considered as having a negative effect on all three aspects, particularly the environment, but now they are expected to have a positive effect. Consumers expect this from large companies, but also from smaller ones. We must not forget that most companies that operate in the tourism sector are small or medium sized (more than 90% for the Spanish case) and, as [4] pointed out, those firms need to implement strategies and take choices to overcome the limitations faced by small firms.

It is mainly through concern for the environment that the concept of CSR has been incorporated into the tourism industry in general. The hotel industry is relevant not only because of the revenues and employment that it generates worldwide, but also because it produces high levels of carbon dioxide emissions, is highly dependent on energy, and can have a marked effect on natural resources. The implementation of CSR in the Spanish tourism industry has been uneven, because of the types of companies that have begun to introduce it and because of the type of practices that have been implemented [5].

Such diversity in the implementation of CSR is due to the nature of the tourism product itself and to the supply-demand relationship that exists in this sector.

From a market point of view, customers and suppliers have different perceptions of the same reality. Clients tend to see the tourism product (i.e. transport, accommodation, catering, and activities) as a complete package that provides them with a satisfactory experience for which they would pay an all-inclusive price. However, tourist package suppliers tend to think of the product as singular: that is, hotels offer accommodation but have no influence on the rest of the package. In other words, the client has a vision of the tourism product as a "destination package", whereas each individual supplier typically implements CSR in isolation [6].

Furthermore, the buying/selling process has the characteristic of the product being consumed at some distance from the client's home. That is, the client buys the package before traveling to the destination without being able to test the product before consuming it. This characteristic underlies two relevant aspects in our analysis: consumer trust during the purchasing process, and the purchasing channel and its recent evolution. As CSR has grown in relevance, new technologies have also drastically changed the way consumer-tourists behave when obtaining information, choosing a product and undertaking the purchasing process using the new technologies that expand the number of products available. The relentless development of electronic commerce (e-commerce) has had a strong effect on the tourism industry because it has given rise to a new consumer profile. This consumer is highly sensitive to key CSR issues and also has more tools to demand that tourism companies implement CSR. As [6,7] pointed out, in countries with advanced social development, buyers consider the CSR factor as part of the purchasing decision process that is also valued by the consumer, allowing companies to charge extra for the same product.

Although in the tourism sector, as will be discussed in Section 2, studies that have considered the environmental variable of the CSR have been very frequent, recent changes in consumer demands regarding the environmental impact have not been taken into account. In addition, the rapid growth of the hotel industry has also had negative aspects [8]. In this context, and as noted in [9], consumers also take into account the precarious employment situation, as well as working conditions and salary in many jobs, in the hotel industry. A greater social awareness of women's rights and their imbalances in terms of wages and employment opportunities have placed this sector, composed mostly of women, into spotlight. The case of cleaning workers and floor services in Spanish hotels has also been analysed from the point of view of tourism consumer decisions [9].

The aim of this study was to use the perceptions of internet users to analyse the effect of the key dimensions of CSR implemented by hotel establishments. Specifically, by using a database that contains references to the behaviour of e-commerce of these consumers, we can determine the impact on their purchases of accommodation due the way they perceive the efforts of hotel companies in terms of respect for the environment, social integration and economic sustainability. The study was based on a sample selected for the case of Spain.

The rest of this article is organised as follows: Section 2 presents a literature review; in Section 3, we describe the materials and methods; Section 4 describes the quantitative results of the analysis; Section 5 provides a qualitative discussion. Finally, Section 6 presents the main conclusions.

2. Literature Review

The literature on CSR in the hotel industry is scarcer than that for other fields of analysis within the tourism sector, and it is even scarcer when compared to other economic sectors. As Gligor-Cimpoieru et al. [10] pointed out, most studies in this field are limited to environmental issues, and tend to neglect the social and cultural variables of CSR. Thus, it has often been pointed out that tourism makes intensive use of the environment, which is a de facto indispensable element in the tourism product [5,11–13]. Although this view is generally true, not all tourism activities or all tourism segments have such a direct relationship with the environment. For example, holiday hotels are typically located on coasts or in natural areas where the environment is an intrinsic part of the tourism package. Thus, they have to implement specific environmental management measures. However, city hotels mainly cater to business tourists, and are therefore more concerned with the management of human resources and occupational health than with environmental management [14].

However, most large hotel chains have focussed the development of CSR practices on the environmental dimension and have reached higher levels of sustainability. Their objectives are to obtain cost savings and increase their presence in the new market segments that are more demanding regarding environmental issues [6,15–19]. In performing an analysis of CSR in Spanish hotel chains, [5] did an in-depth analysis of the literature and found that most studies have addressed the types of CSR practices implemented in hotel companies, the publication of CSR reports, and the economic effect of CSR. The latter aspect has been widely analysed by other authors [20–23]. Some of these authors have suggested that increased CSR investment leads to short-term improvements (i.e. increased profitability) and long-term improvements (i.e. increased company value). Therefore, investment in CSR benefits the organization ([24,25]) by improving its competitiveness and performance [17]. It also improves employee commitment, motivation, and loyalty to the company ([26–28]). It has also been suggested that clients are willing to paying more for sustainable measures [29]. Other authors have suggested that the change in hotel management has been driven and will continue to be driven by the demand from customers who currently show greater concern for the cultural and natural heritage, and by the increase in environmental protection and ecotourism practices ([30,31]).

In relation to the size of the company, in the literature, it seems that only large hotel companies adopt proactive policies in terms of CSR. However, some authors such as [32], taking Eurobarometer data, point out that small hotel companies which consider environmental concerns to be among their objectives have a greater increase in sales and go beyond environmental legislation. To the best of our knowledge, nobody has done this type of study for the Andalusian hotel industry. However, we could take as a proxy the work of [33], who has analysed the environmental strategy and performance in small companies in the Andalusian automotive sector, concluding that these firms vary their environmental compromise from reactive regulatory compliance to proactive prevention of pollution and environmental leadership, the latter being those that obtain the highest economic performance.

Not everything that glitters in CSR is gold, and some authors who have published articles on the lodging sector have expressed doubts concerning the concept or even whether CSR actually exists, at least for accommodation companies. Thus, [34] criticised the marked confusion regarding the concept of CSR and sustainability in the business world. Some authors as [35] suggested that CSR is nothing more than a way by which to gain a competitive advantage in the market. Others, such as [36], have suggested that the prevailing approaches to CSR are so fragmented and disconnected from business and strategy that they mask great opportunities for companies to benefit society.

Regarding the demand side, there is little research on what sustainability means to consumers, which aspects are most valued, and what they would most like to change regarding company behaviour

([35,37]). Some authors have suggested that from the perspective of consumers, CSR has only two dimensions: society and the environment [38].

Several studies conducted in Spain, and specifically in Andalusia, have shown that environmental quality standards, such as ISO 14001, help improve hotel productivity and performance and customer perceptions of the establishment. The study addressed four-star hotels and aspects related to cleaning, attention to detail, and comfort [39]. In their analysis of the ethical responsibility in some tourism subsectors, [40] suggested that advertising aimed at highlighting the ethical behaviour of organizations has a positive influence on the perceived quality of tourism products and intentions to purchase.

However, [37] suggested that despite the acknowledged influence of CSR on customer loyalty, the topic remains relatively unexplored. These authors also suggested that customers are likely to believe that socially responsible companies operate in a more honest way and that they are willing to use companies that implement CSR actions. Thus, some CSR initiatives can be effective instruments to increase the level of trust between hotel companies and their clients.

Some authors have suggested that real commitment to sustainability can only come through consumer pressure, and that innovation and improved quality and corporate image is determined by customer pressure ([39,40]). Thus, hotels wishing to build loyalty in some segments by implementing CSR should focus their attention on designing policies and strategies that would lead customers to perceiving them as socially responsible brands. This approach would require mechanisms by which to provide consumers with credible information about the companies' CSR activities [38].

Needless to say, in the interests of brevity (all the papers have a limit of words for publication), we have centred our analysis in the literature related to both the tourism sector and the European Union Countries. However, CSR has been analysed in very different sectors and countries. For instance, [41] did a cross country analysis between the UK and Italy before the introduction of non-financial reporting directive comparing and obtaining as main result the importance of national and sub-national CSR policies to implement corporate social disclosure.

The lack of transparency on firm's websites is analysed, among others, in [2,42]. That first paper expands the conceptual framework of dialogic communication on social media by incorporating a social dimension via social presence of firms' CEOs. In a very interesting paper, [2] study a critical issue in CSR implementations: the communication firm-consumer by the analysis of web-bases CSR communications in the Czech Republic and Ukraine, concluding that TOP 100 companies operating in these countries communicate economic and environmental responsibility activities in the greatest scope, and ethical responsibility activities the least, a fact which corresponds to the frequently exclusively philanthropic approach to the concept of CSR in these countries.

Also, in Czech Republic, [43] tried to identify socially responsible practices applied by the statutory cities this country in order to analyse and evaluate the scope and structure of socially responsible activities performed by them and communicated on the internet obtaining similar results that the obtained before for Czech companies. In Romania, [44] analysed the correlation between profit and the decision to do CSR activities and tried to identify the correlations between the level of CSR activities and the dimension of profit, obtaining that the companies which implement CSR activities in a greater extent are more profitable in economic terms.

The concept of stakeholder engagement has been also analysed. [45] analyse this aspect of the CSR in the European banking sector concluding highlighting areas in banking that can be strengthened to improve SE processes; [46] concludes demonstrating that whilst specific types of value may vary according to the OC context, culture and purpose, our investigation of the dynamics of OC value creation in terms of stakeholder engagement (cognitive, emotional and behavioural), when linked to the causal mechanisms used to generate profit, yields new and relevant insights.

This brief review of the literature shows that most CSR studies have focussed on company behaviour. We add to the scarce literature on consumer perceptions by addressing consumer behaviour in the face of CSR practices. The aim was to better understand the perceptions of consumers regarding CSR actions and to what extent they value these actions. We also analysed whether CSR actions have a positive influence on the consumers' perceptions of hotel services and on their final decision when contracting hotel accommodation.

3. Materials and Methods

This study analysed an Andalusian population of internet users who make purchases through the internet. According to the Survey on Equipment and Use of Information and Communication Technologies in Households 2017 published by the Spanish National Institute of Statistics, 2 795 986 Andalusian internet users between 16 and 74 years old used e-commerce for private or household purposes in 2017. This figure represented 44.43% of the Andalusian population in this age range in 2017, and was more than 5 percentage points below the Spanish average for this population group. Three of the e-commerce products most in demand by Andalusian users are accommodation services (43% of internet users), tickets for shows (36.5%), and travel services such as public transport tickets and car rental (35.2%). These percentages are around 10% less than the averages for the Spanish population (i.e. 54.1% for accommodation services, 46.6% for tickets for shows, and 44.7% for travel services). It seems reasonable to assume that some special factors differentiate Andalusian e-commerce users from Spanish e-commerce users as a whole when they make purchases in the tourism sector, and more specifically, in the accommodation sector. The study included a sample of 412 individuals, which was statistically representative of the Andalusian population between 16 and 74 years old that uses e-commerce, which implies a maximum error of 4.85% for a confidence level of 95%. The individuals in the sample were selected among users of opinion websites such as Trip Advisor and Booking, among others. We have mainly used these two opinion websites because they are the most important in the Spanish market. The distribution of individuals by age, sex and province segments has been determined by probabilistic sampling by proportional affixation. Individuals in the random sample were provided with an online questionnaire for the collection of statistical information. The data collection period has been developed between March and May 2018.

We investigated the effects of some CSR actions on demand, based on the relevance customers give to such CSR actions.

The different dimensions used in the present work have been previously analysed in the literature, converting the social, environmental and economic dimensions into the three pillars of social responsibility that should be considered in future decision-making.

Social dimension: it is subject to a lesser analysis than the rest of the dimensions in the specialized literature. The behaviour patterns of the organizations have been analysed and identified [47]. Thus, communication efforts aimed at highlighting the ethical and social behaviour of organizations have a positive influence on the perceived quality of tourism products and the intention to purchase. In the case of Spain [48] and specifically in Andalusia, some case studies show how certain quality standards (obtained through external certifications to companies) help improve the hotel's productivity [11].

Environmental dimension: some works identify the increase in consumer sensitivity to environmental issues [49]. The study of environmentally proactive behaviours is repeated in the specialized literature, making it necessary to give greater emphasis on how economic and social objectives can be combined with environmental objectives to achieve greater efficiency [50], and thus, to reduce uncertainty towards these dimensions [51].

Economic dimension: this dimension constitutes one of the engines of economic development [52], with the appearance of different interest groups, perspectives and economic dimensions in the analysis [53]. The hotel industry is not immune to the different dimensions of analysis [54]. The location of the hotels (coast, city or natural places), conditions the perspectives of consumers, although those located in natural landscapes use the environment as a tourist claim resource, those located on the coast or urban environments are obliged to implement specific environmental management measures.

We investigated the latent factors related to the three dimensions of CSR that may affect consumer perceptions using a statistically validated 26-item questionnaire (Table 1) developed in previous studies. The work has a confirmatory character, based on those previous studies. The Likert scale is used to measure the importance of the different variables. For optimal inclusion, a preliminary test of the questionnaire was carried out among professionals (academic researchers and tourism consultants) to determine possible errors in the design of the questionnaire and/or in the transcription of the data that had to be collected, to guarantee the quality of the information obtained, analyse the absence of data and observe the level of coherence in the answers given.

Table 1. Latent Factors.

Latent Factor	Item
Customers' perception of hotel services (CPH)	CPH1 Quality of the facilities (comfort, cleanliness, design, etc.)
	CPH2 Quality of the food & drink (breakfast, dinner, lunch)
	CPH3 Perceived image of the establishment's website
	CPH4 Free Wifi service
	CPH5 Supplementary services: swimming pool, gymnasium, spa, meeting rooms, etc
Economic (CSR-Ec)	EC1 The hotel endeavours to obtain as much economic profit as possible to guarantee its continuity
	EC2 The hotel tries to guarantee its own economic success in the long term
	EC3 The hotel tries to control its production costs
Environment (CSR-En)	EN-1 The hotel suggests a system for the customers to establish when they think it is necessary to change the towels and sheets instead of changing them on a daily basis
	EN-2 The hotel is equipped with water-saving devices, such as gauges and water timers, high-pressure and low-flow showerheads, mixer taps, dual flush cisterns, etc
	EN-3 The hotel equips communal zones, such as toilets, corridors or exteriors, with light gauges and timers
	EN-4 The hotel equips the rooms with automatic systems for disconnecting the air-conditioning when doors and windows are open
	EN-5 The hotel makes the customers aware of their commitment to the environment, and asks for collaboration when they are staying in the hotel, by making small gestures that the customers themselves can carry out.
	EN-6 The hotel provides information in the rooms about good practice codes for the customers (e.g. taking a shower instead of a bath, keeping the air-conditioning system at the recommended temperature, not throwing waste down into lavatory, etc)
Social (CSR-S)	S1 The hotel has an ethical code of conduct and declares that it respects human rights
	S2 The hotel endeavours to treat its employees fairly because it has a non-discriminatory contracting policy, equal pay policy, reconciles the employees' professional and family lives, etc
	S3 The hotel has procedures for only contracting suppliers who implement environmental and sustainability measures and policies
	S4 The hotel publishes annual sustainability reports
	S5 The hotel is equipped with facilities for the disabled (menus in braille, round tables in restaurants, etc)
	S6 The hotel sponsors educational, cultural and public health activities
	S7 The hotel makes economic donations to good causes
	S8 The hotel tries to improve the quality of life of the local communities in which it operates
	S9 The hotel supports world initiatives such as the Global Compact, the Ethical Tourism Code, Global Reporting Initiative or EMAS

Note: All questions are scored from 1 to 7, where 1 indicates that the item has no relevance to the respondent and 7 has very high relevance.

We formulated three main hypotheses on the effect of the three CSR dimensions implemented by hotels on consumers' perceptions of their accommodation services:

Hypothesis 1 (H1): The social dimension of CSR (CSR-S) has a direct effect on customer perceptions of hotel services (CPH).

Hypothesis 2 (H2): The environmental dimension of CSR (CSR-En) has a direct effect on the economic dimensions of CSR (CSR-Ec) and CSR-S.

Two sub-hypotheses of H2 were formulated: H2.1: CSR-En has a direct effect on CSR-S; H2.2: CSR-En has a direct effect on CSR-Ec.

Hypothesis 3 (H3): CSR-Ec has a direct effect on CPH.

We tested these hypotheses using a reflective model in which each latent variable is the cause of the corresponding observed variable. The observed variables (i.e. measures) are therefore a reflection of the dimensions of CSR and consumer perceptions. The data were analysed using partial least squares (PLS) methodology, which is a methodology that combines two techniques of multivariate analysis: principal components analysis and the multiple linear regression.

There are multiple advantages in the use of the Partial Least Squares (PLS) technique ([55–57]), among which the following can be highlighted:

- Predictive character that allows the planning and future decision making of the agents involved.
- A very large sample size is not necessary.
- A lower initial requirement in the distribution of the variables that are integrated in the sample.
- The PLS methodology does not assume variable normality and estimates least squares recursively.
- It is also more suitable than the maximum likelihood method for predictive models or for the exploratory and developmental stages of a theory.

The main disadvantage of this technique, which does not invalidate its use as confirmed by the extensive literature in this field, is that the PLS regression is a correlative rather than a causal model, in the sense that the models obtained do not offer fundamental information about the phenomenon studied, since you do not work with the original variables.

The structural sub model to be estimated was based on four latent factors and their respective indicators included in the reflective measure sub model. The reflective model provided the basis for the four hypotheses that were finally tested. The variable that represented the customers' perceptions of services and quality was considered an exogenous variable, which could thus affect other factors. The foregoing aspects were based on previous literature in this field of research [58]. Figure 1 shows a nomogram representing PLS estimations using the SmartPLS 3 software package [59]. We draw attention to the results of individual item reliability testing, which has been used in similar contexts [55]. In any case, a cut off of < 0.4 was applied using an item-trimming process [60].

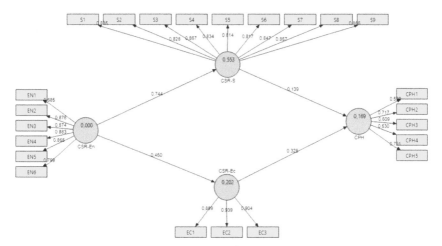

Figure 1. Structural Sub-Model.

4. Results

The results shown in Figure 1 confirm the appropriateness of the indicators selected. Similarly, the reliability measures shown in Table 2 confirm the validity of the questionnaire used to assess the four latent dimensions proposed. The index of goodness-of-fit proposed by [61] as the geometric mean of the average communality and the average R^2 had a value of 0.451. This index is a working solution to the problem of the lack of optimization of scalar functions in PLS modelling and can provide an overall validation of the model.

Table 2. Reliability Measurements.

	AVE	Composite Reliability	R^2	Cronbach's Alpha	Communality	Redundancy
CPH	0.4164	0.7767	0.1689	0.6485	0.4164	0.0609
CSR-Ec	0.8299	0.9360	0.2023	0.8975	0.8299	0.1668
CSR-En	0.6945	0.9312		0.9103	0.6945	
CSR-S	0.7068	0.9559	0.5528	0.9481	0.7068	0.3895

As shown in Table 2, the indicators used to verify the reliability of the measuring instruments and internal consistency (i.e. Cronbach's alpha and the composite reliability indexes) were in all cases more than 0.7 or very close to 0.7. Therefore, the reliability of the constructs was confirmed by their fulfilling the criterion proposed by [62]. In addition, the higher values of the composite reliability index in the PLS model have the advantage over Cronbach's alpha values of there being no need to assume that all indicators have the same weighting [63].

According to the criteria established by [63] to obtain convergent validity, the values of the average variance extracted (AVE) for the four constructs were more than or very close to 0.5. In addition, the items are placed on the latent variable, where together they increase its quantitative load and the criterion proposed by these authors to test discriminant validity was also fulfilled. That is, a comparison of the amount of variance captured by the construct (AVE_j) and the shared variance with other constructs (ρ_{ij}) for the four latent variables (Table 3) showed that the values of the square root of the AVE of each construct were more than the estimated correlation between them (1):

$$\sqrt{AVE_j} \geq \rho_{ij} \forall\, i \neq j, \tag{1}$$

Table 3. Correlation Matrix of Latent Variables.

	CPH	CSR-Ec	CSR-En	CSR-S
CPH	(0.6453)			
CSR-Ec	0.3923	(0.9110)		
CSR-En	0.2287	0.4498	(0.8334)	
CSR-S	0.2937	0.4735	0.7435	(0.8407)

In the case of the predictive capacity of the structural sub-model (see Table 2), the estimated values of the R^2 statistic were more than 0.1 for all latent and significant variables. Therefore, the acceptability criterion proposed by [64] was fulfilled.

Table 4 shows the estimations of the direct and total effects between the latent variables of the study model. As shown, the dependency relationships in the proposed model were verified, and they also confirm the study hypotheses. These results are in line with those obtained by [58] for a sample of Spanish consumers. However, CSR-S had a weaker effect on Andalusian CPH than it did on Spanish CPH.

Table 4. Direct and Overall Effects Between Latent Variables.

Direct Effects					Overall Effects				
	CPH	CSR-Ec	CSR-En	CSE-S		CPH	CSR-Ec	CSR-En	CSR-S
CPH					CPH				
CSR-Ec	0.326				CSR-Ec	0.326			
CSR-En		0.450		0.744	CSR-En	0.250	0.450		0.744
CSR-S	0.139				CSE-S	0.139			

With the aim of confirming the theoretical assumptions on which the hypotheses are based, Table 5 shows the estimations of the standardized regression coefficients of the constructs and their corresponding t-statistics using bootstrapping with 5000 samples. The estimated values confirm the statistical significance of the coefficients related to each of the proposed relationships. The signs of these values also confirm the primary and secondary study hypotheses.

Table 5. Tests of the Hypotheses of Direct Effects Between Latent Variables.

	Standardized B	t-Statistic
CSR-Ec → CPH	0.0676	4.8314 *
CSR-En → CHP	0.0415	6.0348 *
CSR-En → CSR-Ec	0.0499	9.0173 *
CSR-En → CSR-S	0.0354	21.0157 *
CSR-S → CPH	0.0710	1.9600 *

Nots: see [64].

The results presented in Table 5 show the relevance to Andalusian clients of the three dimensions of the CSR initiatives (i.e. economic, environmental, and social) implemented by hotels. It is noteworthy that the relevance of the economic and environmental dimensions reached 99%.

The PLS model provides an assessment of the predictive capacity of our model, by indicating the variance explained by the predictor variables of the endogenous construct in the model. Although its predictive capacity was weak in the case of the social dimension, it was moderate or strong in the other two cases [65].

5. Discussions

This study used a sample of 412 individuals, which was statistically representative of the Andalusian population between 16 and 74 years old that uses e-commerce. We analysed the covariance structure of the factors related to the different dimensions of CSR and to the services provided by hotel establishments, following the methods describes in [58]. The results of the questionnaire used to create the study database show that customer perceptions of hotel services are influenced by four latent factors. The relationships established between those latent factors provided the basis for formulating the three main hypotheses and two sub-hypotheses. All these hypotheses were confirmed.

Firstly, H1 was confirmed, despite CSR-S having the weakest positive effect on customer perceptions (0.139), with Andalusian customers having lower scores than Spanish customers. This result contradicts, in the Andalusian case, the results suggested by [40] or, for the case of Peru by [7], but is in line with the conclusions of [9] for the case of Mexico, where it states that both consumers as the managers of the hotel companies do not know how to recognize hotels' efforts in social matters, especially due to the difficulty of specific certifications since the existing ones tend to value the quality [66] but not how it has managed to reach that certain level quality. As [67] pointed out, many companies report their CSR goals, but only a few of them provide details of specific initiatives which they have undertaken. As we show in the literature review, communication of the CSR efforts seems to be the "Achilles heel" for companies, as [3] and [45] demonstrated for the case of UK and Italy, [42] for the United States, [46] for the case of Australia and [2] in Czech Republic. In this last country, some authors obtained similar results on this issue for different sectors of the country: [68] for the gambling sector, [69] for the chemical industry and [70] for sugar companies.

If companies pay more attention to this, and according to the results obtained in [71] for the case of Colombia and suggested by [44] for Romania, consumers would be willing to pay a higher price if the company meets certain characteristics in its management, such as commitment to the environment, good treatment of workers and support for anti-poverty programs, among other variables; that is, they would be willing to pay more for business attributes linked to social responsibility.

Secondly, H2 was confirmed in that CSR-En had a positive effect on CSR-S (0.744) and CSR-Ec (0.450). Furthermore, the two sub-hypotheses were confirmed in that CSR-En had an indirect positive effect on customers' perceptions of hotel services (0.250). These results show that environmental commitment on the part of hotel establishments, and therefore their greater environmental awareness, is highly relevant to Andalusian consumers. These results come to confirm those already obtained for the Spanish case by [15–17], among others, or for the international case by [22] or [72], which reinforces our own investigation.

Thirdly, H3 was confirmed in that CSR-Ec had direct positive effect on customers' perception of hotel services (0.326). This result was as expected according to the relevant literature in this section [20–23].

In summary, the study hypotheses were confirmed, showing that the model was useful in determining the effect of the different dimensions of CSR on consumer perceptions of hotel services. Nevertheless, the model showed that the economic and environmental factors of CSR are more relevant to consumers than the social components of CSR.

6. Conclusions

It appears reasonable to conclude that customers of hotel services have an increasing interest in business attitudes that promote the greater involvement of hotel establishments in their environmental, social, and economic setting. The results should be taken into account by those responsible for hotel offers, because their involvement in activities related to CSR can be determinant of customer acquisition and loyalty. The strong predictive capacity of the model could be useful to managers by allowing them to adjust the different dimensions of the CSR to the individualized management of the establishments. But, particularly, our findings obtained for the environmental issue could be of interest to hotel managers to guide their investment strategies, which could help them differentiate the services they offer from those of the competition.

Another interesting element to be considered by managers of accommodation companies is the fact that it is difficult for consumers to perceive the efforts of these companies in everything related to the social dimension. The creation of some type of certification that allows such recognition (as in the case of quality certifications, for example) would be an element to be considered by companies. As [71] and [72] pointed out, in the Spanish tourism sector any of the quality models and certifications studied (including ISO 9001 and ISO 14001, EMAS and others), only the Spanish Q-Mark certificate is significantly awarded for consumers.

Also, the participation of employees and even suppliers in promotion campaigns of the establishment, as is common practice among many companies in other sectors, could be a signal to consumers that they are satisfied with their participation in the company and that the behaviour of the company is guided by ethical standards. The communication of the CSR measures implemented by firms and institutions is an issue of critical importance. Efforts in this field are useless if there is no communication between the stakeholders or if it is not running in the correct way.

Finally, this study is limited by the fact that data were not available on consumer socioeconomic variables, such income level, employment status, or cultural level. Some studies on CRS have demonstrated the relevance of these variables for a more detailed analysis [73–76]. Had these data been available, the study could have provided more specific conclusions. Nevertheless, this limitation could act as a stimulus for future studies using other methodologies.

Author Contributions: All authors have contributed equally to each parts of this paper.

Funding: This research received no external funding.

Conflicts of Interest: The authors declare no conflict of interest.

References

1. Bowen, H.R. *Social Responsibilities of the Businessman*; Harper & Brothers: New York, NY, USA, 1953.
2. Tetrevova, L.; Patak, M.; Kyrylenko, I. Web-based CSR communication in post-communist countries. *Appl. Econ. Lett.* **2019**, *26*, 866–871. [CrossRef]
3. Caputo, F.; Pizzi, S. Ethical firms and web reporting: Empirical evidence about the voluntary adoption of the Italian "legality rating". *Int. J. Bus. Manag.* **2019**, *14*, 36–45. [CrossRef]
4. Buffa, F.; Franch, M.; Rizio, D. Environmental management practices for sustainable business models in small and medium sized hotel enterprises. *J. Clean. Prod.* **2018**, *194*, 656–664. [CrossRef]
5. Rodríguez, J.M.; Alonso, M.; Celemín, M. Responsabilidad social corporativa en las cadenas hoteleras españolas. Un estudio de casos. *Revista de Responsabilidad Social de la Empresa* **2013**, *13*, 15–50.
6. Sánchez-Ollero, J.L.; García-Pozo, A.; Marchante-Lara, M. The environment and competitive strategies in hotels in Andalusia. *Environ. Eng. Manag. J.* **2011**, *10*, 1835–1843. [CrossRef]
7. Bernal Peralta, J.; Leo Rossi, E.; Navarrete Álvarez, M. Responsabilidad Social Empresarial de los servicios hoteleros: Valoración de los consumidores. *Revista Académica y Negocios* **2019**, *4*, 107–114.
8. Vargas, E.E. *Responsabilidad Social Empresarial y gestión ambiental en el sector hotelero*; Universidad Autónoma del Estado de México: Ciudad de Mexico, Mexico, 2015.
9. Hernández Sánchez, A.R.; Vargas Martínez, E.E.; Castillo Nechar, M.; Zizumbo Villarreal, L. Responsabilidad Social Empresarial en la hotelería. Un enfoque ético. *Gestão Regionalidade* **2018**, *34*, 43–57. [CrossRef]
10. Gligor-Cimpoieru, D.C.; Partenie-Munteanu, V.; Nitu-Antonie, R.D.; Schneider, A.; Preda, G. Perceptions of Future Employees toward CSR Environmental Practices in Tourism. *Sustainability* **2017**, *9*, 1631. [CrossRef]
11. Sánchez-Ollero, J.L.; Ons-Cappa, M.; Febrero-Paño, E. An analysis of environmental proactivity and its determinants in the hotel industry. *Environ. Eng. Manag. J.* **2016**, *15*, 1437–1445. [CrossRef]
12. Soler, I.; Gémar, G.; Sánchez-Ollero, J.L. Are green hotels expensive? The impact of eco-friendly policies on hotel prices in Spanish cities. *Environ. Eng. Manag. J.* **2016**, *15*, 1511–1517. [CrossRef]
13. García-Pozo, A.; Sánchez-Ollero, J.L.; Ons-Cappa, M. Eco-innovation and economic crisis: A comparative analysis of environmental good practices and labour productivity in the Spanish hotel industry. *J. Clean. Prod.* **2016**, *138*, 131–138. [CrossRef]
14. Rodríguez-Antón, J.M.; Alonso-Almeida, M.M.; Celemín, M.; Rubio, L. Use of different sustainability management systems in the hospitality industry. The case of Spanish hotels. *J. Clean. Prod.* **2012**, *22*, 76–84. [CrossRef]
15. Álvarez-Gil, M.J.; Burgos-Jiménez, J.; Céspedes-Lorente, J.J. Analysis of environmental management, organizacional context and performance of Spanish hotels. *Omega* **2001**, *29*, 457–471. [CrossRef]
16. Carmona-Moreno, E.; Céspedes-Lorente, J.; Burgos-Jiménez, J. Enviromental strategies in Spanish hotels: Contextual factors and performance. *Serv. Ind. J.* **2004**, *24*, 101–130. [CrossRef]
17. Molina, J.F.; Claver, E.; Pereira, J.; Tarí, J.J. Environmental practices and firm performance: An empirical analysis in the Spanish hotel industry. *J. Clean. Prod.* **2009**, *17*, 516–524. [CrossRef]
18. López-Gamero, M.D.; Molina-Azorín, J.F.; Claver-Cortés, E. The whole relationship between environmental variables and firm performance: Competitive advantage and firm resources as mediator variables. *J. Environ. Manag.* **2009**, *90*, 3110–3121. [CrossRef]
19. Alonso, M.M.; Rodríguez, J.M. Organisational behaviour and strategies in adoption of certified management systems. An analysis of the Spanish hotel industry. *J. Clean. Prod.* **2011**, *19*, 1455–1463.
20. Boluk, K. Using CSR as a tool for development: An investigation of the fairhotels scheme in Ireland. *J. Qual. Assur. Hosp. Tour.* **2013**, *14*, 49–65. [CrossRef]
21. Garay, L.; Font, X. Doing good to do well? Corporate social responsibility rea-sons, practices and impacts in small and medium accommodation enterprises. *Int. J. Hosp. Manag.* **2012**, *31*, 329–337. [CrossRef]
22. Inoue, Y.; Lee, S. Effects of different dimensions of corporate social responsibility on corporate financial performance in tourism-related industries. *Tour. Manag.* **2011**, *32*, 790–804. [CrossRef]

23. Kang, K.H.; Lee, S.; Huh, C. Impacts of positive and negative corporate social responsibility activities on company performance in the hospitality industry. *Int. J. Hosp. Manag.* **2010**, *29*, 72–82. [CrossRef]
24. Lee, S.; Park, S. Do socially responsible activities help hotels and casinos achieve their financial goals? *Int. J. Hosp. Manag.* **2009**, *28*, 105–112. [CrossRef]
25. Salzmann, O.; Ionescu-Somers, A.; Steger, U. The business case for corporate sustainability: Literature review and research options. *Eur. Manag. J.* **2005**, *23*, 27–36. [CrossRef]
26. Fu, H.; Ye, B.H.; Law, R. You do well and I do well? The behavioral consequences of corporate social responsibility. *Int. J. Hosp. Manag.* **2014**, *40*, 62–70. [CrossRef]
27. Kim, H.; Lee, M.; Lee, H.M.; Kim, N. Corporate social responsibility and employee–company identification. *J. Bus. Ethics* **2010**, *95*, 557–569. [CrossRef]
28. Branco, M.; Rodrigues, L. Corporate social responsibility and resource-based perspectives. *J. Bus. Ethics* **2006**, *69*, 111–132. [CrossRef]
29. García-Pozo, A.; Sánchez-Ollero, J.L.; Marchante-Mera, A. Environmental sustainability measures and their impacts on hotel room pricing in Andalusia (southern Spain). *Environ. Eng. Manag. J.* **2013**, *12*, 1971–1978. [CrossRef]
30. Mondéjar-Jiménez, J.; Mondéjar-Jiménez, J.A.; Vargas-Vargas, M.; Gázquez-Abad, J.C. Personal attitudes in environmental protection. *Int. J. Environ. Res.* **2012**, *6*, 1039–1044.
31. Villanueva Álvaro, J.J.; Mondéjar-Jiménez, J.; Sáez Martínez, F.J. Rural tourism: Development, management and sustainability in rural establishments. *Sustainability* **2017**, *9*, 818. [CrossRef]
32. González-Moreno, A.; Díaz-García, C.; Sáez-Martinez, F. Environmental responsibility among SMEs in the hospitality industry: Performance implications. *Environ. Eng. Manag. J.* **2016**, *15*, 1527–1532. [CrossRef]
33. Aragón-Correa, J.A.; Hurtado-Torres, N.; Sharmac, S.; García-Morales, V.J. Environmental strategy and performance in small firms: A resource-based perspective. *J. Environ. Manag.* **2008**, *86*, 88–103. [CrossRef]
34. Ayuso, S. Adoption of voluntary environmental tools for sustainable tourism: Analysing the experience of Spanish hotels. *Corp. Soc. Responsib. Environ. Manag.* **2006**, *13*, 207–220. [CrossRef]
35. Jones, P.; Hillier, D.; Comfort, D. Sustainability in the global hotel industry. *Int. J. Contemp. Hosp. Manag.* **2014**, *26*, 5–17. [CrossRef]
36. Porter, M.E.; Kramer, M.R. The link between competitive advantage and corporate social responsibility. *Harv. Bus. Rev.* **2006**, *84*, 78–92.
37. Martínez, P.; Rodríguez Del Bosque, I. CSR and customer loyalty: The roles of trust, customer identification with the company and satisfaction. *Int. J. Hosp. Manag.* **2013**, *35*, 89–99. [CrossRef]
38. Martínez, P.; Perez, A.; Rodríguez Del Bosque, I. CSR influence on hotel brand image and loyalty. *Academia Revista Latinoamericana de Administración* **2014**, *27*, 267–283. [CrossRef]
39. Peiró-Signes, A.; Segarra-Ona, M.; Verma, R.; Mondéjar-Jimenez, J.; Vargas-Vargas, M. The impact of environmental certification on hotel guest ratings. *Cornell Hosp. Q.* **2014**, *55*, 40–51. [CrossRef]
40. Marchoo, W.; Butcher, K. The influence of ethical responsibility initiatives on perceived tour program quality and tour booking intention. In Proceedings of the International Hospitality and Tourism Conference, Kuala Lumpur, Malaysia, 3–5 September 2012.
41. Venturelli, A.; Caputo, F.; Leopizzi, R.; Pizzi, S. The state of art of corporate social disclosure before the introduction of non-financial reporting directive: A cross country analysis. *Soc. Responsib. J.* **2018**. [CrossRef]
42. Men, L.R.; Tsai, W.H.S.; Chen, Z.F.; Ji, Y.G. Social presence and digital dialogic communication: Engagement lessons from top social CEOs. *J. Public Relat. Res.* **2018**, *30*, 83–99. [CrossRef]
43. Tetrevova, L.; Jelinkova, M. Municipal Social Responsibility of Statutory Cities in the Czech Republic. *Sustainability* **2019**, *11*, 2308. [CrossRef]
44. Hategan, C.D.; Sirghi, N.; Curea-Pitorac, R.I.; Hategan, V.P. Doing Well or Doing Good: The Relationship between Corporate Social Responsibility and Profit in Romanian Companies. *Sustainability* **2018**, *10*, 1041. [CrossRef]
45. Venturelli, A.; Cosma, S.; Leopizzi, R. Stakeholder engagement: An evaluation of European banks. *Corp. Soc. Res. Environ. Manag.* **2018**, *25*, 690–703. [CrossRef]
46. Wilkin, C.L.; Campbell, J.; Moore, S.; Simpson, J. Creating value in online communities through governance and stakeholder engagement. *Int. J. Account. Inf. Syst.* **2018**, *30*, 56–68. [CrossRef]
47. Jones, P.; Hillier, D.; Comfort, D. Sustainability in the hospitality industry: some personal reflections on corporate challenges and research agendas. *Int. J. Contemp. Hosp. Manag.* **2016**, *28*, 36–67. [CrossRef]

48. Secondi, L.; Meseguer-Santamaría, M.L.; Mondéjar-Jiménez, J.; Vargas-Vargas, M. Influence of tourist sector structure on motivations of heritage tourists. *Serv. Ind. J.* **2011**, *31*, 1659–1668. [CrossRef]

49. Chan, E.S.W.; Hawkins, R. Attitude towards EMSs in an international hotel: An exploratory case study. *Int. J. Hosp. Manag.* **2010**, *29*, 641–651. [CrossRef]

50. Chasin, F. Sustainability: Are we all talking about the same thing? State-of-the-art and proposals for an integrative definition of sustainability in information systems. In Proceedings of the 2014 Conference ICT for Sustainability, Stockholm, Sweden, 24–27 August 2014; pp. 342–351.

51. Glavic, P.; Lukman, R. Review of sustainability terms and their definitions. *J. Clean. Prod.* **2007**, *15*, 1875–1885. [CrossRef]

52. Johnston, P.; Everard, M.; Santillo, D.; Robert, K. Reclaiming the definition of sustainability. *Environ. Sci. Pollut. Res.* **2007**, *14*, 60–66.

53. Souza, R.G.; Rosenhead, J.; Salhofer, S.P.; Valle, R.A.B.; Lins, M.P.E. Definition of sustainability impact categories based on stakeholder perspectives. *J. Clean. Prod.* **2015**, *105*, 41–51. [CrossRef]

54. Melissen, F. Sustainable hospitality: A meaningful notion? *J. Sustain. Tour.* **2013**, *21*, 810–824. [CrossRef]

55. Barclay, D.; Higgins, C.; Thompson, R. The Partial Least Squares (PLS) Approach to Causal Modeling: Personal Computer Adoption and Use as an Ilustration. *Technol. Stud.* **1995**, *2*, 285–309.

56. Chin, W.W.; Marcolin, B.L.; Newsted, P.R. A partial least square latent variable modeling approach for measuring interaction effects: Results from a Monte Carlo simulation study and an electronic mail emotion/adoption study. *Inf. Syst. Res.* **2013**, *14*, 189–217. [CrossRef]

57. Henseler, J.; Ringle, C.M.; Sinkovics, R.R. The Use of Partial Least Squares Path Modeling in International Marketing. In *Advances in International Marketing*; Emerald JAI Press: Bingley, UK, 2009; Volume 20, pp. 277–319.

58. Mondéjar Jiménez, J.; Sevilla-Sevilla, C.; García-Pozo, A. Environmental, Social and Economic Dimension in the Hotel Industry and its Relationship with Consumer Perception. *Environ. Eng. Manag. J.* **2016**, *15*, 1519–1526. [CrossRef]

59. Ringle, C.M.; Wende, S.; Becker, J.M. *SmartPLS3*; University of Hamburg: Hamburg, Germany, 2013; Available online: http://www.smartpls.com (accessed on 19 December 2018).

60. Urbach, N.; Ahlemann, F. Structural equation modeling in information systems re- search using partial least squares. *J. Inf. Technol. Theory Appl.* **2010**, *11*, 5–40.

61. Tenenhaus, M.; Vinzi, V.E.; Chatelin, Y.M.; Lauro, C. PLS path modeling. *Comput. Stat. Data Anal.* **2005**, *48*, 159–205. [CrossRef]

62. Nunnally, J.C.; Bernstein, I.H. The Assessment of Reliability. *Psychom. Theory* **1994**, *3*, 248–292.

63. Fornell, C.; Larcker, D. Evaluating structural equations models with unobservable variables and measurement error. *J. Mark. Res.* **1981**, *18*, 39–50. [CrossRef]

64. Falk, R.; Miller, N. *A Primer for Soft Modeling*; University of Akron Press: Akron, OH, USA, 1992.

65. Hair, J.F., Jr.; Hult, G.T.M.; Ringle, C.; Sarstedt, M. *A Primer on Partial Least Squares Structural Equation Modeling (PLS-SEM)*; Sage Publications: Los Angeles, CA, USA, 2014.

66. Benavides-Velasco, C.; Quintana-García, C.; Marchante-Lara, M. Total quality management, Corporate Social Responsibility and performance in the hotel industry. *Int. J. Hosp. Manag.* **2014**, *41*, 77–87. [CrossRef]

67. De Grosbois, D. Corporate social responsibility reporting by the global hotel industry: Commitment, initiatives and performance. *Int. J. Hosp. Manag.* **2012**, *31*, 896–905. [CrossRef]

68. Tetrevova, L. Communicating CSR in High Profile Industries: Case Study of Czech Chemical Industry. *Eng. Econ.* **2018**, *29*, 478–487. [CrossRef]

69. Tetrevova, L.; Patak, M. Web-Based Communication of Socially Responsible Activities by Gambling Operators. *J. Gambl. Stud.* **2019**. [CrossRef]

70. Tetrevova, L. Communication of socially responsible activities by sugar-producing companies. *Listy Cukrov. Repar.* **2017**, *133*, 394–396.

71. García-Pozo, A.; Sánchez-Ollero, J.L.; Marchante-Mera, A. Environmental Good practices, quality certifications and productivity in the Andalusian hotel sector. *Int. J. Environ. Res.* **2014**, *8*, 1185–1194.

72. Sánchez-Ollero, J.L.; García-Pozo, A.; Marchante-Lara, M. Measuring the effects of quality certification on labour productivity. An analysis of the hospitality sector. *Int. J. Contemp. Hosp. Manag.* **2015**, *27*, 1100–1116. [CrossRef]

73. Marquina, P.; Reficco, E. Impacto de la Responsabilidad Social Empresarial en el comportamiento de compra y disposición a pagar de consumidores bogotanos. *Estudios Gerenciales* **2015**, *31*, 373–382. [CrossRef]

74. Enz, C.A.; Siquaw, J.A. Best hotel environmental practices. *Cornell Hotel Restaur. Adm. Q.* **1999**, *40*, 72–77. [CrossRef]

75. Hernández, A.R.; Vargas, E.E.; Delgado, A.; Rodríguez, F. Responsabilidad Social en la Hotelería. Una percepción desde el turista de negocios. *Investig. Adm.* **2017**, *46*, 119.

76. Rangel Lyne, L.; Hernández Ángel, F.; Ochoa Hernández, M.L.; Garza Arroyo, M.A. El efecto de la Responsabilidad Social Corporativa percibida en el comportamiento de compra de los nuevos consumidores dominantes. In *Global Conference on Business and Finance Proceedings 2018*; The Institute for Business and Finance Research: San Jose, CR, USA, 2018; Volume 13, pp. 309–318.

Article

Perception of Sustainability of Spanish National Parks: Public Use, Tourism and Rural Development

Esteban Pérez-Calderón [1,*], Jorge Manuel Prieto-Ballester [2], Vanessa Miguel-Barrado [3] and Patricia Milanés-Montero [1]

[1]   Faculty of Economics, University of Extremadura, 06006 Badajoz, Spain; pmilanes@unex.es
[2]   Faculty of Business, Finance and Tourism, University of Extremadura, 10071 Cáceres, Spain; jmprieto@unex.es
[3]   Faculty of Law, University of Extremadura, 10071 Cáceres, Spain; vmiguelb@alumnos.unex.es
*   Correspondence: estperez@unex.es

Received: 21 January 2020; Accepted: 9 February 2020; Published: 12 February 2020

Abstract: In the last decade, tourism activity associated with natural areas has stood out as a driver for economic development. Thus, it is a key factor for the economic and social sustainability of the community near a protected area. This paper analyses, considering the tourist exploitation and the public use of the National Park in the last decade, the perception about the sustainability of its geographical area closest. A questionnaire was used and sent to the authorities of the villages closest to each of the 15 National Parks. The structural equation model was used for the design and analysis of the model. The results confirmed significant relationships between the perception of economic development and quality of life, but not with social development. A positive relationship between quality of life and social development is also demonstrated. The three dimensions analysed, economic, social and quality of life, are influencing the perception of sustainability of the geographical area closest to the protected natural area. The legal limitations to the public use of these natural protected areas have been considered in the assessments made by the respondents. In conclusion, National Park managers, local entrepreneurs and institutional authorities (local, regional and national) are encouraged to better coordinate the resources of the protected natural area. The dynamization of tourist activities should be encouraged while respecting the biological value of the park, as has been done so far.

Keywords: rural development; National Parks; nature tourism; public use

---

1. Introduction

The tourism business is a very important factor in economic and social development. In 2018 it contributed to 10.4% of the world's GDP, which was 3.9% higher than the previous year [1]. Spain is a tourist power and is positioned as the second-largest tourist destination in the world in terms of visitor reception [2].

Tourist activity can be particularly interesting in rural areas due to the deterioration of their main sources of wealth generation, agriculture and livestock [3,4]. The economic marginalisation of these rural areas and the ageing of their residents are causing their impoverishment and depopulation [5]. In particular, nature tourism is strongly associated with these rural areas. This type of tourism has shown constant growth in recent years, both in the world and in Spain. Thus, nature tourism can contribute to the development of rural areas that have a natural environment that is institutionally recognised for its high biological value [6].

In Spain, the figure with the greatest biological recognition and legal protection are the National Parks. This country has 15 National Parks that represent 0.76% of its territory. Likewise, this figure is the best known by society among all the protection categories and has a great tourist attraction, registering millions of visits annually [7,8]. Furthermore, Spanish National Parks represent exceptional environments with their own culture and biological personality, due to the authenticity of their resources, which is one of the country's distinguishing characteristics [9].

In accordance with the above, protected areas are considered an appropriate means of combining traditional activities with new business niches associated with rural and nature tourism, with the aim of promoting sustainable development in the area of influence of the protected natural area [10–13]. In this sense, public use of National Parks cannot be limited only to activities such as contemplation or preservation [14]. Consequently, these wonderful natural spaces must extend their potential to the social and economic sphere, and it is advisable to design sustainable development strategies [15–19].

Economic development in the areas of influence of protected natural environments should not be understood as a form of over-exploitation [19]. Achieving the self-sufficiency and sustainability of the areas bordering these natural spaces would achieve the objective set by the legal norm, since these areas of influence are usually economically disadvantaged rural areas due, among other factors, to the decline of agriculture and the limitations on the use of natural resources as a result of the declaration of a protected space [20,21].

In the previous literature, you can find quite a few studies on rural development and sustainable tourism from an economic and social perspective using macroeconomic indicators. This paper contributes to the previous literature since there are very few studies referring to the perception of sustainability of this type of tourist destinations. In addition, the controversy that justifies this study would be the one that occurs when a National Park is declared and regulated by a law where an important set of limitations to its public use are related. At the same time, the main objectives include the enjoyment of the protected area and the development of its area of socioeconomic influence. These aims will be achieved through the appropriate exploitation of the attraction of the tourist destination, which is a privileged natural environment.

Thus, analysing the limited public use, recognized by law, of the National Parks and the tourist exploitation carried out in the last ten years, the study aims to answer the following question: do the residents near the National Parks perceive that their community is sustainable? According to the above, the main objective of the paper is the analysis of the perception of the economic and social development and the quality of life of the residents in the villages closest to the National Park. In addition, the relationships that are occurring between these latent factors will be measured, and also between these factors and the villagers' perception of the sustainability of their environment.

This paper is structured as follows. In Section 2, the legal framework affecting the public use of Spanish National Parks is analysed, as well as its evolution. In Section 3, the conceptual framework referring to the importance of nature tourism in the socio-economic development of a given geographical demarcation is analysed; here, too, the study hypotheses are defined. In Section 4, the sample and methodology used are detailed. In Section 5, the results of the study are drawn up. Finally, the conclusions and limitations of the paper are shown.

2. Literature Review

2.1. Protected Natural Areas. Public Use of Spanish National Parks

A protected natural area is a clearly defined geographical area recognised, dedicated and managed, through legal or other effective means, to achieve the long-term conservation of nature and associated cultural values [22].

The beginning of the international protectionist trend dates back to 1872 when Yellowstone National Park was declared in the United States [23,24]. The objective of this first declaration was based on the preservation of natural space for the enjoyment of people, due to the devastating effect of human actions on natural resources [25–27]. Focusing on the European landscape, Russia, Switzerland and Spain were the first to regulate the protection of National Parks [28,29].

The concepts of National Park and public use are closely linked and are in constant evolution, as can be seen in Table 1.

Table 1. Evolution of the concept of public use.

Period	The Function of Public Use	Role of the Administration
Late 19th century–1930s	Recreation and contemplative enjoyment	Facilitating access
1930s–1960s (USA)	Environmental education and interpretation	Promote activities
The 1970s	Recreational conditioning	Build reception facilities (picnic areas, barbecues, etc.)
The 1980s	First actions in environmental education and interpretation in protected natural areas	Build equipment for environmental education and interpretation. Public use as a tool for the management of protected natural areas
1990s–2000	Social function Socio-economic vision Construction of visitor centres Extension to tourism and leisure	Planning in an orderly fashion First studies on visitors First evaluations Opportunity to the private sector for equipment management
2001–2014	A Driver of socio-economic development Multiple vision of public use (culture, training, health...) Transcendence of securities Involvement of society	Planning with network vision Public use at the network level Cascade planning (governance) Public use as a communication strategy (means of preservation) Actions in favour of the quality of public use (Quality Q and CETS)

Source: Authors [30].

Table 1 shows that the mere conservationist approach has been evolving towards a model in which the relationship of the human being with nature is promoted through the harmonization of the objectives of preservation and socioeconomic development, turning the National Parks into authentic drivers of sustainable development [26,31].

In particular, in the case of Spain, the protective regime of the National Parks has undergone a significant evolution until today [28]. At the beginning, the public use of the National Parks was only related to environmental interpretation and education [20], while, at present, public use is understood as the set of activities, services and infrastructures whose aim is to bring visitors to protected natural areas closer to their natural and cultural values, from an orderly management that guarantees the conservation of these resources and the enhancement of values such as environmental education and sustainable development [32,33].

After a review of the Spanish regulations that allow the recognition of a National Park, from the first law approved in 1916 to the last one in force since 2014, we can see how two objectives are repeated, such as the biological preservation of the protected area and paying attention to the socio-economic development of the park's area of influence. Currently, the Autonomous Communities are competent in regulatory matters and the management of their own protected areas [34]. The basic regime for public use of the National Parks is the responsibility of the State and is regulated by Law 30/2014, currently in force.

2.2. Nature Tourism: Effects on Sustainable Rural Development

As previously argued, the tourism sector is one of the most prominent in the global economy, due to its capacity to generate income, employment and taxes [35,36]. This wealth-generating power can also be seen in the form of nature tourism, as it is an activity that is fully compatible with environmental preservation, allowing the promotion of traditional values and the improvement of the quality of life of the local residents [37]. All of the above can have a positive effect on the attitude of the residents of the tourist destination's area of influence, which in turn has an impact on the sustainability of the destination [38]. In this sense, the perceptions of local residents are shown to be a key factor in the development of sustainable tourism [39–42].

In the last decade, nature tourism has achieved great importance in international tourism [43]. Nowadays, there has been an increase in the number of tourists who are looking for tranquillity, a link with nature, the practice of sports activities or recreational value in the open air [26,30,44–46].

Tourism in National Parks can be of great socio-economic value to them and their respective areas of influence [21,47]. Among the benefits generated by nature tourism are: increased income; greater job creation; improved financing of the protected environment; or a higher level of environmental education and, consequently, a greater appreciation of the natural and cultural heritage by human beings [44,48,49].

On the contrary, nature tourism can also generate important negative impacts, such as the undermining of environmental conservation, seasonal unemployment, loss of tranquillity, increased pollution, the alteration of local customs, or the increase in prices of local products and services [26,44,50]. In addition, the declaration of National Parks carries with it a significant limitation on the use of the occupied land demarcation and traditional activities rooted in the area that can be detrimental to local development [21,50]. In particular, current Spanish legislation limits certain activities such as hunting, fishing, certain extractions, building, among others [51].

The National Parks in Spain have become important tourist destinations. Thus, the number of visits has grown considerably since 1991, exceeding 15.44 million in 2017, as shown in Figure 1 [52]. Nature tourism, through an adequate management model, constitutes a valuable tool through which multiple benefits can be obtained [13,19,32,53,54]. This approach represents one of the great challenges of the current panorama, that is, the search for a balance between public use for recreational purposes, the socio-economic development of the area of influence of the National Park and the conservation of the ecosystem [27,31,55].

Figure 1. Evolution of visitors to National Parks in Spain [49].

In addition to the clear relationship between economic development and the sustainable development of a rural area, a number of other factors associated with the sustainability of that tourist destination can be distinguished. Thus, the perception of social development and quality of life would be factors that influence the decision to maintain residence in the village and, moreover, can have an impact on an active contribution to the maintenance of the area's resources, including those related to tourism and the biological value of the area [11,56,57]. According to the above, the preservation of natural and cultural heritage in villages can be reinforced by policies that involve greater community empowerment [41].

Considering the externalities caused by tourism in protected areas, as well as the legal limitations on public use implicit in the declaration of National Parks, it is necessary to determine the effects on the perception of environmental sustainability caused by the declaration of Spanish National Parks in their respective areas of influence. Through this study, we will be able to ratify whether the declaration of these spaces has generated a positive perception of the sustainability of the environments from a triple perspective: economic, social and quality of life. This would be an indicator of the sustainability of the area near the National Park as a tourist destination.

Several studies have demonstrated the facilitating role of economic development in social development. In particular, tourist activity can be a tool for keeping alive the customs and authenticity of a village if they are properly managed as products of interest to a tourist destination [45,58].

In this way, previous studies researching the local community's perceptions of the sustainability of tourism can be consulted in the literature, taking the theory of social exchange as a starting point. According to this theory, local residents who perceive positive effects derived from tourism will agree with the development of tourism, and vice versa. Aspects such as community attachment, participation and capacity to influence society in the management of tourism, improvement of the quality of life or low negative impact in the environmental scope result in positive perceptions towards tourism and, consequently, its success and sustainability [39–42]. In this sense, tourism activities related to the traditions and culture of the destination involve greater participation by residents and are presented as an opportunity to strengthen the identity of the local community, which also translates into a positive perception of sustainable tourism development and greater support for tourism development by local residents [39].

In the previous literature, there are many references that have demonstrated the influence of economic development on the residents' quality of life [57,59]. Thus, in the study, there is a hypothesis that reflects this relationship between the perceptions of the quality of life associated with the residents' perception of economic development.

Therefore, the perception of economic development, in addition to influencing the sustainability of the environment, maybe influencing the other latent factors. Thus, the following hypotheses can be put forward, all of which refer to the perceptions of the residents of the villages closest to a National Park:

Hypothesis 1 (H1). *Hypothesis 1 (H1). The perception of economic development influences the residents' perception of sustainability.*

Hypothesis 2 (H2). *The perception of economic development influences the residents' perception of social development.*

Hypothesis 3 (H3). *The perception of economic development influences the residents' perception of quality of life.*

Confirmation of each of these hypotheses would confirm the effect of the three dimensions analysed on the overall satisfaction of the declaration of a National Park and, therefore, on its sustainability.

Satisfaction with the area of residence, together with the feeling of belonging and pride in the value of the biological space, maybe the motivation that facilitates the social development of the village and also on the perception of their overall satisfaction with the environment [59,60].

Hypothesis 4 (H4). *The residents' perception of quality of life has influence on their perception of social development.*

Hypothesis 5 (H5). *The residents' perception of quality of life has influences on their perception of sustainability.*

In the case of social development, there are also studies that analyse the relationships between social perceptions or attitudes, referring to traditions and customs, with the sustainable development of a tourist destination [11,56,57]. The last hypothesis reflects this relationship:

Hypothesis 6 (H6). *The residents' perception of social development influences the on their perception of sustainability.*

3. Method

The study sample is made up of the villages located within the National Parks' zone of socio-economic influence. The selection was based on the zoning set out in the Master Plan of the National Park Network [61]. The sample totals 169 villages. The questionnaire was sent by email to the highest representatives of the town halls (mayors) and the answers were collected through a google form. In a second round to increase the number of responses, a telephone call was made to those town halls in the towns where there was no response. In the end, 75 responses were obtained, representing 44.38% of the total initial sample. Of the fifteen National Parks, three of them did not receive any answer (Cabrera, Tablas de Daimiel and Timanfaya). The most collaborative National Park was Islas Atlánticas; to a lesser extent, Teide (See Table 2). The fieldwork was carried out in November 2019.

Table 2. Statistics of Spanish National Parks.

National Park	Extension Has.	Residents	Number of Villages	% of Answer
Aigüestortes	14,119	13,564	10	50.00%
Cabañeros	40,856	2171	6	66.67%
Cabrera	90,800.52	414,538	2	-
Doñana	54,252	44,296	4	75.00%
Garajonay	3984	21,136	6	66.67%
Guadarrama	33,960	146,603	34	52.94%
Islas Atlánticas	8480	370,376	4	100.00%
Monfragüe	18,396	12,520	14	50.00%
Ordesa	15,696.20	1843	6	66.67%
Picos de Europa	67,127.59	14,492	11	45.45%
Sierra Nevada	85,883	69,014	44	29.55%
Tablas de Daimiel	3030	30,912	3	-
Taburiente	4690	45,094	9	55.56%
Teide	18,990.00	275,416	14	21.43%
Timanfaya	5107.50	22,408	2	-
Total	465,371.81	1,484,383	169	-

The indicators of the socio-economic development of the villages have been those detailed below (see Table 3). Some of these variables were already used in studies such as those by Mosammam et al. [62], Woo et al. [63] and Ristić et al. [13].

IBM SPSS Statistics Version 21.0 was used to perform a descriptive analysis of the data. In addition, this software was used to check the normality of the data.

The proposed model was analysed by modelling structural equations using Partial Least Squares (PLS). This is one of the most used methodologies when the cause-effect relationships need to be analysed [7,64,65] since it informs us of the sign and intensity of these relationships. A PLS path model consists in two components. Firstly, there is a structural model (the inner model) which illustrates the specified constructs and focuses on the relationships (paths) between them. Secondly, the measurement models (the outer models) show the relationships between the factors (constructs) and the indicators. While structural and measurement models are present in all types of SEMs with latent constructs, the weighting scheme represents the third specific component of the PLS approach and is used for estimating the inner weights linking latent constructs [66].

Table 3. Questionnaire used to collect the data [1].

Perception of Economic Development (ED)
ED1. The level of wealth of the village, in general, has increased since the declaration of the N. Park
ED2. The village has a greater number of services related to tourism (directly or indirectly)
ED3. The subsidies received have led to an improvement in the environment in terms of signalling
ED4. You think the number of tourists in your area has increased
ED5. The municipality has increased its recreational use and has more tourist activities
ED6. Conflicts exist between tourism and the exploitation of activities related to agriculture and livestock, mineral extraction... (primary sector)
Perception of Social Development (SD)
SD1. The number of residents in the village has been maintained
SD2. Local culture and traditions have been preserved
SD3. The culture and traditions of your village are exploited as a tourist attraction
SD4. Conflicts have arisen between tourism and residents (noise, waste...)
Perception of Quality of Life (QL)
QL1. The subsidies received have led to an improvement in the area of residence in terms of infrastructure for travel to the area
QL2. An improvement in communication technologies has been noted, with greater mobile phone coverage and greater data transmission capacity
QL3. Residents would not prefer to live in another community
QL4. Since the declaration of the National Park, efficiency in resource consumption has been enhanced. For example, promoting the use of renewable energy systems to save water consumption
QL5. Residents are more environmentally friendly
QL6. You have improved the quality of life of the residents of your village
Perception of Global Satisfaction (SG)
GS1. Residents are more aware of the opportunity for the town to be in the National Park's zone of influence
GS2. The expectations generated by economic and social opportunities due to the proximity to a National Park have been fulfilled
GS3. The park has meant that the residents of this town are proud to live in this community and not in another
GS4. The park has meant that local customs and traditions are still alive
GS5. Rate your overall satisfaction with the declaration of National Park, by the economic impact it has had on your village

[1] The following instructions were given in the questionnaire heading: Please answer briefly or rate on a scale of 1 to 7 your perception of the impact of tourism exploitation and public use of the National Park near your village over the past 10 years.

4. Results

In a first descriptive analysis (see Table 4) we can see how the perception of sustainable development, depending on the effect of the declaration of the National Park near that village, obtains an average rating (3.60 out of 7). A medium-high perception of tourist activity and visitors is recognised (3.84 and 4.56). An average score is also obtained for the perception of legal limitations on public use associated with the traditional activity of these villages (3.92), in line with the low score given to the question about the increase in wealth (3.23). With respect to the social construct, the item referring to the maintenance of traditions and customs was the most valued (4.21). In the quality of life (QL), an average score was reached by declaring no preference for living elsewhere (4.27); furthermore, the deficient scores on ease of travel, access to ICTs or actions to respect the environment were highlighted (QL1, QL2, and QL4, respectively).

Table 4. Evaluation of the measurement model (starting elements).

Latent Variables and Their Indicators	Mean	S. Desv.	Loading	Composite Reliability	AVE
Perception of Economic Development (ED)	-	-	-	0.8540	0.5391
ED1	3.23	1.5902	0.8460	-	-
ED2	3.84	1.7323	0.8467	-	-
ED3	3.89	1.5987	0.5274	-	-
ED4	4.56	1.7876	0.8611	-	-
ED5	3.77	1.6404	0.8825	-	-
ED6	3.92	1.9225	0.0575	-	-
Perception of Social Development (SD)	-	-	-	0.7924	0.5036
SD1	3.75	1.8678	0.8804	-	-
SD2	4.81	1.6165	0.7044	-	-
SD3	4.27	1.7578	0.7587	-	-
SD4	3.16	1.6687	0.4092	-	-
Perception of Quality of Life (QL)	-	-	-	0.8409	0.5084
QL1	2.94	1.6406	0.6956	-	-
QL2	2.63	1.4024	0.8007	-	-
QL3	4.27	2.0110	0.0501	-	-
QL4	2.97	1.559	0.7969	-	-
QL5	4.05	1.692	0.7875	-	-
QL6	3.17	1.6795	0.8171	-	-
Global Satisfaction Perception (GS)	-	-	-	0.9323	0.7339
GS1	3.36	1.5124	0.8209	-	-
GS2	2.72	1.4384	0.8913	-	-
GS3	3.57	1.8756	0.8905	-	-
GS4	2.64	1.6655	0.8347	-	-
GS5	3.60	1.6925	0.8436	-	-

A test of normality was then done. The results showed that all variables have a normal distribution. Reliability was evaluated by considering a standardized external load greater or slightly less than 0.70 (see Table 4). The elimination of these indicators resulted in an increase in composite reliability or Mean-Variance Extracted (AVE), as suggested by Hair et al. [67].

The model reliability indicators are shown below, once the elements that do not exceed the reliability cut have been eliminated. The AVE values (defined as the great average of the square of the indicators associated with the constructions), exceed 0.60, thus demonstrating the convergent validity for all cases. The composite reliability of the 4 constructs is also satisfactory as the values ranged from 0.85 to 0.93 (see Table 5).

Table 5. Evaluation of the measurement model (final elements).

	AVE	Composite Reliability	R Square	Cronbach's Alpha
ED	0.7586	0.9263	-	0.8936
SD	0.6643	0.8551	0.2134	0.7553
QL	0.6092	0.8559	0.5232	0.8396
GS	0.7340	0.9323	0.8348	0.9090

Discriminant validity assessed using the criteria defined by Fornell and Larcker [68], which compares the square root of the AVE values with the correlation of the latent variable, was also satisfactory. In fact, as shown in Table 6, the square root of the AVE of each construct is greater than its correlation with any other construct.

Table 6. Matrix of correlation between latent variables.

	QL	ED	SD	GS
QL	0.7805			
ED	0.7233	0.8710		
SD	0.4611	0.3526	0.8151	
GS	0.8460	0.8288	0.5254	0.8567

To evaluate the structural model, the R-square for each dependent construct was analysed, as well as the meaning of the trajectories, using Bootstrapping [67]. Figure 2 shows the results of the estimation of the trajectory coefficients describing the relationships between the different perceptions of the respondents. The standard errors were bootstrapped by considering 2,500 sub-samples, created with observations randomly drawn from the original set of data (with replacement).

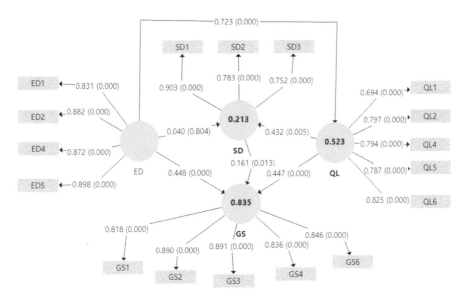

Figure 2. Estimation of the structural equation model. Notes: ED, Economic Development; SD, Social Development; QL, Quality of Life; GS, Global Satisfaction.

According to the results shown in Table 7, the latent endogenous variables of the model have a weak to moderate explanatory power. The model can explain 21.3% of the residents' perceptions of social development, 51.3% of those related to the quality of life and 83.5% of those associated with the sustainability of the village in terms of public use of the National Park (see Figure 2).

The results of the direct structural relations reveal that all the hypothetical relations are statistically significant, except the one referred to in Hypothesis 2. Four hypotheses are significant at a level of 1% (value $p < 0.01$), hypothesis 6 is significant at 5% (value $p < 0.05$). Social development (SD) is influenced by the quality of life (QL) but not by economic development (ED). On the other hand, QL is strongly influenced by ED (0.723). The results also show the positive and significant effects of ED and

QL constructs, with very similar importance (0.448 and 0.447, respectively), and to a lesser extent of SD (0.161).

Table 7. Tests of hypotheses for direct effects between latent variables.

	Original Sample	Standard Dev.	T-Statistic	*p* Values
H1. ED→GS	0.4484	0.0670	6.6884	0.0000
H2. ED→SD	0.0400	0.1671	0.2415	0.8108
H3. ED→QL	0.7233	0.0472	15.3085	0.0000
H4. QL→SD	0.4322	0.1586	2.7796	0.0055
H5. QL→GS	0.4475	0.0817	5.4785	0.0000
H6. SD→GS	0.1609	0.0627	2.5686	0.0114

5. Conclusions

The study analyses the effects of public use of National Parks in Spain on the perception of sustainability in their immediate geographical area. The evaluations of indicators associated with three dimensions of community sustainability are compiled: economic and social development and the quality of life of its people. The assessments are carried out by some of the main stakeholders such as the mayors of the villages. One advantage of choosing this type of participant is that we have the opinion of a person with quality information on the reality of each village. The villages selected are those included in what is known as the park's zone of influence, legally defined according to the criteria of geographical proximity to the protected natural area [61]. Both the choice of the respondents and the choice of the villages contribute to what has been done in the previous literature.

According to the results of the analysis, the perception of economic development conditions the perception of the quality of life, not being the same for the case of social development. Likewise, quality of life is influencing the perception of social development. The three dimensions analysed are affecting the community's perception of sustainability, with the social development dimension doing so to a lesser extent. The other two factors have a very similar average impact.

Once the results have been analysed, the park managers are encouraged to improve coordination between the resources of the protected natural environment and its area of influence. That is, greater collaboration between National Park managers, local companies, village authorities and public administrations. This, applied to current funding resources or their possible extension, would lead to the recommendation of the development of new activities and initiatives aimed at making these destinations more dynamic for tourism. Villagers and local businesses should be more involved in such initiatives. In this way, in addition to boosting their economy, it will be possible to develop an attitude and a feeling of pride in the intangible property of the natural resource that will have an impact on the sustainability of the resource and the environment itself.

In accordance with Eagles et al. [44], and Job et al. [54], the goals of sustainable tourism in protected areas include, in addition to offering the contemplation of the natural and cultural heritage of that environment through efficient long-term management, the implementation of management practices that minimize the negative impacts of the public use that is made and the maximization of the positive effects at the social, cultural, ecological and economic levels. The above will be done taking into account the evaluation of the indicators of each dimension analysed in this study and other previous ones [38,69].

Some advisable actions aimed at increasing the assessment of the perception of the sustainability of the National Park would be the following:

- To monitor the subsidies received by the localities in order to ensure the return of this investment and to redirect them if necessary in the future.
- A greater dynamization of the tourist activities associated with the traditions and customs of the localities. Here a benchmarking activity and the success stories in protected natural environments can be good references to propose new initiatives or improve the current ones.

- To carry out investments or redirect funds to improve the villagers' quality of life in terms of access to information and communication technologies, movement within the area and with other nearby villages/towns/cities, improvement of signposting of infrastructures, monuments or natural points of special interest in the area.

In accordance with this study, it is essential to stress the need for a sustainable tourism management model in Spanish National Parks that combines the perspective of environmental conservation with that of economic and social development and the quality of life of their closest villagers. The management model that would be most beneficial for the sustainability of National Parks and protected natural areas, in general, would be one that, from the conservation of natural resources, promotes public use of these areas in order to positively influence the economic growth of their closest area of influence.

Therefore, a more dynamic use of the public area near the park will cause an improvement in the economic indicators and this will be perceived as such by the residents of these areas. Once this improvement in the economic situation occurs, the direct and indirect effects on overall satisfaction with the protected area will increase. In addition, better use of public resources that provide infrastructure and communications will increase the quality of life of residents and directly and indirectly increase their satisfaction. This satisfaction will be key to the sustainability of the protected environment.

The results obtained in this paper for the National Parks can serve as an example for the rest of the areas and figures of protected spaces. Parks are the natural spaces with the greatest limitation in terms of public use. Thus, if sustainable management of the space is achieved, it will be the best proof that the sustainability of this type of environment can be achieved by generating sustainable development for its areas of influence while safeguarding its biological value.

Finally, the results of this study invite us to improve the work carried out and to continue investigating this interesting subject. It is true that it was decided to send a questionnaire with a few questions in order to get a high number of answers. Thus, the paper could be improved by increasing the number of items, that is, the detail of the components of each factor. In addition, in order to increase the number of responses, it might have been preferable to conduct a personal interview rather than using the telephone and the web form.

As future lines of work, it is proposed to carry out a characterisation of the managers, entrepreneurs and local authorities in those National Parks or other protected natural environments that are proving to be a successful tourist destination. This will help to focus on funds and efforts on the development of these characteristics in the National Parks and their nearest villages.

In addition, the perception of sustainability of other very important stakeholders for the sustainable development of these communities taking into account the public use that has been given in recent years and the potential that still presents for the future. Thus, the local business mass or the villagers themselves should be taken into account in future work.

Author Contributions: Conceptualization, J.M.P.-B. and V.M.-B.; methodology, E.P.-C. and P.M.-M.; software, E.P.-C.; validation, P.M.-M.; data collection and treatment, V.M.-B.; preparation of the original draft of the manuscript, J.M.P.-B. and V.M.-B.; review and editing of the manuscript, E.P.-C. and P.M.-M.; supervision, E.P.-C. All authors have read and agreed to the published version of the manuscript.

Funding: This research was funded by European Regional Development Fund, European Union "A way of making Europe", and by Council of Economy and Infrastructure, Regional Government of Extremadura (Spain), grant number GR18128.

Una manera de hacer Europa

Unión Europea   Fondo Europeo de Desarrollo Regional - FEDER

JUNTA DE EXTREMADURA
Consejería de Economía e Infraestructuras

Conflicts of Interest: The authors declare no conflict of interest.

References

1. World Travel & Tourism Council. *Travel & Tourism Economic Impact 2019 World*; WTTC: London, UK, 2019.
2. Organización Mundial de Turismo. *Turismo, Comercio y La OMT [Comunicado de Prensa]*; OMT: Madrid, Spain, 2018.
3. MacDonald, R.; Jolliffe, L. Cultural Rural Tourism: Evidence from Canada. *Ann. Tour. Res.* **2003**, *30*, 307–322. [CrossRef]
4. Jaafar, M.; Rasoolimanesh, S.M.; Lonik, K.A.T. Tourism Growth and Entrepreneurship: Empirical Analysis of Development of Rural Highlands. *Tour. Manag. Perspect.* **2015**, *14*, 17–24. [CrossRef]
5. Li, Y.; Westlund, H.; Liu, Y. Why Some Rural Areas Decline While Some Others Not: An Overview of Rural Evolution in the World. *J. Rural Stud.* **2019**, *68*, 135–143. [CrossRef]
6. Hall, D. Rural Tourism Development in Southeastern Europe: Transition and the Search for Sustainability. *Int. J. Tour. Res.* **2004**, *6*, 165–176. [CrossRef]
7. Cordente-Rodríguez, M.; Mondejar-Jimenez, J.A.; Villanueva-Alvaro, J.J. Sustainability of Nature: The Power of the Type of Visitors. *E Environ. Mag.* **2014**, *13*, 2437–2447. [CrossRef]
8. EUROPARC-España. *Anuario 2018 Del Estado de Las Áreas Protegidas En España*; EUROPARC-España: Madrid, Spain, 2019.
9. Rada, B. Parques Nacionales: Razones Para Una Ley. *Ambienta* **2014**, *106*, 4–15.
10. Thomas, L.; Middleton, J. *Guidelines for Management Planning of Protected Areas*; IUCN: Gland, Switzerland, 2003. [CrossRef]
11. Kim, K.; Uysal, M.; Sirgy, M.J. How Does Tourism in a Community Impact the Quality of Life of Community Residents? *Tour. Manag.* **2013**, *36*, 527–540. [CrossRef]
12. Weaver, D.B.; Lawton, L.J. A New Visitation Paradigm for Protected Areas. *Tour. Manag.* **2017**, *60*, 140–146. [CrossRef]
13. Ristić, D.; Vukoičić, D.; Milinčić, M. Tourism and Sustainable Development of Rural Settlements in Protected Areas—Example NP Kopaonik (Serbia). *Land Use Policy* **2019**, *89*. [CrossRef]
14. Rodary, E.; Aubertin, C. *Protected Areas, Sustainable Land?* Ashgate Publishing: Milano, Pennsylvania, 2012.
15. Font, X.; Garay, L.; Jones, S. Sustainability Motivations and Practices in Small Tourism Enterprises in European Protected Areas. *J. Clean. Prod.* **2016**, *137*, 1439–1448. [CrossRef]
16. Naughton-Treves, L.; Holland, M.B.; Brandon, K. The Role of Protected Areas in Conserving Biodiversity and Sustaining Local Livelihoods. *Annu. Rev. Environ. Resour.* **2005**, *30*, 219–252. [CrossRef]
17. West, P.; Igoe, J.; Brockington, D. Parks and Peoples: The Social Impact of Protected Areas. *Annu. Rev. Anthropol.* **2006**, *35*, 251–277. [CrossRef]
18. Mose, I. *Protected Areas and Regional Development in Europe*; Shgate Publishing: Aldershot, UK, 2007.
19. Saviano, M.; Di Nauta, P.; Montella, M.M.; Sciarelli, F. Managing Protected Areas as Cultural Landscapes: The Case of the Alta Murgia National Park in Italy. *Land Use Policy* **2018**, *76*, 290–299. [CrossRef]
20. Hidalgo, S. *Uso Público En Parques Naturales. Análisis Comparado de Andalucía y de Castilla y León (Tesis Doctoral)*; Universidad de Granada: Granada, Spain, 2006.
21. Ghoddousi, S.; Pintassilgo, P.; Mendes, J.; Ghoddousi, A.; Sequeira, B. Tourism and Nature Conservation: A Case Study in Golestan National Park, Iran. *Tour. Manag. Perspect.* **2018**, *26*, 20–27. [CrossRef]
22. Dudley, N. *Guidelines for Applying Protected Area Management Categories*; UICN: Gland, Switzerland, 2008.
23. Smith, L. *The Evolving National Park Idea: Yellowstone National Park, 1872–1890 (Doctoral Dissertation)*; College of Letters & Science—Bozeman: Bozeman, Montana, 1999.
24. Foresta, R.A. *America's National Parks and Their Keeper*; Resources for the Future: Washington, DC, USA, 2011.
25. Nash, J. *Wilderness and the American Mind*; Yale: New Haven, CT, USA, 1997.
26. Bell, J.; Stockdale, A. Evolving National Park Models: The Emergence of an Economic Imperative and Its Effect on the Contested Nature of the "national" Park Concept in Northern Ireland. *Land Use Policy* **2015**, *49*, 213–226. [CrossRef]
27. Austin, R.; Thompson, N.; Garrod, G. Understanding the Factors Underlying Partnership Working: A Case Study of Northumberland National Park, England. *Land Use Policy* **2016**, *50*, 115–124. [CrossRef]
28. Iniesta, P. Parques Nacionales: Crónica Bibliográfica de Su Régimen Jurídico. *Obs. Medioambient.* **2001**, *4*, 407–414.
29. Watson, J.E.M.; Dudley, N.; Segan, D.B.; Hockings, M. The Performance and Potential of Protected Areas. *Nature* **2014**, *515*, 67–73. [CrossRef]

30. Gómez-Limón, J.; García, D. *Capacidad de Acogida de Uso Público En Los Espacios Naturales Protegidos*; Organismo Autónomo Parques Nacionales (OAPN): Madrid, Spain, 2014.

31. DeFries, R.; Hansen, A.; Turner, B.L.; Reid, R.; Liu, J. Land Use Change around Protected Areas: Management to Balance Human Needs and Ecological Function. *Ecol. Appl.* **2007**, *17*, 1031–1038. [CrossRef]

32. Pulido, J.I. Criterios Para Una Política Sostenible En Los Parques Naturales de Andalucía. Ph.D. Thesis, Universidad de Jaén, Jaén, Spain, 2005. [CrossRef]

33. Das, M.; Chatterjee, B. Ecotourism: A Panacea or a Predicament? *Tour. Manag. Perspect.* **2015**, *14*, 3–16. [CrossRef]

34. Vozmediano, J. Incidencia de La Doctrina Del Tibunal Constitucional En La Gestión de Los Parques Nacionales. *Rev. Jurídica Castilla Y León* **2005**, *7*, 13–62.

35. Choi, H.S.C.; Sirakaya, E. Sustainability Indicators for Managing Community Tourism. *Tour. Manag.* **2006**, *27*, 1274–1289. [CrossRef]

36. Dwyer, L.; Forsyth, P. Economic Measures of Tourism Yield: What Markets to Target? *Int. J. Tour. Res.* **2008**, *10*, 155–168. [CrossRef]

37. Baum, J.; Cumming, G.S.; De Vos, A. Understanding Spatial Variation in the Drivers of Nature-Based Tourism and Their Influence on the Sustainability of Private Land Conservation. *Ecol. Econ.* **2017**, *140*, 225–234. [CrossRef]

38. Jurowski, C.; Uysal, M.; Williams, D.R. A Theoretical Analysis of Host Community Resident Reactions to Tourism. *J. Travel Res.* **1997**, *36*, 3–11. [CrossRef]

39. Olya, H.G.T.; Gavilyan, Y. Configurational Models to Predict Residents' Support for Tourism Development. *J. Travel. Res.* **2016**, *56*, 893–912. [CrossRef]

40. Alipour, H.; Olya, H.; Forouzan, I. Environmental Impacts of Mass Religious Tourism: From Residents' Perspectives. *Tour. Anal.* **2017**, *22*, 167–183. [CrossRef]

41. Olya, H.G.T.; Alipour, H.; Gavilyan, Y. Different Voices from Community Groups to Support Sustainable Tourism Development at Iranian World Heritage Sites: Evidence from Bisotun. *J. Sustain. Tour.* **2018**, *26*, 1728–1748. [CrossRef]

42. Olya, H.G.T.; Shahmirzdi, E.K.; Alipour, H. Pro-Tourism and Anti-Tourism Community Groups at a World Heritage Site in Turkey. *Curr. Issues Tour.* **2017**, *22*, 763–785. [CrossRef]

43. Balmford, A.; Beresford, J.; Green, J.; Naidoo, R.; Walpole, M.; Manica, A. A Global Perspective on Trends in Nature-Based Tourism. *PLoS Biol.* **2009**, *7*, e1000144. [CrossRef]

44. Eagles, P.F.J.; Mccool, S.F.; Haynes, C.D. *Sustainable Tourism in Protected Areas: Guidelines for Planning and Management*; IUCN, Ed.; UICN: Gland, Switzerland, 2002. [CrossRef]

45. Ramkissoon, H.; Weiler, B.; Smith, L.D.G. Place Attachment and Pro-Environmental Behaviour in National Parks: The Development of a Conceptual Framework. *J. Sustain. Tour.* **2012**, *20*, 257–276. [CrossRef]

46. Reinius, S.W.; Fredman, P. Protected Areas as Attractions. *Ann. Tour. Res.* **2007**, *34*, 839–854. [CrossRef]

47. Benayas, J.; Muñoz, M. Nuevos Retos y Oportunidades Para La Financiación de Los Servicios de Uso Público En Los Espacios Naturales Protegidos. *Ecosistemas* **2007**, *16*, 125–136. [CrossRef]

48. Baral, N.; Stern, M.J.; Bhattarai, R. Contingent Valuation of Ecotourism in Annapurna Conservation Area, Nepal: Implications for Sustainable Park Finance and Local Development. *Ecol. Econ.* **2008**, *15*, 218–227. [CrossRef]

49. Ryan, C.; Gu, H.; Zhang, W. The Context of Chinese Tourism—An Overview and Implications for Research. In *Tourism in China: Destination, Cultures and Communities*; Ryan, C., Gu, W., Eds.; Routledge: Nueva York, NY, USA, 2009; pp. 327–336.

50. Park, D.B.; Lee, K.W.; Choi, H.S.; Yoon, Y. Factors Influencing Social Capital in Rural Tourism Communities in South Korea. *Tour. Manag.* **2012**, *33*, 1511–1520. [CrossRef]

51. Ley 30/2014, de 3 de Diciembre, de Parques Nacionales. Available online: https://www.boe.es/buscar/pdf/2014/BOE-A-2014-12588-consolidado.pdf (accessed on 17 January 2020).

52. Ministerio Para la Transición Económica MITECO. Datos de Visitantes a los Parques Nacionales (1996–2017). Available online: https://www.miteco.gob.es/es/red-parques-nacionales/la-red/gestion/visitasppnn_tcm30-67283.pdf (accessed on 11 January 2020).

53. Aparicio, M. El Reto Del Turismo En Los Espacios Naturales Protegidos Españoles: La Integración Entre Conservación, Calidad y Satisfacción (Tesis Doctoral), 2012. Open Academic Production of the UCM. Available online: https://eprints.ucm.es/20836/ (accessed on 11 February 2020).

54. Job, H.; Becken, S.; Lane, B. Protected Areas in a Neoliberal World and the Role of Tourism in Supporting Conservation and Sustainable Development: An Assessment of Strategic Planning, Zoning, Impact Monitoring, and Tourism Management at Natural World Heritage Sites. *J. Sustain. Tour.* **2017**, *25*, 1697–1718. [CrossRef]

55. Frost, W.; Hall, C. *Tourism and National Parks: International Perspectives on Development, Histories and Change*; Routledge: Oxon, MD, USA, 2009.

56. Lee, T.H. Influence Analysis of Community Resident Support for Sustainable Tourism Development. *Tour. Manag.* **2013**, *34*, 37–46. [CrossRef]

57. Jeon, M.M.; Kang, M.(Michelle); Desmarais, E. Residents' Perceived Quality Of Life in a Cultural-Heritage Tourism Destination. *Appl. Res. Qual. Life* **2016**, *11*, 105–123. [CrossRef]

58. Nunkoo, R.; Gursoy, D. Residents' Support for Tourism. An Identity Perspective. *Ann. Tour. Res.* **2012**, *39*, 243–268. [CrossRef]

59. Nunkoo, R.; So, K.K.F. Residents' Support for Tourism. *J. Travel Res.* **2015**, *55*, 847–861. [CrossRef]

60. Liang, Z.X.; Hui, T.K. Residents' Quality of Life and Attitudes toward Tourism Development in China. *Tour. Manag.* **2016**, *57*, 56–67. [CrossRef]

61. Real Decreto 389/2016, de 22 de Octubre, por el que se Aprueba el Plan Director de la Red de Parques Nacionales. Available online: https://www.boe.es/diario_boe/txt.php?id=BOE-A-2016-9690 (accessed on 17 January 2020).

62. Mosammam, H.M.; Sarrafi, M.; Nia, J.T.; Heidari, S. Typology of the Ecotourism Development Approach and an Evaluation from the Sustainability View: The Case of Mazandaran Province, Iran. *Tour. Manag. Perspect.* **2016**, *18*, 168–178. [CrossRef]

63. Woo, E.; Kim, H.; Uysal, M. Life Satisfaction and Support for Tourism Development. *Ann. Tour. Res.* **2015**, *50*, 84–97. [CrossRef]

64. Mondéjar-Jiménez, J.; Mondéjar-Jiménez, J.A.; Vargas-Vargas, M.; Gázquez-Abad, J. Personal Attitudes in Environmental Protection. *Int. J. Environ. Res.* **2012**, *6*, 1039–1044.

65. Fritzsche, D.; Oz, E. Personal values' influence on the ethical dimension of decision making. *J. Bus. Ethics* **2007**, *75*, 335–343. [CrossRef]

66. Monecke, A.; Leisch, F. SemPLS: Structural equation modeling using partial least squares. *J. Stat. Softw.* **2012**, *48*, 1–32. [CrossRef]

67. Hair, J.F.; Ringle, C.M.; Sarstedt, M. PLS-SEM: Indeed a Silver Bullet. *J. Mark. Theory Pract.* **2011**, *19*, 139–151. [CrossRef]

68. Fornell, C.; Larcker, D.F. Evaluating Structural Equation Models with Unobservable Variables and Measurement Error. *J. Mark. Res.* **1981**, *18*, 39. [CrossRef]

69. Campón-Cerro, A.M.; Folgado-Fernández, J.A.; Hernández-Mogollón, J.M. Rural Destination Development Based on Olive Oil Tourism: The Impact of Residents' Community Attachment and Quality of Life on Their Support for Tourism Development. *Sustainability* **2017**, *9*, 1624. [CrossRef]

Article

Radon Gas as an Indicator for Air Quality Control in Buried Industrial Architecture: Rehabilitation of the Old *Británica* Warehouses in Alicante for a Tourist Site

Carlos Rizo-Maestre [1,*], Víctor Echarri-Iribarren [1], Raúl Prado-Govea [1] and Francisco Pujol-López [2]

1   Department of Architectural Constructions, University of Alicante, 03690 Alicante, Spain
2   Department of Computer Science and Technology, University of Alicante, 03690 Alicante, Spain
*   Correspondence: carlosrm@ua.es

Received: 9 July 2019; Accepted: 14 August 2019; Published: 28 August 2019

Abstract: The infrastructure of the *Británica* warehouses in Alicante is a very important industrial architectural element in the history of Spain, although it is unknown to almost all of the inhabitants of the city. The former fuel refinery is located in the Serra Grossa Mountains and served much of the country until 1966. This research is based on the plans of the city of Alicante to convert a historical element, the *Británica* warehouses, into a unique tourist site. Currently, the network of storage domes in this facility, which has an approximate footprint of 20,000 m^2 and domes approximately 20 m high, is in a state of neglect, and there are neighborhood initiatives for its rehabilitation to become a cultural or tourist site. Therefore, it is necessary to take into account the quality of the indoor air. Radon gas is analyzed as a control element for future refurbishment of the facility. Alicante is a nongranite area and therefore is not very susceptible to generation of radon gas indoors, but the conditions of a buried and poorly ventilated space make the site appropriate for analysis. Most scientific agencies in the field of medicine and health, including the World Health Organization, consider radon gas to be very harmful to humans. This element in its gaseous state is radioactive and is present in almost all the land in which the buildings are implanted, with granitic type soils presenting higher levels of radon gas. Nongranitic soils have traditionally been considered to have low radon levels. The city of Alicante, where the installation is located, is a nongranitic area and therefore is not very susceptible to generating radon gas in buildings, but the conditions of buried and poorly ventilated places make the site appropriate for analysis to support air quality control and decision-making.

Keywords: healthy architecture; construction materials; environment; radon; underground building; heritage building

1. Introduction

The majority of scientific agencies in the field of medicine and health, including the World Health Organization, consider radon gas to be very harmful to humans. This element in its gaseous state is radioactive, and higher levels of radon gas are present in almost all granitic soils in which buildings are located. Nongranitic soils have traditionally been considered to have low radon levels.

This research is based on the plans of the city of Alicante to convert a historical element, the *Británica* warehouses (Figure 1), into a singular tourist site therefore, the quality of the interior air has to be taken into account. Radon gas is analyzed as a control element for future rehabilitation.

Alicante is in a nongranitic area that is not very susceptible to generation of radon gas in buildings, but the conditions of a buried and poorly ventilated space make the site appropriate for analysis.

Sustainability **2019**, *11*, 4692

Figure 1. Image of the Serra Grossa from the Castle of Santa Bárbara on Monte Benacantil (own source).

1.1. Radon Gas and Health

Radon is a chemical element belonging to the group of noble gases. It is found mainly in the subsoil. The uranium in the soil disintegrates and produces radon, which remains in the soil. When decomposed, it is released to the surface in the form of a gas. In its gaseous form, it is colorless, odorless and tasteless and therefore undetectable [1,2].

Radon gas occurs as a result of the decay of the uranium contained in rocks [3]. Radon emanates from the ground and is concentrated mostly in enclosed spaces [4], so it is highly recommended that homes and workplaces are properly ventilated [5].

Three-quarters of the radioactivity in the environment comes from natural elements [6]. Radon is the major source of natural radioactivity [7], and the public health problem generated by its concentration both inside buildings and in drinking water means that it must be considered for evaluation [8].

Radon decays due to so-called ionizing radiation because, when it enters matter, it usually pulls electrons out of the surrounding atoms by a process known as ionization [9]. If the matter is biological tissue with a high water content, the ionization of the water molecules can give rise to so-called free radicals with a high chemical activity [10], sufficient to alter important molecules that form part of the tissues of living beings [11]. These alterations may include chemical changes in DNA, the basic organic molecule that forms part of the cells that make up our bodies [12]. These changes may lead to the appearance of biological effects, including abnormal cell development [13]. These alterations may be more or less severe depending on the dose of radiation received [14]. The main effect of the presence of radon in the human environment is the risk of lung cancer [15]. This radioactive gaseous element is present in almost all construction materials and in the ground on which buildings are constructed [16].

Different radon-measuring devices are available. Some are active, require electricity and allow continuous recording of radon gas concentrations and fluctuations during the measurement period [17]. Others are passive and do not require electrical current to operate in the sampling environment [18].

Electret ion chambers (CIE) have been used to carry out this research. CIE are passive devices that function as integrating detectors to measure the average concentration of radon gas during the measurement period. The electret functions both as an electric field generator and as a sensor in the ionic chamber. The radon gas enters the chamber by diffusion through an inlet equipped with a filter without allowing the rest of the elements produced during the disintegration process to pass [19]. The radiation emitted by the radon and its disintegration products formed inside the chamber ionize the air inside the chamber by reducing the detector surface voltage [20]. Subsequently, a calibration factor relates this voltage drop to the radon concentration existing in the space and time studied.

The most important source of radon in isolated buildings or ground floors is the radon present in the ground. The radon concentration in the soil is generally between 10 and 50 Bq/kg, although it can reach much higher values. The average value is approximately 40 Bq/kg. The amount of radon entering a building's interior from the soil depends mainly on the concentration of radium-226 in the subsoil and the permeability of the subsoil.

Predictive maps of radon content are available in most countries, based mostly on the igneous compositions of the ground [21]. For example, Sweden has developed maps based on the measurement of the geogenic potential of radon, which indicates the level of risk by area estimated from the concentration of radon in the ground at a depth of 1 meter [22]. Likewise, the usefulness of methods based on other variables, such as the concentration of radium-226 in the soil or the equivalent of uranium (eU), has been proven. In the case of France, for example, the national map has been drawn up on the basis of geological maps and the average uranium content of each geological unit [23]. The German map [24] and the Czech map [25] have also been elaborated using the geogenic potential of radon. All radon gas predictive maps consider granitic soils to be the highest risk in terms of concentrations [26] and consider clay soils to have a low presence of radon gas. In Spain, the Technical Building Code (CTE), as of February 2018, did not regulate the maximum dose of radon allowed in a building and how to contain it [27].

The Spanish Mediterranean coast, where the city of Alicante is located, is mainly clay [28]. In the urban center of the city are the two mountains compared in the study: Monte Benacantil and Serra Grossa. Therefore, they can be considered to have the same igneous composition.

The ventilation of building interiors is essential to define their air quality because the greater the air renewal rate [29], the fewer stale particles remain in the environment [30]. Therefore, the presence of radon gas is used to analyze whether ventilation is adequate inside railway tunnels, i.e., whether the area where the extraction machines are located (Monte Benacantil) has better ventilation than the area where it is excavated in the rough (Serra Grossa) [31].

1.2. Radon Gas Regulations in Spain

In Spain, the National Institute for Occupational Safety and Hygiene, under the Ministry of Labor and Social Affairs, has published two related Technical Protection Standards [32], from which most of the paragraphs in this section have been extracted. The NTPs are guides to good practice and specifications, although they are not obligatory unless they are included in a regulatory provision in force, and they follow the recommendations of the European public body in charge of coordinating nuclear energy research programs, the European Nuclear Energy Community, or EURATOM.

According to NTP 533 "*Radon and its effects on health*", experimental studies carried out on animals that have been irradiated, as well as those carried out on people who, for various reasons, have been subjected to high doses of radiation, have shown that ionizing radiation constitutes a carcinogenic agent. The appearance of cancer usually occurs several years after receiving irradiation, being a late effect, probabilistic or stochastic. The probability evidently increases with the dose.

The first works citing the carcinogenicity of radon in animals (rats and monkeys) exposed by inhalation to concentrations of 27.8×10^6 Bq/m^3 were carried out in 1943. In subsequent acute toxicity studies with the same species for periods of three to seven weeks and with exposure to radon inhalation concentrations between $18.5–740 \times 10^6$ Bq/m^3, the effects found for whole-body irradiation were pulmonary congestion and, frequently, paralysis of the hind limbs. X-rays revealed hyperactivity in the skin, lungs, and adrenal glands [31].

The first epidemiological studies on which the association between exposure to radon and lung cancer is based were carried out in workers in uranium mines, demonstrating an incidence of lung cancer 50 times higher than the average of the unexposed population in the mining population of several countries [33]. Due to insufficient ventilation, the high concentration of uranium (and as a consequence, of radium-226) produced a high concentration of radon and its byproducts, which when inhaled generated lung cancer. Although cancer was initially associated only with inhalation of solid matter, the importance of gas in the induction of the disease was later noted. The latency period of the disease was set at 20 years.

In the absence of sufficient data, estimates of the risk associated with domestic radon exposure were initially based on extrapolation of the results obtained for miners. This extrapolation had a series of limitations, among which the following stand out:

- The absence of data concerning women and children, who obviously did not work in the mines.
- Uncertainties in the effect on health of the dose rate.
- Lack of data on smoking habits in most studies.
- Inadequate control of other confounding variables (such as exposure to gamma radiation or suspended aerosols).

Therefore, to specifically assess the risk of cancer associated with radon exposure in housing, a number of epidemiological studies of varying scope were undertaken from the 1980s onwards. They have shown that the risk associated with household exposures is higher than that predicted by extrapolation from the cohort of miners. According to studies conducted in Europe [34], China [35] and North America [36], an increase of 100 Bq/m^3 in the mean radon concentration in a household leads to a 10% increase in the likelihood of lung cancer.

In short, radon has been considered carcinogenic by the World Health Organization (WHO) since 1998, according to the International Agency for Research on Cancer (IARC) and the U.S. Environmental Protection Agency (EPA), which classify it as a Group 1 and Group A carcinogen, respectively. The main adverse effect of inhaling radon and its breakdown products is the risk of lung cancer.

Radon, as a gas, is not significantly retained in the respiratory tract. However, 90% of its descendants may be attached to aerosol particles present in the air, which, depending on their size, may be retained at different levels of the respiratory system. The smallest, the respirable fraction, will reach the most sensitive areas of bronchial and pulmonary tissue, depositing there, along with the remaining 10% of the disintegration products. The deposition of these particles generates a source of emission of high-density α particles, so that a part of this tissue receives a high exposure, increasing the possibility of developing a carcinogenic process. The dose received in the lung by beta radiation (β) or gamma radiation (γ) is negligible compared to that due to alpha particles (α).

In Spain, the most valuable source of environmental radiological information is the Natural Gamma Radiation Map (Marna) [37]. The Marna evaluates the rate of exposure to terrestrial gamma radiation of natural origin referenced to one meter above ground level, which has an excellent correlation with the content of radium-226, which is the precursor isotope of radon. Because the currently available network of radon measurements in homes is not dense enough, the Marna offers a good alternative for developing a radon exposure predictive map.

2. The *Británica* Warehouses as a Future Tourist Site in the City of Alicante

Inside the Serra Grossa is one of the most important engineering works of the 20th century, unknown to almost all the inhabitants of the city: the storage domes of an old oil refinery that in the past was initially owned by the state and then by the private company Campsa (Figure 2). This infrastructure served a large part of the country until 1966, when a more modern refinery was inaugurated in the port of Alicante. At present, it is in a state of abandonment, and there are neighborhood initiatives for its rehabilitation and for it to become a cultural or tourist site. Therefore, it will house people, and it is vitally important to conduct a study of indoor air quality.

Figure 2. Image of the location of the *Británica* warehouses on the Serra Grossa from a drone flight (own source).

This industrial facility was used for refining oil and its derivatives, from storage to distribution. The installation included surface and other underground constructions excavated in the rock of the Serra Grossa. This complex was internally connected with galleries and tunnels at different heights that connected the interior rooms with the exterior rooms (Figure 3).

Today, despite decades of deterioration, you can still see part of the complex, especially the parts that remain buried in the mountain. In its interior remain part of the elements of the old factory; wagons, rails and electric cables are between dirt and complete abandonment.

The study of indoor air quality within this complex with radon gas as an indicator is presented not only because of its interesting architectural morphology built on the mountain but also because of its importance in the history of the city and the residents' lack of knowledge about the site.

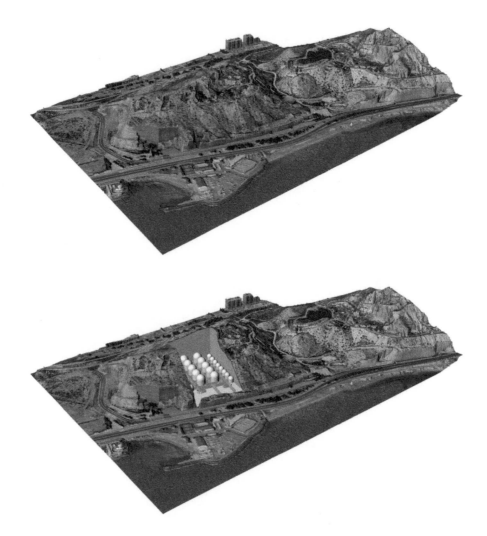

Figure 3. 3D image made with drone photogrammetry of the location of the *Británica* warehouses (own source).

2.1. History of the Place

The city of Alicante is very important at a strategic military level due to its port and Mediterranean location. In the past, the province had two oil refineries, one of them located in Benalúa (from "Industrias Fourcade y Provot") and the other in the southern area of Serra Grossa on the site of an old metallurgical company called "La Británica", from which the *Británica* warehouse complex inherited its name. The *Británica* factory received the crude oil from its own pier, Santa Ana, which later became known as Pichón's Shot. The first company to exploit the refinery was Deutsch y Cía in 1875; later, it was used by the company El León.

The refinery grew as the country required its services due to the increase in population. At the beginning of the 20th century, it supplied 55% of the Spanish market to be used for, among other uses, public lighting and both civil and military vehicles. In 1903, an enormous delimiting wall was erected for the factory, as seen in the photos of the time (Figure 4). In 1915, the refinery was linked to the railroad. In 1929, the pier was destroyed by a storm and was not rebuilt to link to the factory.

Figure 4. Left: Image of the Raval Roig and the boats of the Postiguet in the foreground. The factory is in the background, with the jetty and the chimney. Image from the beginning of the 20th century. Right: Image of the factory in 1909 (source: *Alicante Vivo*).

In 1929, the facility was acquired by the national company Campsa, which had a monopoly on the country's oil. At that time, the factory covered approximately 72,000 m^2. The facility was modernized due to the demand for fuel. With the existing political situation on the verge of warfare, the need for crude oil was growing, and the location of the depots was a concern because it was an area vulnerable to bombardment and easy combustion.

In 1932, an expansion and remodeling project was presented to be able to face the demand for increasing the capacity of the tanks. In 1937, the project for Campsa's underground factory was presented. Excavation continued until the 1950s, and the interior was reinforced with shotcrete to hold the vaults. This process of remodeling the factory was carried out to protect one of the most important assets during the period of wars of the time.

When the Spanish Civil War ended in 1939, the underground factory began to be excavated, the exterior installations were modified, new tanks with more capacity were added, and the employees' homes were removed (Figure 5).

Figure 5. Image of the external tank of the refinery that is still conserved (own source).

The facilities were used uninterruptedly until they were abandoned in 1966, when Campsa moved its operations to the Port of Alicante, in the area now known as Panoramis; they remained there until they were relocated in 1979 to the outskirts of the city (Figure 6).

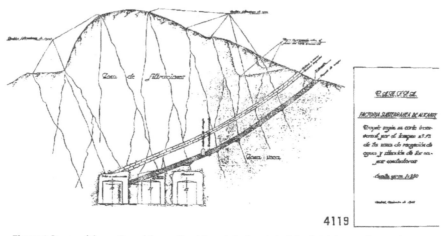

Figure 6. Image of the section of the vaults of the original project of the *Británica* warehouses (source: original project, AMA files).

With the end of its use, all the tools that had served in the factory premises were removed for different reasons. According to testimonies at the time, the cutting of one of the fuel tanks caused a fire that lasted several days, and the smoke produced left the walls of the vaults completely black, as can be seen today.

2.2. Architectural Description of the Complex

In addition to the underground volumes that make up the complex today, there are a few elements that were once part of this important industrial factory in the city. Currently, it is abandoned, and due to its dimensions and historical route, it can be considered within the framing of *industrial archaeology*.

The enclosure consisted of three main galleries and seven secondary galleries, linked in a grid pattern that housed large concrete vaults on their sides in which metal tanks were installed to store the crude oil. The main vaults were approximately 20 m high and 18 m in diameter. The communication galleries had average dimensions of 3 m by 2 m in height and a length of approximately 160 m. The layout can be seen in Figure 7, showing 10 main and 16 secondary vaults. The total footprint of the subterranean facility is located in a rectangle of 170 by 120 m.

The main entrance to the complex was the high central gallery, where maintenance and repair work was carried out. The fuel tanks were filled by means of large pipelines that came to the surface and connected with the external plants for distillation and refining of crude oil.

Figure 7. 3D reconstruction of the tanks (own source).

On the lower level, there were different outbuildings, such as warehouses, workshops, offices, garages, warehouses and even workers' homes. All of this area was demolished and at the moment serves as the Sangueta stop of the Metropolitan Transport of Alicante.

On the next level was the large exterior tank, which is still partially standing, and the chimney, which can be seen in the photos of the period. There were also old exterior gabled naves with masonry walls.

3. Building Materials in *Británica* Warehouses: The Current Complex and Future Proposals for Use

The *Británica* warehouses were a work of considerable technical difficulty for the time as they were underground tanks holding the fuel reserves for part of the country and were located inside the mountain, which is now called the quarry. This area was the origin of San Julian's stone, which was highly valued for ancient and important buildings in the city, such as the city hall and the Cathedral of St. Nicholas.

The underground installation consists of a set of circular naves with domes excavated from the rock and reinforced with reinforced concrete connected by long corridors. All this construction was calculated to be able to contain the weight of the mountain and, in case of enemy attack, to keep the fuel well protected. During tank inspections, in addition to radon analyses, samples of different construction materials were extracted for further analysis.

As described, the complex has been in disuse since 1966, and no work has been carried out to reconvert or clean up the site. The refinery has been used for shooting films but has not had a subsequent use due to the low level of conservation that it has had during the last 50 years. Various proposals have been made to rehabilitate the complex, including for a leisure and cultural park that would take advantage of the underground enclosures and high domes as an auditorium area.

The municipal Special Archaeological Protection Plan of Alicante has collected the proposals but did not grant any type of protection. A report by the Directorate General of Heritage of the Department of Culture of the Valencian Community recommended that the facilities be declared a "Property of

Local Relevance". Figure 8 shows one of the entrances to the complex from the Sangueta stop that was finally built.

Figure 8. Image of the southern entrance to the complex, which was used as access to make the measurements taken from the stop of the TRAM de la Sangueta. It is trellised and in a deteriorated state such as the rest of the accesses (own source).

During the study of the layout for the new metro line crossing the Serra Grossa to the north, consideration was given to the possibility of cutting through the factory as part of the excavation of the tunnel, which would have meant the total loss of the site. This idea was discarded by the Conselleria de Infraestructuras y Transportes, which makes later rehabilitation possible to enable viable approaches of recovery similar to the aforementioned ones.

4. Study of the Quality of the Air in the *Británica* Warehouses

The study carried out inside the old fuel tanks of the *Británica* warehouses lasted two days, beginning on 7 September 2016. The entrance to the site was made through the south door, which is currently partially closed with damaged grilles that do not impede passage. Through this door, access was gained to carry out the study. In the mountain, there are other hidden entrances that connect with the large galleries, but they are closed and have not been explored during the work in the complex.

The measurement areas of the study in the old *Británica* deposits were as follows, as shown in Figure 9:

1. Zone 1
2. Zone 2
3. Zone 3
4. Zone 4
5. Zone 5
6. Zone 6

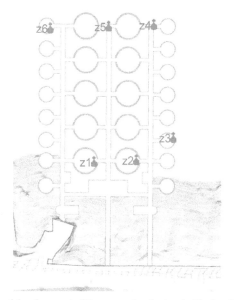

Figure 9. Plant image of the placement of the measuring devices inside the old tanks (own source).

The design of this work allows the communication of all of the rooms. The only ventilation comes from the main entrances and some elements that emerge at the top of the mountain that in the past served the factory to treat the fuel, so the air renewal is virtually null.

This old factory is very interesting for the study of the amount of radon gas because of its location in the Serra Grossa and the type of construction. In addition, due to its activity, it played a tremendous role in the supply of petroleum products for the whole country, and its underground structure is the product of engineering more than 60 years ago, having endured although the mountain rests on it, with domes close to 20 m high.

4.1. Radon Measuring System

The radon gas measuring system used in the study was a **short chamber** and **short electret** of the *Eperm System* for two days (Figure 10). The complex morphology of the site means that all the rooms studied have similar conditions of low ventilation.

Figure 10. Image of the data collection phase inside the tanks (own source).

4.2. Climatology during the Study

The average temperatures recorded in the city of Alicante during the time of the study were between 23 °C and 32 °C, and there was no precipitation, although that would not have considerably impacted the underground tanks.

The temperature inside the tanks is similar to that recorded inside the tunnel that passes a few meters into Serra Grossa itself, with average values close to 17 °C.

4.3. Results Obtained in the Study

The equipment introduced into the tanks was placed for two days in different rooms with a unique combination of **short-short camera-electret**. The results obtained in the six previously chosen zones are shown in Figure 11.

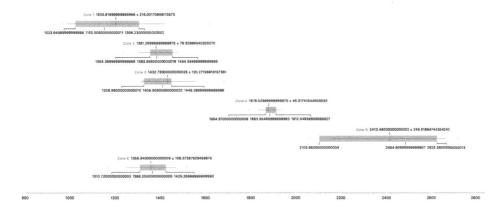

Figure 11. Measurements carried out in the *Británica* tanks (own source).

5. Discussion of Results

The representation of the radon gas results in the environment of the *Británica* tanks obtained using the combination of **short chamber** and **short electret** is provided in a comparative table that shows the different measurement areas and the obtained average environmental concentrations of the gas in Bq/m^3. Table 1 and Figure 12 show the dispersion of the results in each of the zones.

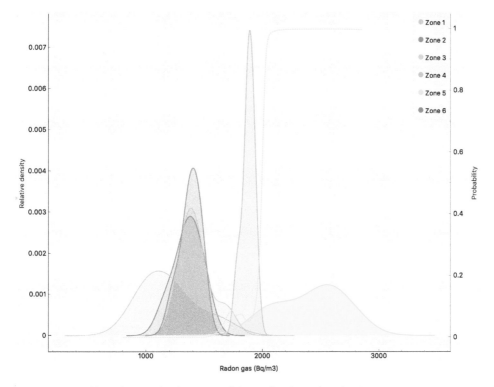

Figure 12. Chart showing the dispersion of the results obtained in the six measurement zones (own source).

Table 1. Summary of the measurements carried out in the *Británica* tanks (own source).

Zone	Place	Number of Samples	Average Gas Concentration Radon (Bq/m^3)
Zone 1	Dome 1	6	1203,62
Zone 2	Dome 2	6	1381,27
Zone 3	Dome 3	6	1432,73
Zone 4	End of Corridor 1	6	1878,53
Zone 5	Aisle 2	6	2413,48
Zone 6	Dome 4	6	1358,94

The results obtained in the installation show a high average amount of radon gas inside, which is explained by the limited air movement that occurs and the contact with the ground. In the different measurements, the radon gas accumulation obtained varied between 1203.62 and 2413.48 Bq/m^3, quadrupling the threshold of 300 Bq/m^3 in the most favorable case. Thus, this study has established a value from which it is necessary to take corrective ventilation measures. A heat map of the results is shown in Figure 13.

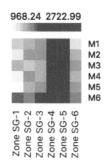

Figure 13. Heat map of the results obtained (own source).

6. Conclusions

The infrastructure of the *Británica* warehouses of Alicante is a very important industrial architectural element in the history of Spain, although it is unknown to almost all the inhabitants of the city. The former fuel refinery is located in the Serra Grossa and served much of the country until 1966.

As an element for the future accommodation of people, it is necessary to carry out an air quality study with radon gas as an indicator. The results obtained in the installation show a high average amount of radon gas inside, which is explained by the limited air movement and its contact with the ground. The values in the eleven measurement zones varied between 1203.62 and 2413.48 Bq/m^3, quadrupling the threshold of 300 Bq/m^3 in the most favorable case, and establishing values for which corrective ventilation measures must be taken.

The old *Británica* warehouses exhibit radon values much higher than those estimated for constructions in Alicante, if we consider the Marna map, where the area of the Levante is considered low risk. When this area is rehabilitated as recently proposed, the observation of high amounts of radon gas inside must be addressed and solutions adopted. These must be oriented to better renew the interior air by means of mechanical processes to avoid making more openings in the mountain that would distort the landscape and weaken the structure. It is for this reason that the current conditions should not be considered suitable for accommodating people until remodeling projects that include adequate ventilation of the installation have been carried out.

Author Contributions: The work presented here was developed in collaboration among all the authors. All of the authors have contributed to, seen and approved the manuscript.

Acknowledgments: The authors of this paper thank the University of Alicante for the grant that allowed part of this research.

Conflicts of Interest: The authors declare no conflicts of interest.

References

1. Leccese, F.; Salvadori, G.; Barlit, M. Ventilated flat roofs: A simplified model to assess their hygrothermal behaviour. *J. Build. Eng.* **2019**, *22*, 12–21. [CrossRef]
2. Leccese, F.; Rocca, M.; Salvadori, G. Fast estimation of speech transmission index using the reverberation time: Comparison between predictive equations for educational rooms of different sizes. *Appl. Acoust.* **2018**, *140*, 143–149. [CrossRef]
3. Lavi, N.; Steiner, V.; Alfassi, Z.B. Measurement of radon emanation in construction materials. *Radiat. Meas.* **2009**, *44*, 396–400. [CrossRef]
4. Maestre, C.R.; Yepes, S.C. Detection and importance of the presence of Radon Gas in buildings. *Int. J. Eng. Tech. Res. (IJETR)* **2016**, *4*, 67–70.
5. Cuvier, A.; Panza, F.; Pourcelot, L.; Foissard, B.; Cagnat, X.; Prunier, J.; van Beek, P.; Souhaut, M.; Roux, G.L. Uranium decay daughters from isolated mines: Accumulation and sources. *J. Environ. Radioact.* **2015**, *149*, 110–120. [CrossRef]
6. Szabó, K.Z.; Jordan, G.; Ákos Horváth.; Szabó, C. Mapping the geogenic radon potential: Methodology and spatial analysis for central Hungary. *J. Environ. Radioact.* **2014**, *129*, 107–120. [CrossRef]
7. Collignan, B.; Powaga, E. Impact of ventilation systems and energy savings in a building on the mechanisms governing the indoor radon activity concentration. *J. Environ. Radioact.* **2017**. [CrossRef]
8. Miguel, M.G.T.S.; Matarranz, J.L.M.; de Mingo, R.G.; Cadierno, J.P.G.; Mahou, E.S. El Mapa Predictivo de Exposición al Radón en España; Editor Consejo de Seguridad Nuclear. Available online: https://www.foronuclear.org/es/publicaciones-y-documentacion/recomendaciones-bibliograficas/120471-el-mapa-predictivo-de-exposicion-al-radon-en-espana (accessed on 6 August 2019).
9. United Nations Scientific Committee on the Effects of Atomic Radiation. *Sources and Effects of Ionizing Radiation: United Nations Scientific Committee on the Effects of Atomic Radiation: UNSCEAR 2000 Report to the General Assembly, with Scientific Annexes*; United Nations: New York, NY, USA, 2000.
10. Cristobo, J.J.J.L. Medición de la Concentración de Gas 222Rn en el Interior de Edificios; USC Departamento de Física de las Partículas. Available online: http://fpsalmon.usc.es/Diplomas/DEA_JJLLerena.pdf (accessed on 6 August 2019).
11. Boerma, M.; Sridharan, V.; Mao, X.W.; Nelson, G.A.; Cheema, A.K.; Koturbash, I.; Singh, S.P.; Tackett, A.J.; Hauer-Jensen, M. Effects of ionizing radiation on the heart. *Mutat. Res. Rev. Mutat. Res.* **2016**, *770*, 319–327. [CrossRef]
12. Bhattacharya, S.; Asaithamby, A. Ionizing radiation and heart risks. *Semin. Cell Dev. Biol.* **2016**, *58*, 14–25. [CrossRef]
13. Ravanat, J.L.; Douki, T. UV and ionizing radiations induced DNA damage, differences and similarities. *Radiat. Phys. Chem.* **2016**, *128*, 92–102. [CrossRef]
14. Amber, I.; O'Donovan, T.S. Natural convection induced by the absorption of solar radiation: A review. *Renew. Sustain. Energy Rev.* **2018**, *82*, 3526–3545. [CrossRef]
15. Maestre, C.R.; Yepes, S.C. Radon Gas. Hazardous element for human life really found in the environment. In Proceedings of the 2nd International Conference on Green Materials and Environmental Engineering, Phuket, Thailand, 20–21 December 2015; Atlantis Press: Paris, France, 2015; pp. 60–62.
16. De Seguridad Nuclear, C. Dosis de Radiación; Editor Consejo de Seguridad Nuclear. Available online: https://www.csn.es/documents/10182/914805/Dosis%20de%20radiaci%C3%B3n (accessed on 6 August 2019).
17. Barbosa-Lorenzo, R.; Ruano-Ravina, A.; Caramés, S.C.; Barros-Dios, J.M. Radón residencial y cáncer de pulmón. Un estudio ecológico en Galicia. *Med. Clin.* **2015**, *144*, 304–308. [CrossRef]
18. Nastro, V.; Carnì, D.L.; Vitale, A.; Lamonaca, F.; Vasile, M. Passive and active methods for Radon pollution measurements in historical heritage buildings. *Measurement* **2018**, *114*, 526–533. [CrossRef]
19. Li, P.; Zhang, R.; Gu, M.; Zheng, G. Uptake of the natural radioactive gas radon by an epiphytic plant. *Sci. Total Environ.* **2018**, *612*, 436–441. [CrossRef]
20. Zeeb, H. International Radon Project. Survey On Radon Guidelines, Programmes and Activities; WHO HSE/PHE/RAD. Available online: https://www.who.int/ionizing_radiation/env/radon/IRP_Survey_on_Radon.pdf (accessed on 6 August 2019).

21. Duval, J.S. *Use of Aerial Gamma-Ray Data to Estimate Relative Amounts of Radon in Soil Gas*; U.S. Geological Survey: Reston, VA, USA, 1971; pp. 155–161.

22. Amgarou, K. *Long-Term Measurements of Indoor Radon and Its Progeny in the Presence of Thoron Using Nuclear Track Detectors a Novel Approach*; Universitat Autònoma de Barcelona: Barcelona, Spain, 2003.

23. Cambeses, A.; Garcia-Casco, A.; Scarrow, J.H.; Montero, P.; Pérez-Valera, L.A.; Bea, F. Mineralogical evidence for lamproite magma mixing and storage at mantle depths: Socovos fault lamproites, SE Spain. *Lithos* **2016**, *266–267*, 182–201. [CrossRef]

24. Tanner, A.B. Methods of Characterization of Ground for Assessment of Indoor Radon Potential at a Site. Available online: https://books.google.co.th/books?id=Vc1RAQAAMAAJ&pg=PA1&lpg=PA1&dq=Methods+of+Characterization+of+Ground+for+Assessment+of+Indoor+Radon+Potential+at+a+Site;+1991&source=bl&ots=h8OPlDzW2n&sig=ACfU3U0hIJZSJ5xQFanQOkFt0B0BmJXwAw&hl=en&sa=X&ved=2ahUKEwjRzZOOrKXkAhWBP48KHVw9D2UQ6AEwAHoECAYQAQ#v=onepage&q=Methods%20of%20Characterization%20of%20Ground%20for%20Assessment%20of%20Indoor%20Radon%20Potential%20at%20a%20Site%3B%201991&f=false (accessed on 6 August 2019).

25. Ielsch, G.; Cushing, M.E.; Combes, P.; Cuney, M. Mapping of the geogenic radon potential in France to improve radon risk management: methodology and first application to region Bourgogne. *J. Environ. Radioact.* **2010**, *101*, 813–20. [CrossRef]

26. Kemski, J.; Siehl, A.; Stegemann, R.; Valdivia-Manchego, M. Mapping the geogenic radon potential in Germany. *Sci. Total Environ.* **2001**, *272*, 217–30. [CrossRef]

27. Neznal, M.; Matolín, M.; Barnet, I.; Mikšová, J. *The New Method for Assessing the Radon Risk of Building Sites*; Prace Ceskeho Geologickeho Ustavu; Czech Geological Survey: Brno-střed-Staré Brno, Czechia, 2004; pp. 7–47.

28. Buttafuoco, G.; Tallarico, A.; Falcone, G. Mapping soil gas radon concentration: A comparative study of geostatistical methods. *Environ. Monit. Assess.* **2007**, *131*, 135–151. [CrossRef]

29. Olaya, M.; Borja, F. El Código Técnico de la Edificación en España (CTE) Medidas Correctoras Destinadas a Frenar la Entrada de Radón en los Edificios. Investigación de Campo como Experiencia Piloto en España. Available online: https://docplayer.es/22067449-El-codigo-tecnico-de-la-edificacion-en-espana-cte-medidas-correctoras-destinadas-a-frenar-la-entrada-de-radon-en-los-edificios.html (accessed on 6 August 2019).

30. Cepedal, A.; Fuertes-Fuente, M.; Martín-Izard, A.; García-Nieto, J.; Boiron, M.C. An intrusion-related gold deposit (IRGD) in the NW of Spain, the Linares deposit: Igneous rocks, veins and related alterations, ore features and fluids involved. *J. Geochem. Explor.* **2013**, *124*, 101–126. [CrossRef]

31. Maestre, C.R.; Iribarren, V.E. The radon gas in underground buildings in clay soils. The plaza balmis shelter as a paradigm. *Int. J. Environ. Res. Public Health* **2018**, *15*, 1004. [CrossRef]

32. Maestre, C.R.; Iribarren, V.E. The importance of checking indoor air quality in underground historic buildings intended for tourist use. *Sustainability* **2019**, *11*, 689. [CrossRef]

33. Krewski, D.; Lubin, J.H.; Zielinski, J.M.; Alavanja, M.; Catalan, V.S.; Field, R.W.; Klotz, J.B.; Letourneau, E.G.; Lynch, C.F.; Lyon, J.I.; et al. Residential radon and risk of lung cancer: A combined analysis of 7 North American case-control studies. *Epidemiology* **2005**, *16*, 137–145. [CrossRef] [PubMed]

34. 440, N. Radón en Ambientes Interiores. Available online: http://insht.es/InshtWeb/Contenidos/Documentacion/FichasTecnicas/NTP/Ficheros/401a500/ntp_440.pdf (accessed on 6 August 2019).

35. 533, N. El radón y sus Efectos Sobre la Salud. Available online: https://www.insst.es/InshtWeb/Contenidos/Documentacion/FichasTecnicas/NTP/Ficheros/501a600/ntp_533.pdf (accessed on 6 August 2019).

36. Darby, S.; Hill, D.; Auvinen, A.; Barros-Dios, J.M.; Baysson, H.; Bochicchio, F.; Deo, H.; Falk, R.; Forastiere, F.; Hakama, M.; et al. Radon in homes and risk of lung cancer: collaborative analysis of individual data from 13 European case-control studies. *BMJ* **2005**, *330*, 223. [CrossRef] [PubMed]

37. Mahou, E.S.; Ángel Fernández Amigot, J.; Espasa, A.B.; Bonito, M.C.M.; del Pozo, J.M.; del Busto, J.M.L. Proyecto Marna (Mapa de Radiación Gamma Natural en España); Editor Consejo de Seguridad Nuclear. Available online: https://www.csn.es/mapa-de-radiacion-gamma-natural-en-espana-marna (acccessed on 6 August 2019).

Article

Spatial Imbalance Between Tourist Supply and Demand: The Identification of Spatial Clusters in Extremadura, Spain

María Cristina Rodríguez Rangel and Marcelino Sánchez Rivero *

Faculty of Economics and Business, Universidad de Extremadura, 06006 Badajoz, Spain; mcrisrod@unex.es
* Correspondence: sanriver@unex.es

Received: 17 December 2019; Accepted: 20 February 2020; Published: 22 February 2020

Abstract: The techniques provided by spatial analysis have become a great ally of tourist planning as they allow the carrying out of exhaustive territorial analyses. The greater availability of georeferenced databases together with the more and more extensive use of GIS (Geographic Information Systems) is materialising in the proliferation of studies analysing the distribution patterns of tourist territories. The present study uses these techniques to study the degree of equilibrium in the distribution of places and its level of occupation in a region where the use of expansionary policies of growth of the tourism sector has been able to cause a strong imbalance in said activity, i.e., the case of the region of Extremadura. To verify this, both global contrasts, global Moran's I and G (d) of Getis and Ord, are used, as well as local contrasts, to map LISA (Local Indicators of Spatial Association). The results obtained confirm the existence of strong imbalances in the effectiveness of the places created while allowing the identification of different clusters of high and low values. These findings represent an important output for the strategic planning of the territory in order to develop a strategy that allows the sustainable tourism development of the territory.

Keywords: spatial statistics; spatial clusters; Moran's I; Getis–Ord G (d); LISA; Extremadura

---

1. Introduction

The inclusion of the space variable in economic analyses is becoming an increasing habitual practice, especially in the case of activities, which, owing to their very nature, have a close relationship with their development in a given territory, as with tourism. As pointed out by Sánchez [1], a tourist destination cannot be analysed in isolation without taking into account the influence on it of proximal destinations and vice versa. The presence of a tourist business in a certain location will determine aspects as essential as the resources available; these are understood to be the presence of attractions and their exploitation [2,3], as at the same time this affects the occupation level, that of seasonality, and that of competitive intensity, among others [4]. Moreover, the satisfactory progress of tourist activities will also be influenced by factors such as accessibility or the supply of accommodation or complementary services [5].

The ways in which the location of an establishment in a given geographical area may influence the satisfactory progress of the activity are therefore diverse. For this reason it is not surprising that the conceptualisation of distance must be included in the statistical analyses to be performed in order to obtain an exhaustive vision of the tourist situation, and this is possible thanks to the application of the techniques of spatial statistics. This statistical tool is characterised by going further than conventional statistical analyses, including the space variable and spatial relations gathered by means of the design of a matrix of spatial weights as another parameter to be taken into account in the analysis to be performed; its use in social science is becoming more and more frequent.

This growth in the use of techniques of spatial statistics has not occurred in isolation but has been encouraged by the greater dissemination of geographic information systems (GIS) in the field of economic analysis in general and in particular, in the case of tourism. As pointed out by Anselin [6], the application of techniques of spatial statistics together with GIS extends the limits of the types of analysis that may be carried out in a realistic environment, such as those orientated towards supporting the analysis of policies or the making of decisions. It is therefore possible to synthesise the factors which have had an influence on the fact that the space variable is becoming more important in social science in the following ways: the greater importance of spatial interaction in social science, the greater availability of georeferenced databases, and the development of GIS software including specific modules allowing the statistical analysis of spatial data [7].

For all these reasons, GIS are beginning to be recognised as valuable tools for arranging, analysing, and expounding large volumes of data for any local and regional planning activities; their use is becoming imperative in tourist planning and management [8]. The main advantage of the application of GIS technology in tourist analysis is that it allows the acquiring of greater knowledge of the structure and the operation of the tourist system in a given area, either for the purpose of planning or with the objective of monitoring the development of the existing activity [9].

The analysis of the distribution patterns of the variables related to tourism, identifying whether the variables tend to be concentrated or dispersed in the space, the finding of groups with characteristics similar to those of proximal locations, or on the contrary, the finding of observations of behaviour clearly differentiated from that of their neighbours, are some of the possibilities of spatial analysis. In other words, by means of spatial statistical analyses, two important spatial effects can be observed: dependence or autocorrelation and spatial heterogeneity, which will have important implications for tourist management.

The main implications of the finding of interdependence relationships in space lie in the geographic spillovers associated with them. This interdependence between regions has been analysed under the agglomeration economies approach [10–12], which is based on the premise that the concentration or spatial proximity of economic activities can be beneficial due to externalities of the agglomeration for the whole economy as well as for the sectors and companies grouped in a particular location, highlighting the improvement of productivity, investments, labor market, knowledge transfer, among other aspects [13]. In this line, the works carried out by Majewska [14,15] and Majewska & Trusklolaski [16], which, based on this premise, analyse the geograhics spillovers of tourism activity in Poland and countries of central Europe, identifying the existence of different hot spots that represent essential knowledge for proper planning of these destinations.

In the same way, the works carried out by Yang and Wong [17] that, with the object of study being China, identified the presence of different hot spots in coastal areas, mountainous regions, gateway cities or higher-hierarchy cities within the country that extend its effects beyond natural borders, as well as the existence of certain areas that constitute cold spots with a low level of tourism development. Alongside these, other works carried out for the same purpose stand out: the identification and description of the spatial pattern of tourism activity in particular territories [1,5,8–32].

As a general conclusion of all these works, it can be confirmed that the distribution of tourist activities in a region is not homogeneous [5,9,20,25,27,29,33,34]. On the contrary, this spatial distribution is characterised by a series of patterns which must be identified and taken into account for the correct management and planning of a destination.

In general terms, in analysing the distribution of the demand from travellers in the territory, it can be expected that there will be a certain preference for those locations which have the most tourist attractions. In accordance with this premise, it can be anticipated that tourist lodgings have a greater supply of beds in those locations which are more attractive to the demand, or what amounts to the same, that the beds are concentrated in the locations of greater preference of the demand. This has been the approach used by a large proportion of the studies carried out to date to analyse the distribution of tourist activity in space, i.e., assimilating that supply and demand have the same distribution pattern. Therefore, the lack of specific details allowing the analysis of the behaviour of travellers may be compensated for by a detailed study of the behaviour of the supply [1,5,9,25].

It must, however, be taken into account that the creation of beds for tourists is not always a response to the prior existence of interest from the demand. This could be the case of the creation of beds in locations which lack a strong tourist tradition but which see in the development of this activity a good opportunity to generate wealth and employment.

This paper aims to investigate the degree of adjustment between supply and demand in a territory where, due to the particularities of the growth model implemented based on expansive policies, it has given rise to a strong imbalance between supply and demand, the region of Extremadura [1,5,25,28,32] that needs to be studied and analyzed in order to implement the appropriate strategies to achieve growth sustainable tourism in the region.

The principles on which sustainable tourism development rests based on various institutional declarations of the World Tourism Organization (UNWTO) according to Cánoves, et. al [35] can be synthesized as follows: giving optimum use to environmental resources, maintaining and helping to conserve natural resources and biological diversity, respect the cultural authenticity of host communities, conserve their cultural and architectural assets and their traditional values, and ensure long-term viable economic activities that benefit all agents and report socio-economic benefits. Therefore, the mere creation and provision of housing capacity is not enough, but for a truly sustainable economic system to be constituted, it is necessary that the distribution of these be adjusted correctly to the preferences of the demand, or what is the same, that these places obtain a sufficient occupancy rate to generate an economic benefit that allows the continuity of the business without exceeding maximum saturation levels that hinder the correct conservation of the main tourist attractions.

In this sense, the analysis of the occupation level seems to be a good option to generate knowledge from which to design development strategies that allow fulfilling the necessary objectives so that the sustainable tourism development of the area under study is possible.

Moreover, as some of the previous studies underline, one of the main weaknesses of the technique used is that the use of administrative boundary affects the results obtained [14,15], so some of the geographic spillovers could be covered up; in order to avoid this problem, it has been decided to use a global positioning system (GPS) coordinate reference unit for each of the observation units, that is, this analysis is performed from a territorial perspective disaggregated at the highest possible level, the very location of each establishment. This study uses in total as a sample, a set consisting of 270 accommodation establishments for which data are available on their beds and occupation levels for July 2015; all these establishments are located in the region of Extremadura. The use of the establishment itself as a unit of analysis will allow the identification of a set of lodgings with similar behaviour (spatial clusters), which in view of the management of the territory, allows the definition of joint planning strategies.

The novelty of the approach used in this article must be sought in the combination of the methodology and destination used. Most of the work done to date to analyse the distribution pattern is carried out at an intra-urban scale [36,37], also selecting destinations that are in the maturity phase. The peculiarity of the analysed destination lies in the fact that it is an emerging interior destination that, due to the characteristics of tourism products with development potential in these destination, requires sustainable tourism management. Therefore, using an analysis focused on the efficiency of the territory measured through the occupation level as a proxy indicator of tourism pressure is an important temporary spatial tool to locate possible locations that could present problems of excess load capacity. In the same way, it is essential to establish the appropriate development policies for the identification of possible locations that in the space and time analysed make less efficient use of their available resources. Therefore, it is considered that the analysis performed is a valuable tool for public and private managers in order to manage the destination that allows its sustainable development.

In order to achieve its objective, this study is structured as follows: after this introduction, the next section details what is meant by exploratory spatial data analysis (ESDA) and what has been its application in the field of tourism. The third section serves as a guide to the reader in the enumeration of some characteristics of the geographical scope of this study, the region of Extremadura. Subsequently, we describe in detail the methodology used in this research. Section five describes the results obtained, and finally this research is completed with a synthesis of the main conclusions and implications for the management of the results.

2. The ESDA and Its Application to the Tourist Sector

The tourist industry is characterised by a growing need for planning, which in its turn requires techniques capable of monitoring and analysing the flows of tourists [38]. One of the characteristics traditionally attributed to tourism is its territorial dimension, which is also characterised by an unequal distribution within and between destinations [27]. For this reason, finding out the distribution pattern of the data in a given territory is an essential task in the field of tourist management and planning.

The ESDA is a good tool for this purpose when no clear signs are present in the distribution patterns of a variable. The ESDA can be defined as a set of techniques which describe and visualise spatial distributions and at the same time identifies atypical locations (spatial outliers), discovers schemes of spatial association, groupings (clusters), or hotspots and also suggests spatial structures and other forms of spatial heterogeneity [39].

The importance of GIS in this process lies in the possibility which GIS offer for statistical analysis using graphs, which gives rise to what some authors term "scientific visualisation" [40].

By means of the exploratory study of spatial data, the so-called spatial effects can be identified: autocorrelation or dependence and spatial heterogeneity. Spatial heterogeneity can be defined as the variation of relationships in space. It is determined either by the presence of structural instability caused by the lack of stability in the space of the behaviour of the variable under study or by the presence of heteroscedasticity [41]. The second of these effects, the so-called spatial dependence or autocorrelation, is confirmed when there is a relation between what occurs at a given point in the space and what occurs in other points of the same space [42]. It is therefore in line with the contents formulated in the "first law of geography" of Tobler [43], according to which "everything is related to everything else, but near things are more related than distant things".

This study of dependence or spatial autocorrelation may result in three possible scenarios.

The first of these consists of the finding of the lack of spatial autocorrelation, i.e., when it is confirmed that the values of the variable are distributed at random in the territory analysed (random pattern of distribution).

The second of these scenarios is associated with the confirmation of positive spatial autocorrelation. This occurs when there is a direct relationship between similar values of a variable. It implies that the presence of a given phenomenon in a region means that it extends to other nearby regions [44]. In the specific case of tourism, the presence of this type of autocorrelation involves the presence of similar values of the tourist variable among nearby destinations, which means that a "contagion" effect therefore exists [1].

Finally, the third possible scenario is when the presence of negative spatial autocorrelation is confirmed. This occurs when nearby destinations present very different values of a variable, or what amounts to the same thing, when the presence of a phenomenon in a region prevents or hinders its appearance in neighbouring regions [44]. In the specific field of tourism, this case generates what is known as the effect of the "absorption" of a given geographical space [1].

Moreover, it must be taken into account that the study of spatial autocorrelation can be approached from two different perspectives: at a global level or a local level. The contrast from a global perspective pursues the objective of identifying spatial trends or structures in a specific geographical space, including the total of the observations of the variables in said space. In order to do so, the indicators proposed by Moran [45] and Getis and Ord [46] will be used. The main differentiating characteristic of these contrasts from local contrasts is that they allow the summarising of a general scheme of dependence on a single indicator [41].

For its part, the local contrast of spatial dependence or autocorrelation is characterised because an indicator is calculated for each of the observation units, owing to which they allow the identification of in which of them higher (or lower) values than those expected in a homogenous distribution are concentrated. The most popular indexes for confirming the presence of local spatial autocorrelation include the local indicators of spatial association (LISA) proposed by Anselin [47] and the G_i family of statistics of Getis and Ord [46] and Ord and Getis [48].

Although both tests can be considered complementary, their approach can be clearly differentiated. While the Getis–Ord G_i test concentrates on locating groupings of similar high or low values of the variable which are in accordance with the values of their neighbouring locations, Anselin's local I test expands these results to locate not only these two types of groupings but also those other entities presenting anomalous values compared with those taken by their neighbouring locations. This test may therefore give rise to five different results: groupings of high or low values with neighbouring locations taking similar values (HH or LL), high-value groupings surrounded by low values (HL), low-value groupings surrounded by neighbours with high values (LH), and finally entities in which no significant relationship can be identified.

As can therefore be seen, the results obtained by the application of Moran's local I test enriches the analysis and it is for this reason that this option has been selected to perform the analysis of local spatial distribution in this study.

On the other hand, the joint use of both types of contrasts, local and global, will allow the obtaining of exhaustive results in the spatial analysis carried out. In this sense, several authors point out that these are complementary techniques, as one of the main limitations of global autocorrelation tests is their incapacity to detect local spatial structures, hotspots or coldspots that may or may not extend to the global pattern structure [44,46,47,49–52].

At the same time, both types of test, local and global, have a common problem which must be correctly approached and resolved prior to the application of these techniques; deciding what will be the conceptualisation of the relationship of proximity, i.e., how to distinguish which entities are to be considered neighbouring. In order to do so, various criteria have been established, which in turn will vary depending on the approach used: the lattice perspective or the geostatistical perspective.

In the specific case of the geostatistical perspective, which will be the approach used in this research, the relationship of proximity can be established by means of any of the following criteria: inverse distance, square inverse distance, and fixed distance band. In general terms, the fixed distance band criterion is the most frequently used in the existing literature [53,54]. Authors such as Sánchez et al. [28] point out that it should be taken into account that each of the criteria listed establishes a relationship of proximity which has a significant effect on the results obtained; owing to this it is necessary to be cautious and carry out different tests before deciding on a criterion so as to ascertain which is best suited to the study area.

With regard to the possibilities of the application of these techniques to the specific field of tourism, it should be pointed out that this will allow the identification of the distribution pattern followed by the variable in the area analysed, with the implications for tourist planning which these findings involve. In this way the identification of a positive spatial autocorrelation pattern in a given region indicates the existence of a contagious effect among neighbouring destinations, which would make possible the existence of a common strategy for tourist development in neighbouring regions. At the same time, the existence of spatial autocorrelation at a local level will allow the identification of groups of municipalities with common characteristics regarding their tourist situation and therefore with similar needs as to the designing of strategies for future development.

The following section provides a series of characteristic features of the evolution of the tourist sector in Extremadura together with a reference to some studies carried out in this region which allow the reader to obtain further knowledge on the tourist situation of the region.

3. Case Study: Space and Tourism in Extremadura, Spain

Extremadura is a Spanish region in the southwest of the Iberian Peninsula which consists of the two largest provinces in Spain: Cáceres and Badajoz. The total surface area of the region is 41,633 km^2. Its economy has traditionally been characterised by a strong dependence on agro-forestry activities and by being that of the Spanish region with the lowest gross domestic product (GDP) per capita [55]. Moreover, this is combined with a high rate of unemployment which was 19.68% in the third quarter of 2019 [56]. Given this situation, the region has been obliged to create new productive activities to provide economic development by means of the creation of wealth and employment and has seen in the development of tourist activities a good ally to achieve this.

The potential of tourist activities for contributing to economic development, reducing regional asymmetries, creating employment, and generating positive external elements affecting other economic activities has been traditionally accepted [57]. This characteristic becomes particularly relevant in the case of regions which owing to a geographically isolated location see in the tourist sector their only possibility of growth [58] by means of the diversification of the existing incomes.

It is as a result of all this that at a European level a series of programmes have been developed with the ultimate aim of the diversification of economic activities in areas with a low level of economic development. The LEADER, LEADER II, and PRODER programmes are a good example of this, and their impact is particularly noteworthy in the region under study, Extremadura.

The result of these subsidies has been the rapid growth of the accommodation capacity of the region, especially in the case of rural lodgings. This growth has not been matched by a parallel increase in the number of visitors, which has therefore created considerable imbalances which must be analysed exhaustively in order to understand the current situation of the tourist sector in the region [5].

In the year under study, the region had a total of 1296 accommodations that offered a total of 38,940 places. Of these, a total of 19,837 places were offered by the 471 hotel accommodations installed in the territory, the rest, 19,103 places, are the result of the offer of beds made by the 827 non-hotel accommodations located in the region in that year according to data provided by the Tourism Observatory of Extremadura. We find, therefore, a region that keeps a good balance between the number of places offered by hotel and non-hotel accommodation. However, the own peculiarities of extra-hotel accommodations, which offer on average a smaller number of places, entail a greater representativeness with respect to the number of accommodations, which in turn allows a better distribution throughout the territory.

The studies which have been carried out to date in order to find out the pattern of distribution of tourist activity in this space have taken as a reference variable the number of beds available, with these studies being limited to the analysis of the beds offered by rural tourism lodgings. In this way it has been possible to confirm the existence of different clusters of municipalities offering a high number of beds in comparison with what would be expected in a homogeneous distribution of the variable [1,5,25,28].

There is no doubt that these studies have helped to stress the importance of the analysis of spatial distribution patterns of tourism in the region as their results confirm the existence of groups of municipalities with a similar accommodation capacity and which can therefore develop common strategies of development and planning. As is stressed by the authors themselves, the existence of these similarities among territories allows a bid for joint policies to cover extensive proximal territories [5].

However, up to now, the findings on the spatial behaviour of the tourist supply in the region have only served to emphasise the need for carrying out exhaustive spatial analyses of tourist activities and in particular to provide information on the behaviour of the demand from travellers to the region and its adjustment with respect to the places offered.

One of the common conclusions of the studies carried out to date on the distribution of the beds for tourists in the region is that the expansive policies used as strategies for developing the sector have given rise to unequal growth between the supply and the demand, with the result being the generation of imbalances in the activity [1,5,25,28]. This situation of imbalance appears to be preventing these beds from fulfilling their function of generating the economic growth for which they were created.

This imbalance may be represented by one of the variables habitually used in order to characterise the satisfactory performance of tourist activities, the occupation level. The occupation level of an accommodation establishment can be defined as the quotient between the beds which have actually been occupied in relation to those available. This variable can therefore be considered a good proxy indicator of the level of adjustment between the supply of and the demand for tourist activities in a given territory. The spatial analysis of the occupation level variable will allow us on the one hand to find out whether there is a general pattern of the grouping of the variable in the space and on the other to discover groups of lodgings showing similar behaviour in the space, i.e., having a satisfactory adjustment in their supply of beds (hotspot) or on the contrary, poor adjustment between supply and demand (coldspot).

The importance of the findings which we aim to discover with the performing of this analysis lies in the fact that as a consequence of the same it will be possible to group together those accommodation establishments which are near to each other and show similar behaviour; this in turn will allow the generalisation of the tendency identified in the territory in which they are located. In short, the groupings identified by this kind of analysis will permit the regional administration to establish common development strategies, making use of the synergy effect and the consequent scale economies, and designing joint planning to cover extensive territories with a similar characterisation and initial situation.

Given that the objective of this research is to help the regional administration to identify territories in which tourist lodgings are located that have an equal occupation level different from that to be expected in a homogeneous distribution of the activity, we decided to use as a reference the territorialisation created by the regional administration for the strategic planning of the region. Since the establishment of the Extremadura Observatory Tourism in 2013, the regional administration responsible for tourism has opted to use a territorial division that allows combining tourist regions that, because they have similarities in terms of their portfolio of tourism products, have been considered optimal to perform a joint analysis. It should be noted that this division is carried out on the basis of knowledge of each of the regions subject to territorialization but that it is not based on any study that has used ESDA techniques that have allowed us to verify the spatial grouping of accommodation whose behavior is similar and different from that expected under a homogeneous distribution pattern, and that therefore, supports the feasibility of using joint planning that allows optimizing the results of the policies implemented for joint development.

In the same way, the sample used to perform this analysis is that proposed by the Extremadura Tourism Observatory and guarantees the correct representation of the supply of beds existing in each of the territories used. Specifically, for the reference month and year, the sample consisted of a total of 270 lodgings that offered 15,966 places in the region. According to the total accommodation capacity indicated above formed by 38,940 places distributed among a total of 1298 accommodations, the sample obtained represents 20.8% of the establishments and a total of 41.0% of the total places. In addition, it should be noted that, as specified in the different reports published by the Tourism Observatory, the representativeness of the sample was determined for each of the territories, and given that sample is the sample used by the agency that is responsible for carrying out the official statistics of the region, and it is confirmed, the selected sample is considered representative of the tourist activity of Extremadura.

Figure 1 shows both the distribution of the sample of accommodation establishments used and the location of each of the territories which will subsequently be analysed.

Once the sample to be analysed has been presented, the following section explains in detail the methodology used to achieve the proposed objectives of this research.

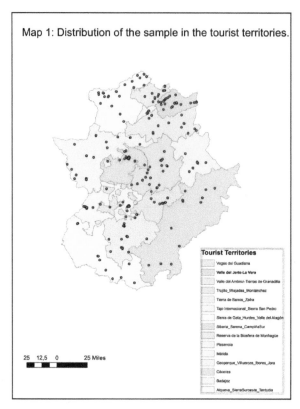

Figure 1. Distribution of the sample in the tourist territories. Source: Own material from calculations made with ArcGIS ver. 10.3.

4. Methodology

This study fits in with the techniques of the ESDA, concentrating particularly on the analysis of the phenomenon of spatial dependence or autocorrelation. In order to achieve this we have used the ArcGIS software in its 10.3 version, which from a geostatistical perspective allows the analysis of spatial dependence or autocorrelation by means of the most commonly used indexes.

The variables to analyse are on the one hand the beds offered by the various types of accommodation establishments in the region of Extremadura, and on the other hand the occupation level of the region, using for the purpose a sample consisting of a total of 270 tourist lodgings which provided their occupation details to the Extremadura Tourist Observatory in July 2015.

The month and year selected for carrying out this study depend on a strategic criterion within the general objective pursued by the authors. In this sense it should be emphasised that this study is part of a more extensive research project which aims to analyse the spatial patterns of distribution over a three-year period from 2015 to 2017. In this way the decision was made to perform the analysis using the first year of reference and within this year, July was chosen for being the first month of the quarter (the third of the year) recording the highest occupation levels in most of the territories to analyse. Also, this month is characterized by being among the two that present the highest occupancy, July and August, which has a lower variability. Once the reference quarter has been selected, the objective is to see which month meets the requirement to position itself as a month that presents a good performance for most of the territories under analysis and, in turn, does not present a great variability between the different months under study. For this, the study carried out on tourist seasonality between the different territories is taken as a reference [59]. This study analyzes, among other aspects, the tourist density for the different tourist territories in which the region is divided and it is obtained that although August, together with the month of July, are the months that present maximum values for the greater part of the territories, August is also established as a minimum month for any of them; the same not happening with the month of July. Therefore, although the final objective is to analyze the tourism efficiency pattern in the territory in the entire annuity, it is decided to use the month of July to start as a basis for analysis and confirm if, depending on the results obtained after this first analysis between the different territories, it is worth extending the analysis to an annual scale.

The findings of this research therefore not only generate exhaustive knowledge of the distribution pattern of the supply and its satisfactory adjustment to the tourist demand in the region during the month and year selected but also allow the laying down of the methodological foundations for the analysis of the remainder of the period of time considered.

Within the range of the possible variables available for measuring tourist activities, the decision was made to select the two variables considered most suitable for the characterisation of tourist activities as a whole, as in this way the distribution pattern of the supply can be analysed and in turn, the satisfactory adjustment between supply and demand measured by the occupation level of each of the lodgings.

The study of the autocorrelation or spatial dependence of the variables mentioned in the territory of Extremadura is moreover analysed from a double perspective: global and local. The objective of the contrast of spatial dependence in the global perspective is to identify spatial trends or structures in a specific geographical space. The indicators proposed by Moran [45] and Getis and Ord [46] are used for this purpose. These indicators are the first formulations proposed in the literature as statistical measurements of the spatial autocorrelation effect. Moreover, they are characterised by their capacity to summarise a general outline of dependence in a single indicator [44].

Both contrasts assume an objective statistical criterion which allows the confirmation or rejection of the presence of trends or spatial structures in the distribution of a variable. In both cases, the null hypothesis to confirm is the lack of spatial dependence, i.e., the randomness of the distribution of the variable in the territory selected.

Moran's I test (1948) is given by the following, Equation (1):

$$I = \frac{N}{S_0} \frac{\sum_{ij}^{N} w_{ij} \times (y_i - \overline{y}) \times \left(y_j - \overline{y}\right)}{\sum_{i=1}^{N} (y_i - \overline{y})} \quad i \neq j, \tag{1}$$

where

w_{ij} is the element of the matrix of spatial weights corresponding to par (i, j);
S_0: the sum of the spatial weights $\sum_i \sum_j w_{ij}$;
$\overline{y}$: the average or expected value of the variable;
N: the number of observations.

Once one proceeds to standardisation by rows of the matrix of spatial weights $S_0 = N$, the statistic I takes the form of the following, Equation (2):

$$I = \frac{\sum_i \sum_j w_{ij} \times (y_i - \overline{y}) \times \left(y_j - \overline{y}\right)}{\sum_{i=1}^{N} (y_i - \overline{y})}. \tag{2}$$

According to Cliff & Ord [60], when the sample is large enough this statistic is distributed as a standard rule N (0.1). The inferential process uses the standardised values (Z) of each of them, which are obtained by the quotient between the difference of the initial value and the theoretical average and the deviation, i.e.,

$$z = \frac{I - E[I]}{SD[I]}. \tag{3}$$

The values obtained by the test will be interpreted as follows: non-significant values of test I will involve the non-rejection of the null hypothesis of the random distribution of the variable in the space studied. For their part, significant values of the variable and positive values (values exceeding 1.96 at a significance level of 5%) will indicate the presence of positive spatial autocorrelation, i.e., they will identify values of the variable (high or low) specially grouped in the space to a greater extent than would be expected if they were following a random distribution pattern. The significant and negative values of the variable (values lower than −1.96 at a significance level of 5%) will reflect the existence of negative spatial autocorrelation, or what amounts to the same they will identify a non-grouping pattern of similar values (high or low) of the variable which is higher than normal in a random spatial pattern.

In order to complete the global analysis of the distribution of the variables, the family of indicators proposed by Getis and Ord [46] is also used. They stand out by using a criterion which is different to those used up to now to measure spatial autocorrelation based on the distance or spatial concentration statistics.

The calculation of the statistic requires the definition of a critical distance (d), as from this distance a radius of influence is established from which it is determined which units are neighbours to others depending on whether they are within the radius of influence determined by the critical distance.

It is given as follows:

$$G(d) = \frac{\sum_{i=0}^{n} \sum_{j=0}^{n} w_{i,j}(d) y_i y_j}{\sum_{i=0}^{N} \sum_{j=0}^{N} y_i y_j} \text{ for } i \neq j, \tag{4}$$

where two pairs of spatial units i and j are neighbours if they are found within a determined distance d, taking the w_{ij} value of 1 when this is so or 0 when it is not.

The statistical significance is checked by means of the standardised statistic Z which is distributed at an asymptotic level according to a rule N (0.1). The interpretation of this test in those cases with statistical significance will be as follows: a positive (or negative) z value exceeding 1.96 for the absolute value will indicate a tendency to the concentration of similar high (or low) levels.

One of the main limitations of global autocorrelation tests is they are incapable of detecting local spatial structures, hotspots or coldspots, which may or may not extend to the global pattern structure [41,46–52]. It was in order to overcome this limitation that local spatial autocorrelation tests were developed. The objective of these tests is the detection of particularly high or low values (hotspots or coldspots) of a variable in comparison with its average values. They are characterised by being calculated for each of the spatial units to analyse, owing to which they allow the detection of those concentrating higher or lower values than what can be expected in a homogeneous distribution.

The analysis of local spatial autocorrelation may present two different scenarios in contrast to global spatial autocorrelation as is pointed out by Vayá and Suriñach [52]. In the first place, it may occur that in a specific space as a whole a distribution pattern of the concentration or dispersal of values at a global level is not detected and indeed there are small clusters in which high (or low) values of the variable are concentrated. Secondly, it may also occur that given the existence of a global distribution pattern, some spatial units contribute to a greater extent to that global indicator.

For this reason, the analysis of autocorrelation at a local level constitutes a good complement to the study of global distribution.

The local indicators of spatial association (LISA) proposed by Anselin [47] and the G_i family of statistics of Getis and Ord [46] and Ord and Getis [48] are the most frequently used indicators for the study of spatial autocorrelation at a local level. In this study, as is explained in section two, we decided to use the LISA maps of Anselin [47] as a criterion as we consider that the results of this test give a wider interpretation.

Anselin [47] proposes a set of local indicators of spatial association with the objective on the one hand of the determination of significant local spatial groupings (clusters) and on the other the detection of pockets of spatial instability, understood as the presence of atypical values.

Among the indicators proposed by the author, Moran's local I_i statistic stands out; its equation is as follows:

$$I_i = \frac{z_i}{\sum_i z_i^2 / N} \times \sum_{j \in j_i} w_{ij} z_j, \tag{5}$$

where z_i is the standardised value of the spatial unit i and j_i the set of spatial units proximal to i.

According to a random distribution hypothesis, the probability of the statistic is:

$$E_A(I_i) = -\frac{w_i}{N-1}, \tag{6}$$

where w_i is the sum of all the elements corresponding to the row of unit i.

The hypothesis assumed is that the standardised I_i statistic is distributed as an N (0.1) rule.

The standardised statistic is interpreted as follows: a high positive value (z-score) exceeding 1.96 at 5% of significance will indicate the presence of clusters of high or low values of the variable. For its part, a significant negative value (less than −1.96 at 5% of significance) indicates the existence of spatial outliers.

For each of the tests listed up to now, and as has been revealed in section two of this study, it is necessary to choose a proximity criterion that adjusts satisfactorily to the particularities of the area under study. In order to be able to make this choice, various tests have been carried out with each of the three possible criteria in accordance with the geostatistical perspective used. After they were carried out it was decided to use the criterion most frequently followed in the literature to date, the fixed band distance criterion; the distance used is that established by the programme by default to ensure that all spatial units have at least one neighbour, 15.79 miles.

Once the different contrasts to be used in this study have been presented, the following section gives the main results obtained from the analysis of spatial autocorrelation at both a local and global level of the variables of the beds available and the occupation level of the region of Extremadura.

5. Results

As has been mentioned, the final aim of this research is to determine the level of adjustment between tourist supply and demand in the region of Extremadura, describing the distribution pattern of this region and identifying groupings of establishments in a similar situation. In order to do so it uses a sample consisting of a total of 270 tourist establishments, which in July 2015 provided their occupation data to the Extremadura Tourism Observatory. Given the different data provided, it was decided to use two of the most representative variables with the aim of measuring tourist activities: on the one hand, the total number of beds offered by the various accommodation establishments during the period analysed, and on the other the average occupation level of each establishment (as an indicator of a satisfactory balance between the beds offered and those actually occupied).

Moreover, the study is carried out from a double perspective: on the one hand the existence of a global pattern of distribution of the variables being studied is contrasted and on the other the possible existence of local distribution patterns is examined. For the first objective we used the two most commonly used indexes, Moran's global I test and the Getis–Ord general G (d) statistic.

The results obtained for the first variable analysed, the number of beds available, can be seen in Figure 2.

As can be seen in graph 1, Moran's global I statistic takes a value of 0.0271, with the score z being equal to 1.7239, owing to which at a significance level of 10% we can affirm that a pattern exists of the concentration of the values of the variable in the space. It is therefore confirmed that there is a slight tendency towards the concentration of the beds available in the space studied.

For its part, the Getis–Ord general G (d) test gives a value of the statistic G of 0.0829, which gives a score z of 1.6091, owing to which we cannot reject the null hypothesis of the random distribution of the variable in the space at a confidence level of 95%. In other words, with the results obtained in this test we cannot affirm that the beds for tourists are not distributed at random in the space analysed.

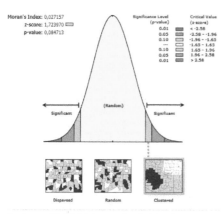

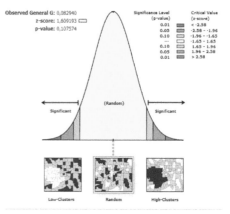

(a) **Moran`s Global I test**

(b) **Getis-Ord general G(d) test**

Figure 2. Results of Moran's gGlobal I Test and the Getis–Ord general G (d) test on beds available in Extremadura. Source: Own material from calculations made with ArcGIS 10.3.

From the results obtained for each of these tests the lack of coincidence can be appreciated; this may be due to the weak relationship of the variable which means that this relationship is not maintained in all the tests carried out. In turn, this weak relationship may be a sign of an equal bid on the part of the public administration of Extremadura for the development of accommodation infrastructures apart from the resources and the tourist potential of each tourist territory in the region.

On the other hand, the study carried out up to now only takes into account the analysis of the beds at a global level, i.e., considering the whole of the target territory. The fact that a global distribution pattern is not identified, or that if it is identified it is weak, does not imply that it is impossible for there to be groups of lodgings at a local level with values of the variable which are very different from the average values of their neighbours. For this reason, Moran's local I test has been calculated; this will allow us to obtain further knowledge on the distribution of beds for tourists at a local level. The results obtained can be observed in Figure 3.

In view of Figure 3, it can be concluded that certain areas exist in which groups of accommodation establishments offer a higher number of beds than those located in neighbouring areas. In the case of the two main towns of the region, both of which are provincial capitals, the existence of several accommodation establishments with high values of the variables in comparison with the value of neighbouring locations can be observed. In these two locations, therefore, one can speak of the existence of two clusters of high values of the variables, i.e., of two clusters in which the accommodation establishments offer a higher number of beds than those located in neighbouring areas.

In the same way, this technique will allow the identification of atypical spatial entities, i.e., those with a high (or low) value of the variable which are surrounded by low (or high) values. In this case, one can observe the existence of three accommodation establishments with a high number of beds compared with the average offered by neighbouring establishments. In turn, there are also two accommodation establishments which offer a small number of beds and are surrounded by neighbouring establishments offering on average a higher number. Finally, two isolated lodgings were also identified with a high number of beds in comparison with the average. In all cases, the results obtained will not be taken into consideration in the analysis performed as we are here concerned with findings related to isolated accommodation establishments, which although they are significant in terms of the administration of the same, do not allow the forming of accommodation groups which suggest that the results can be extended to the entire territory.

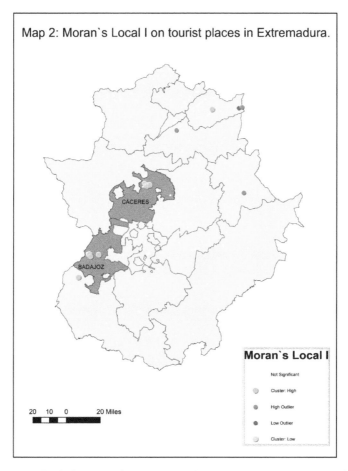

Figure 3. Moran's local I for tourist places in Extramadura. Source: Own material from calculations made with ArcGIS 10.3.

Once the analysis of the distribution of the variable of the beds available in the territory of the region has been completed, it can be concluded in the first place that there is a slight tendency towards the concentration of the values of the variable in the total space of the region. Secondly, the existence is confirmed of two groups of accommodation clusters offering a high number of beds in comparison with the average for the territory and which are located in the two main centres of population: Badajoz and Cáceres.

Subsequently, we proceed to repeat the analysis performed for the second variable which is the subject of this study, the occupation level, which will allow the identification of the level of adjustment existing between supply and demand for the region of Extremadura.

Figure 4 shows the results obtained for Moran's global I test and the Getis–Ord general G (d) test.

As can be seen in Figure 4, statistic I has a value of 0.1594, which means a score z of 8.7278; it can therefore be confirmed that at a significance level of 1% there is a pattern of the concentration of the variable in the space. In other words, at a confidence level of 99% it is confirmed that the similar values of the variable have a tendency towards concentration in the space.

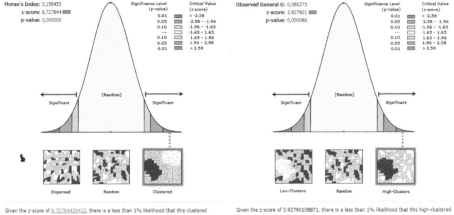

Given the z-score of 8.72794429412, there is a less than 1% likelihood that this clustered pattern could be the result of random chance.

Given the z-score of 3.92790108871, there is a less than 1% likelihood that this high-clustered pattern could be the result of random chance.

Figure 4. Moran's global I test and the Getis–Ord general G (d) test on the occupation level in Extremadura. Source: Own material from calculations carried out with ArcGIS 10.3.

For its part, the Getis–Ord general G (d) test gives a statistic with a value of 0.0863, with the score z being 3.9279, and a p-value of practically zero. This implies that a significance level of 1% confirms that the variable tends to concentrate in the space and moreover is concentrated at high values.

As we can see, both results coincide and confirm the existence of a global pattern of the concentration of the occupation level variable in high values of the same. However, the contrast of the two results obtained with respect to the global distribution of the variables allows us to confirm the initial suspicions regarding the results of the expansionary growth policies used as development strategies in the region. These have allowed the tourist places in the region to have a practically homogeneous distribution pattern, thus only obtaining confirmation of a weak tendency to concentrate in the high value space that is not confirmed in the totality of the tests performed. On the other hand, the results obtained for the occupation level do confirm the existence of a strong tendency to group high values in the region, which suggests the existence of a serious imbalance in terms of the efficiency of these places that should be studied in an exhaustive way with the objective of being able to create strategic lines that fit the reality of each of the territories in which the region is divided, with the ultimate goal of achieving sustainable tourism development throughout the territory.

The local analysis of the variable by means of Moran's local *I* test allows determining whether groups with similar behaviour are created and their locations. The results of this analysis can be seen in detail in Figure 5.

In view of the results obtained, the presence of different groupings of spatial clusters with similar values as to the occupation level is confirmed, i.e., they show a high or low level of adjustment between supply and demand in comparison with the average value to be expected in the space analysed.

Firstly, we can observe the presence of three clusters of high values of the occupation level variable located in the towns of Badajoz, Mérida, and Cáceres. These three territories are therefore characterised by the presence of a high number of lodgings with higher occupation levels than would be expected from the average value of their neighbouring territories. If we take the occupation level as a proxy indicator, we find that these are the three territories in the region with the best adjustment between supply and demand.

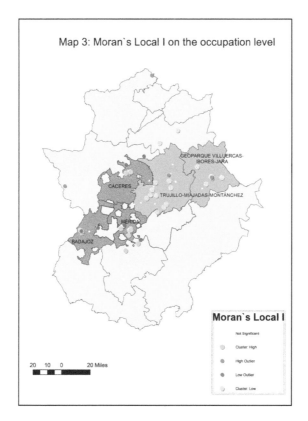

Figure 5. Moran's Local I for the occupation level. Source: Own material from calculations carried out with ArcGIS 10.3.

For their part, the presence of two clusters of low values is observed in the territories of Trujillo-Miajadas-Montánchez and the Villuercas-Ibores-Jara Geopark. In these territories, therefore, we find a set of accommodation establishments with the common characteristic of a low occupation level with regard to the average value to be expected in the month and territory analysed. In accordance with the above reasoning, these two territories are those with the worst adjustment between supply and demand, owing to which they must concentrate on developing strategies allowing the increasing of said occupation level so that the creation of the existing beds for tourists fulfils the mission of creating wealth and employment in the territories analysed.

Finally, the presence of different spatial outliers and outlier types is observed, such as high outliers and low outliers. As can be seen, these are not grouped together in any of the territories in question but are rather isolated cases of accommodation establishments with a casuistry causing this situation owing to specific management, or to obtaining better or worst results than those to be expected in the territory in which they are to be found. Although these results could represent a valuable output for each specific accommodation establishment, they go beyond the scope of the global objective of this research, which consists of the location of groupings, which as their situation is similar, can help the administration to characterise them, and as from this starting point to create common lines of strategy which allow the optimum tourist development of each territory analysed.

As a general conclusion of the distribution pattern of the occupation level variable, it should be stressed that in contrast to what occurred with the beds available, on this occasion a strong tendency to the concentration of high values in the space can be observed. This conclusion is confirmed with the existence of various clusters of high and low values, which requires an analysis of the same before carrying out any task of tourist planning in the interests of achieving more efficient management.

6. Discussion and Conclusions

The analytical possibilities of the inclusion of GIS for the application of the techniques of spatial statistics have opened up many options for achieving highly exhaustive analyses in the territories and their spatial dimension. By means of the application of said techniques it is possible to identify spatial distribution patterns of the variables under study in a given territory and also to identify groupings of entities with a similar or different behaviour to that which could be expected in a homogeneous distribution of the variable. The main advantages deriving from the identification of these clusters is that they will allow the joint planning of more extensive territories, in which owing to their characteristics it is possible to analyse the initial situation and at the same time the existing needs to establish a common goal, making use of the advantages of this joint planning regarding management.

It is for this reason that more and more studies are concentrating on analysing the distribution patterns of the variables related to tourism in the space, with the aim of improving the planning and management of the territory. These studies are characterised by being essentially focussed on demand, concentrating their efforts on studying the distribution in the space of the accommodation capacity of the territory.

This study expands this perspective, completing the analysis of the supply with a detailed analysis of the distribution of the occupation level, taking this last variable as a proxy indicator of the satisfactory level of adjustment between supply and demand in the territory. By means of this analysis therefore, the objective of getting to know the efficiency of each territory with regard to the hotel beds offered is achieved, identifying accommodation groupings with similar characteristics in the territory and which therefore can be examined for correct planning and management in a joint manner.

Moreover, this analysis also presents the novelty, regardingthose tudied on the region previously, of using a geostatistical approach which allows the using as an analytical unit the maximum level of territorial disaggregation possible, the location of the establishment itself. As a result, the contributions of this research allow on the one hand exhaustive knowledge of the distribution pattern of the two variables which are the subject of study in the month of reference used, and on the other hand the laying down of the methodological foundations allowing their repetition at different moments in time, allowing in this way the considerable enriching of the results obtained. In this sense, and after performing various tests in accordance with the characteristics of the sample used, the decision was taken to consider as the most suitable neighbourhood criterion a fixed band distance of 15.79 miles.

With regard to the main results obtained from this study, it should be emphasised that the beds available in the total territory analysed have a weak tendency towards the concentration of values in the space. However, given that this relationship is not significant in the Getis–Ord general G (d) test, it cannot be confirmed whether this tendency is the result of the concentration of high or low values of the variable.

From a local perspective, the presence has been detected of two clusters of high values in the main population centres of the region, i.e., in the towns of Cáceres and Badajoz.

The analysis of the global distribution of the occupation level variable identifies a strong tendency towards concentration in the space, and moreover this spatial concentration occurs with high values. It is therefore a variable with the characteristic of a contagion effect which allows the increase of a variable in a given space, favouring also the value taken in its proximal locations, which is a clear indication that joint management has the possibility of benefitting a wider extension than that of the territory itself.

In relation to the study of the distribution of the occupation level at a local scale, the presence is identified of three spatial clusters of high values located in Badajoz, Cáceres, and Mérida. These territories are therefore characterised by concentrating a high number of accommodation establishments with high occupation levels in comparison with what would be expected in a homogeneous distribution of the variable in the territory.

With regard to the administration of this result, it must be taken into account that although these three territories stand out as being the most efficient in relation to the beds they provide, the result only implies that they have a good initial situation as the average occupation level of each of these territories in the month analysed varies from 38.2% in Badajoz, 40.2% in Cáceres, and 60.7% in Mérida as has been calculated from the data available from the Extremadura Tourism Observatory. In all cases it can be observed that there is clearly room for improvement, and that there is no evidence to assume that the same are exceeding the maximum load capacity to ensure sustainable management, owing to which said territories should in the first place find out whether this situation remains constant over time. Secondly, the regional administration should analyse the characteristics of the offer of tourist products, which at the moment places them in this position, and finally analyse the possibilities of the territory in accordance with their allocation of resources so as to improve the initial situation.

On the other hand, the analysis has also allowed the identification of two accommodation clusters with low occupation values in relation to the figures for accommodation in their neighbouring locations; these are the territories of Trujillo-Miajadas-Montánchez and the Villuercas-Ibores-Jara Geopark. The average occupation levels of these territories are 20.7% and 16.7%, respectively. These figures are below the regional average, which is 25.8% of the beds available for the month being studied.

We are therefore concerned with two territories with a demand deficit which they must resolve if the beds they offer are to contribute to the creation of wealth and employment. It would be recommendable to perform an exhaustive analysis on the supply of the type of tourist product these territories currently offer with the aim of determining whether there is a strong dependence on any specific tourist type with a marked seasonality which is causing this situation. If necessary, the existing offer should be diversified with the aim of palliating this deficit and improving the results. In short, once the similarity of the initial situation has been detected, the analysis of the reasons will give rise to a series of common needs which will be those allowing the articulation of the lines of action to bring about the more efficient management of their resources.

To conclude this analysis of the results, it should be pointed out that both in the local analysis of the distribution of the beds available and in the respective occupation level a series of accommodation establishments appear which represent both clusters of similar values (HH or LL) and an outlier of HL and LH values. These results have not been detailed among the main conclusions of this study, as all of them are found in the space in isolation, owing to which said findings, although they may constitute a valuable output for the managers of these establishments, are beyond the scope of this study, the purpose of which is the comprehensive (or global) management of the territory.

One of the main limitations of this research is that the results obtained are restricted to the timeframe used, July 2015. In order to resolve this shortcoming, we propose as a future line of research the extending, by means of the repetition of the methodology proposed, of the results to a wider timeframe, preferably annual to limit the possible effects of seasonality in each of the territories, so as to find out whether the clusters identified are maintained throughout the whole of the tourist season, and also the possibility that new associations may appear so as to expand the knowledge on the region of Extremadura. Likewise, it would be enriching to complete the analysis of the tourist reality of the region and be able to design properly adapted development strategies, disaggregate the results obtained according to the type of accommodation, taken into account variables such size, quality, the profile or ownership, among others, to eliminate the possible effects that the peculiar characteristics of the results might be introducing into each one of them.

Author Contributions: Conceptualization, M.C.R.R. and M.S.R.; methodology, M.C.R.R. and M.S.R.; software, M.C.R.R. and M.S.R.; validation, M.C.R.R. and M.S.R.; formal analysis, M.C.R.R. and M.S.R.; investigation, M.C.R.R. and M.S.R.; resources, M.C.R.R. and M.S.R.; data curation, M.C.R.R. and M.S.R.; writing—original draft preparation, M.C.R.R. and M.S.R.; writing—review and editing, M.C.R.R. and M.S.R.; visualization, M.C.R.R. and M.S.R.; supervision, M.C.R.R. and M.S.R.; project administration, M.S.R.; funding acquisition, M.S.R. All authors have read and agreed to the published version of the manuscript.

Sustainability **2020**, *12*, 1651

Funding: This publication is part of the research carried out within the research project "Análisis de factores críticos para el desarrollo turístico de Extremadura (IB-18015)". This project is funded by the Ministry of Economy and Infrastructure of the Junta de Extremadura and by the European Regional Development Fund (ERDF). The article processing charge (APC) was financed by Junta de Extremadura with ERDF funds (GR18124)

Conflicts of Interest: The authors declare no conflict of interest. The funders had no role in the design of the study; in the collection, analyses, or interpretation of data; in the writing of the manuscript, or in the decision to publish the results.

References

1. Sánchez, M. Análisis espacial de datos y turismo: Nuevas técnicas para el análisis turístico. Una aplicación al caso extremeño. *Rev. Est. Emp.* **2008**, *2*, 48–66.

2. Cawley, M.; Gillmor, D.A. Integrated rural tourism: Concepts and practice. *Ann. Tour. Res.* **2008**, *35*, 316–337. [CrossRef]

3. Hall, M.C. Policy learning and policy failure in sustainable tourism governance: From first- and second-order to third- order change? *J. Sust. Tour.* **2011**, *19*, 649–671. [CrossRef]

4. Lado-Sestayo, R.; Otero-González, L.; Vivel-Búa, M. Impacto de la localización y la estructura de mercado en la rentabilidad de los establecimientos hoteleros. *Tour. Manag. Stud.* **2014**, *10*, 41–49.

5. Sánchez, J.M.; Sánchez, M.; Rengifo, J.I. Patrones de distribución de la oferta turística mediante técnicas geoestadísticas en Extremadura (2004–2014). *Bol. Asoc. Geogr. Esp.* **2018**, *76*, 276–302. [CrossRef]

6. Anselin, L. Interactive techniques and exploratory spatial data analysis. In *Geographical Information Systems: Principles, Techniques, Management and Applications*; Longley, M., Goodchild, D., Maguire, D., Rhind, D., Eds.; Geoinformation International: Cambridge, UK, 1998; pp. 253–266.

7. Anselin, L.; Florax, R. New directions in spatial econometrics: Introduction. In *New Directions in Spatial Econometrics*; Anselin, L., Florax, R., Eds.; Springer: Berlín, Germany, 1995; pp. 3–18.

8. Abomeh, O.; Nuga, O.; Blessing, I. Utilization of GIS technology for tourism management in Victoria island lagos. *Eur. Scientif. J.* **2013**, *9*, 1857–7881.

9. Sarrión, M.D.; Benítez, M.D.; Mora, E.O. Spatial distribution of tourism supply in Andalusia. *Tour. Manag. Perspect.* **2015**, *15*, 29–45. [CrossRef]

10. Marshall, A. *Principles of Economics*, 8th ed.; Macmillian: London, UK, 1920.

11. Hoover, E. *Location Theory and the Shoe and Leather Industries*; Harvard University Press: Cambridge, MA, USA, 1968.

12. Jacobs, J. *The Economy of Cities*; Random House: New York, NY, USA, 1969.

13. Prager, J.C.; Thisse, J.F. *Economic Geography and the Unequal Development of Regions*; Routledge: London, UK, 2012.

14. Majewska, J. Inter-regional agglomeration effects in tourism in Poland. *Tour. Geogr.* **2015**, *17*, 408–436. [CrossRef]

15. Majewska, J. GPS-based measurement of geographic spillovers in tourism—example of Polish districtis. *Tour. Geogr.* **2017**, *19*, 612–643. [CrossRef]

16. Majewska, J.; Trusklolaski, S. Spatial concentration of economic activity and competitiveness of Central European regions. In *Challenges for International Business in Central and Eastern Europe*; Wach, K., Knežević, B., Šimurina, N., Eds.; Cracow University of Economics: Kraków, Poland, 2017; pp. 47–64.

17. Yang, Y.; Wong, K.F. Spatial distribution of tourist flows to China's cities. *Tour. Geogr.* **2013**, *15*, 338–363. [CrossRef]

18. Polo, A.I.; Chica, J.; Frías, D.M.; Rodríguez, M.A. Market orientation adoption among rural tourism enterprises: The effect of the location and characteristics of the firm. *Int. J. Tour. Res.* **2015**, *17*, 54–65. [CrossRef]

19. Fang, Y.; Huang, Z.; Wang, K.; Cai, B. Spatial pattern of Chinese tourism development and its mechanism based on different spatial-temporal scales: Taking the panel data of China Mainland (1996–2010) for Example. *J. Landsc. Res.* **2015**, *7*, 47–54.

20. García-Palomares, J.C.; Gutierrez, J.; Mínguez, C. Identification of tourist hot spots based on social networks: A comparative analysis of European metropolises using photo-sharing services and GIS. *Appl. Geogr.* **2015**, *63*, 408–417. [CrossRef]

21. Mason, P. *Tourism Impacts, Planning and Management*, 3rd ed.; Routledge: New York, NY, USA, 2016.

22. Grinberger, A.; Shoval, N.; McKercher, B. Typologies of tourists´time-space consumption: A new approach using GPS data and GIS tools. *Tour. Geogr.* **2014**, *16*, 105–123. [CrossRef]

23. Lee, S.H.; Choi, J.Y.; Yoo, S.H.; Oh, Y.G. Evaluating spatial centrality for integrated tourism management in rural áreas using GIS and network analysis. *Tour. Manag.* **2013**, *34*, 14–24. [CrossRef]

24. Rutherford, J.; Kobryn, H.; Newsome, D. A case study in the evaluation of geotourism potential through geographic information systems: Application in a geology-rich island tourism hotspot. *Curr. Iss. Tour.* **2015**, *18*, 267–285. [CrossRef]

25. Sánchez, J.M.; Sánchez, M.; Rengifo, J.I. La evaluación del potencial para el desarrollo del turismo rural: Aplicación metodológica sobre la provincia de Cáceres. *Geofocus* **2013**, *13*, 99–130.

26. Gutierrez, J.; García-Palomares, J.C.; Romanillos, G.; Salas-Olmedo, M.H. Airbnb in touristic cities: Comparing spatial patterns of hotels and peer-to-peer accommodations. *Tour. Manag.* **2017**, *62*, 278–291. [CrossRef]

27. Batista, F.; Marín, M.A.; Rosina, K.; Ribeiro, R.; Freire, S.; Schiavina, M. Analysing spatiotemporal patterns of tourism in Europe at high-resolution with conventional and big data sources. *Tour. Manag.* **2018**, *68*, 101–115. [CrossRef]

28. Sánchez-Martín, J.M.; Rengifo-Gallego, J.I.; Blas-Morato, R. Hot spot analysis versus cluster and outlier analysis: An enquiry into the grouping of rural accommodation in Extremadura (Spain). *J. Geo-Inf.* **2019**, *8*, 176. [CrossRef]

29. Chua, A.; Servillo, L.; Marcheggiani, E.; Vande, A. Mapping Cilento: Using geotagged social media data to characterize tourist flows in southern Italy. *Tour. Manag.* **2016**, *57*, 295–310. [CrossRef]

30. Yang, Y.; Fik, T.J. Spatial effects in regional tourism growth. *Ann. Tour. Res.* **2014**, *46*, 144–162. [CrossRef]

31. Yang, Y.; Fik, T.J.; Zhang, H. Designing a tourism spillover index based on multidestination travel: A two-stage distance-based modeling approach. *J. Trav. Res.* **2016**, *56*, 317–333. [CrossRef]

32. Rodríguez-Rangel, C.; Sánchez-Rivero, M. Analysis of the spatial distribution pattern of tourist activity: An application to the volume of travellers in Extremadura. In *Trends in Tourist Behavior. Tourism, Hospitality & Management*; Artal Tur, A., Kozak, M., Kozak, N., Eds.; Springer: Cham, Germany, 2019; pp. 225–245.

33. Li, M.; Wu, B.; Cai, L. Tourism development of world heritage sites in China: A geographic perspective. *Tour. Manag.* **2008**, *29*, 308–319. [CrossRef]

34. Balaguer, J.; Pernías, J.C. Relationship between spatial agglomeration and hotel prices. Evidence from tourism consumers. *Tour. Manag.* **2013**, *36*, 391–400. [CrossRef]

35. Cánoves, G.; Pérez, M.V.; Herrera, L. Políticas públicas, turismo rural y sostenibilidad: Díficil equilirbio. *BAGE* **2006**, *41*, 199–220.

36. Rogerson, J.M. The economic geography of South Africa's hotel industry 1990–2010. *Urb. For.* **2013**, *24*, 425–446. [CrossRef]

37. Yang, Y.; Luo, H.; Law, R. Theoretical, empirical and operational models in hotel location research. *Int. J. Hosp. Manag.* **2014**, *36*, 209–220. [CrossRef]

38. Williams, S. Issues and approaches in the contemporany geography of tourism. In *Tourism Geography*; Routledge: London, UK, 1998; pp. 1–20.

39. Anselin, L. The future of spatial analysis in the social sciences. *Geogr. Inf. Sci.* **1999**, *5*, 67–76. [CrossRef]

40. Haining, R.; Wise, S.; Signoretta, P. Providing scientific visualization for spatial data analysis: Criteria and an assesment of SAGE. *J. Geograp. Syst.* **2000**, *2*, 121–140. [CrossRef]

41. Moreno, R.; Vayá, E. *Técnicas econométricas para el tratamiento de datos espaciales: La econometría espacial*; University of Barcelona: Barcelona, Spain, 2000.

42. Anselin, L. *Spatial Econometrics: Methods and Models*; Kluwer Academic Publisher: Dordrecht, The Netherlands, 1988.

43. Tobler, W. A computer simulating urban growth in the Detroit región. *Econ. Geogr.* **1970**, *46*, 234–240. [CrossRef]

44. Moreno, R.; Vayá, E. Econometría espacial: Nuevas técnicas para el análisis regional. Una aplicación a las regiones europeas. *J. Reg. Res.* **2002**, *1*, 83–106.

45. Moran, P. The interpretation of statistical maps. *J. R. Stat.* **1948**, *10*, 243–251. [CrossRef]

46. Getis, A.; Ord, J. The Analysis of spatial association by use of distance statistics. *Geogr. Anal.* **1992**, *24*, 189–206. [CrossRef]

47. Anselin, L. Local Indicators of Spatial Association (LISA). *Geogr. Anal.* **1995**, *27*, 93–115. [CrossRef]

48. Ord, J.K.; Getis, A. Local spatial autocorrelation statistics: Distributional issues and an application. *Geogr. Anal.* **1995**, *27*, 286–306. [CrossRef]

49. Anselin, L. The Moran scatterplot as an ESDA tool to assess local instability in spatial association. In *Spatial Analytical Perspective on GIS*; Fisher, M., Scholten, H.J., Unwin, D., Eds.; Taylor & Francis: London, UK, 1996.

50. Openshaw, S. Some suggestions concerning the development of artificial intellegence tools for spatial modelling and analysis in GIS. In *Geographic Information System, Spatial Modelling and Policy Evaluation*; Fisher, M., Nijkamp, P., Eds.; Springer: Berlín, Germany, 1993; pp. 17–33.

51. Tiefelsdorf, M.; Boots, B. A note on the extremities of local Morans's I_i and their impact on global Moran's I. *Geogr. Anal.* **1997**, *29*, 248–257. [CrossRef]

52. Vayá, E.; Suriñach, J. Constrastes de autocorrelación espacial: Una aplicación al ámbito de las provincias españolas. In Proceedings of the X Reunión ASEPELT, Albacete, Castilla la Mancha, Spain, 20–21 June 1996.

53. Babak, O.; Deutsch, C.V. Statistical approach to inverse distance interpolation. *Stoch. Environ. Res. Risk. Assess.* **2009**, *23*, 543–553. [CrossRef]

54. Fei, L.; Zhang, Q.; Deng, Y. Identifying influential nodes in complex networks based on the inverse-square law. *Phys. A Stat. Mech. Appl.* **2018**, *512*, 1044–1059. [CrossRef]

55. Instituto Nacional de Estadística (INE). Available online: https://www.ine.es/dyngs/INEbase/es/operacion.htm?c=Estadistica_C&cid=1254736167628&menu=ultiDatos&idp=1254735576581 (accessed on 17 December 2019).

56. Encuesta de Población Activa (EPA). Available online: https://www.ine.es/dyngs/INEbase/es/operacion.htm?c=Estadistica_C&cid=1254736176918&menu=resultados&idp=1254735976595 (accessed on 17 December 2019).

57. Soukiazis, E.; Proença, S. Tourism as an alternative source of regional growth in Portugal: A panel data analysis at NUTS II and III levels. *Port. Econ. J.* **2008**, *7*, 43–61. [CrossRef]

58. Irvine, W.; Anderson, A.R. Small tourism firms in rural areas: Agility, vulnerability and survival in the face of crisis. *Int. J. Entrepr. Behav. Res.* **2003**, *10*, 229–246. [CrossRef]

59. Rodríguez, C.; Sánchez, M. Estudio de la estacionalidad a nivel de microterritorios: El caso de Extremadura. In *Gran Tour*; Escuela Universitaria de Turismo de Murcia: Murcia, Spain, 2018; ISSN 2172-8690.

60. Cliff, A.; Ord, J. *Spatial Processes, Models and Applications*; Pion Limited: London, UK, 1981.

Article

Spatial Diversity of Tourism in the Countries of the European Union

Michał Roman [1], Monika Roman [1,*] and Arkadiusz Niedziółka [2]

[1] Institute of Economics and Finance, Warsaw University of Life Sciences, 02-787 Warsaw, Poland; michal_roman@sggw.pl

[2] Faculty of Agriculture and Economics, University of Agriculture in Krakow, 31-120 Krakow, Poland; arkadiusz.niedziolka@urk.edu.pl

* Correspondence: monika_roman@sggw.pl

Received: 28 February 2020; Accepted: 27 March 2020; Published: 30 March 2020

Abstract: The aim of the article is to present the spatial diversity of tourism in the countries of the European Union (EU). The main objective of the article can be divided into three immediate goals, each of which is to determine countries that are similar by means of: (1) accommodation base; (2) tourism traffic; and (3) tourism-related expenditures and revenues. In order to group countries, Ward's cluster analysis method is used. The aim is verified with the use of 2017 United Nations World Tourism Organization (UNWTO) and Eurostat data. The analysis covers all EU member states. The research conducted confirms, inter alia, the key role of the accommodation base in the development of tourism in those countries.

Keywords: tourism; spatial analyses; cluster analysis; Ward's method; EU

1. Introduction

The issue of spatial diversity is a subject matter that often draws the attention of economists studying markets. This diversity is often analyzed in regions, macro-regions and countries. The spatial diversity of markets is one of the matters used to assess interrelations and spatial development by the identification of developed and underdeveloped areas. This also applies to the tourism market.

Travel and tourism make up the largest service industry in the world and it is continuing to grow. This industry stimulates Gross Domestic Product (GDP) growth in host countries and contributes substantially to government tax revenues [1]. Worth USD 7.6 trillion, the travel and tourism sector accounts for more than 10% of global GDP and represents 7% of all international trade and 30% of the world's export of services. Tourism receipts provide an important source of foreign exchange for countries around the world, enabling economic growth and investment in a multitude of other sectors. In 2016, tourism grew by 3.1%, outperforming the global economy's growth of 2.5% [2,3].

Tourism is the third largest socio-economic activity in the European Union (EU), and it makes an important contribution to the EU's gross national product and to employment [4]. Europe is also the world's number one tourist destination. Within the global sector, however, Europe is not the fastest-growing region and its market share, in terms of international tourist arrivals and receipts, is shrinking [5]. Europe is ranked as the world's number one destination for international arrivals, USD 713 million in 2018, over half the global total, growing by 6% in 2018. Early indications are that 2019 saw further growth, although at more modest levels than 2018. Tourism creates a surplus for the EU's economy, with international tourism receipts exceeding EU residents' spending on international tourism by USD 27 billion in 2016 [5,6].

Tourism businesses in the EU are confronted with a number of changes in tourists' profiles and behavior. Demographically, tourists in the EU are older than in previous decades. Geographically, a growing number of tourists travelling to the EU come from emerging countries, although the EU's source markets still provide the biggest share of tourists [5,7].

Tourism has an important territorial dimension, with uneven spatial distribution between and within countries, and it delivers localized impacts. The importance of the spatial dimension of tourism is also underscored by findings indicating that tourism growth in one region positively influences tourism in neighboring regions [8], or that public policy can impact the spatial patterns of tourism demand [9]. Therefore, an interesting research issue is the recognition of the spatial diversity of tourism in EU countries. This information may be useful for tour operators, owners of facilities and tourist attractions, and above all for EU and national government leaders. The conducted research will indicate areas with the weakest results, which may constitute valuable information for developing tourism in these countries.

The aim of the article is to present the spatial diversity of tourism in the countries of the EU by means of cluster analysis with the use of Ward's method. Ward's method was selected because of its tendency to produce more evenly sized clusters. Most other measures have a tendency to produce one large and numerous much smaller clusters, which is less useful for spatial diversity in tourism [10]. As part of the main goal, the authors looked for answers to the following questions:

- What is the spatial diversity of the accommodation base in EU countries?
- What is the spatial diversity of tourist traffic in EU countries?
- What is the spatial diversity of expenditures and revenues in EU countries?
- Are countries with similarly developed accommodation facilities characterized by similar tourist traffic?

The individual parts of the article present the theoretical premises for the spatial diversity of tourism, followed by the research part of the spatial analysis. After this, the initial issues of the thesis, theoretical background and research gaps are presented. Section 2 presents an in-depth literature review on how to use data sets to generate tourist statistics, especially spatial relationships. Section 3 discusses the materials and methods. Section 4 deals with the results of the cluster analysis, and is divided into three parts: spatial diversity of the accommodation base, spatial diversity of tourism traffic and spatial diversity of tourism expenditures and revenues. The final part of the thesis concerns the discussion and applications.

2. Literature Review

Tourism is perceived as a spatial phenomenon that has a great impact on society and various sectors of the national economy, inter alia, the construction industry, transport and trade [11]. One of the elements of tourism development is the accommodation base. There are many studies covering analysis of the accommodation base of individual cities or small regions [12–14]. However, there is no research on the spatial diversity of the accommodation base in EU countries. For example, Batista e Silva et al. [9] created a map of tourism capacity in the group of 28 EU countries (EU-28) in 2017 using data from Booking.com and TripAdvisor. They also analyzed tourist density changes in selected months of the year in EU-28 at a city level. Navrátil et al. [15] assessed the impact of various characteristics of the geographic space on the location of tourist accommodation facilities. According to them, hotels create spatial clusters situated mainly in urbanized areas. Hostels are strictly related to towns, and camps and resorts are situated primarily near water resources in warmer areas. This is the reason why they are considered to be a core source for the sustainable competitiveness of a destination. The lack of an accommodation base "acts as a constraint on overnight visitor numbers" [16]. Building up the accommodation capacity is one of the essential parts of the process of planning tourism development for destinations [17]. The location of hotels constitutes part of the development of the regions [18], as well as influencing tourism traffic [19].

Tourist traffic means the spatial movement of people, which is connected with voluntary and temporal changes of residence, environment and the rhythm of life. Within tourist traffic, one can distinguish leisure, sightseeing and specialist tourism [20]. In areas where tourist traffic is developing, in order to satisfy its needs, the natural environment is changed, transport infrastructure is built, and accommodation and catering bases are created [21,22]. As a result, tourism can become a positive and valuable element of the spatial order but also contribute to the degradation of a given area's natural and cultural environment [23–25]. Shoval et al. [19] concluded that hotel location has a profound impact on tourist movements, with a large share of the total tourist time budget spent in the immediate vicinity of the hotel. Further, the study illustrated the impact of geomorphic barriers on tourist movements. Some research has examined the importance of location in hotel site selection, especially for urban destinations [18,26,27]. In this case, it results in the creation of several models of hotel location [28,29].

Table 1 presents a list of the selected publications that are subject to analysis in order to identify methods of using databases to generate tourist statistics, and in particular indicators measuring spatial diversity dependencies and the use of cluster analyses. There is a lot of tourism research, but as Xiao and Smith [30] have pointed out, one of the major limitations of research in tourism is caused by the fact that the research is, in most cases, concerned with a single case, location, nationality, etc. Examples of such research can be found in the work of e.g., Soybali [31], Raun et al. [32], Peng et al. [33], Del Vecchio et al. [34] and Guilarte and Quintans [35].

Table 1. List of publications on tourism spatial diversity and sustainability development (by date of publication).

Authors and Years of Publication	Title	Methodology
Soybali (2005) [31]	Temporal and spatial aspects of tourism in Turkey	Period: 1981–2003 Area: Turkey Methods: Questionnaire techniques, Chi-Square analysis
Papapavlou-Ioakeimidou, Rodolakis, Kalfakakou (2006) [36]	Spatial structure of tourist supply and relations between sub-regions: a case study in a Coastal Region	Period: 10 years Area: Greece—Chalkidiki peninsula Methods: Location Quotient, Coefficient of Location, Coefficient of Specialization, Correlation Analyses
Borzyszkowski, Marczak, Zarębski (2016) [37]	Spatial diversity of tourist function development: the municipalities of Poland's West Pomerania province	Period: 2012 Area: Poland—West Pomerania province Methods: Defert's tourist function index (DTFI)
Raun, Ahas, Tiru (2016) [32]	Measuring tourism destinations using mobile tracking data	Period: 2011–2013 Area: Estonia Methods: Mobile tracking data
Navarro Chavez, Zamora Torres, Cano Torres (2016) [38]	Hierarchical Cluster Analysis of Tourism for Mexico and the Asia-Pacific Economic Cooperation (APEC) Countries	Period: 2013 Area: 20 of APEC countries Methods: Cluster analysis—Ward's method and K-Means method
Peng, Huang (2017) [33]	A Novel Popular Tourist Attraction Discovering Approach Based on Geo-Tagged Social Media Big Data	Period: 2005–2016 Area: Beijing Methods: DBSCAN algorithm
Świstak, Świątkowska (2018) [39]	Spatial Diversity of Accommodation as a Determinant of Tourism in Poland	Period: 2014 Area: Poland Methods: Indicator analysis of accommodation base
Del Vecchio, Mele Ndou, Secundo (2018) [34]	Open Innovation and Social Big Data for Sustainability: Evidence from the Tourism Industry	Period: 2015–2017 Area: Italy—Apulia Methods: Case study
Lascu, Manrai, Manrai, Gan (2018) [14]	A cluster analysis of tourist attractions in Spain. Natural and cultural traits and implications for global tourism	Period: 2017 Area: Spain—17 regions Methods: Cluster analysis
Guilarte, Quintans (2019) [35]	Using Big Data to Measure Tourist Sustainability: Myth or Reality	Period: 1999–2019 Methods: Systematic Literature Review (SLR)

Table 1. *Cont.*

Authors and Years of Publication	Title	Methodology
Gawroński, Król, Gawrońska, Leśniara (2019) [40]	Spatial diversity of tourism attractiveness of the Nowy Sącz district, using the Wrocław taxonomic method	Period: 2015 Area: Poland—Nowy Sącz district Methods: Taxonomic methods
Rodriguez, Sanchez (2019) [41]	Spatial Imbalance Between Tourist Supply and Demand: The Identification of Spatial Clusters in Extremadura, Spain	Period: 2015–2017 Area: Spain—Extremadura Methods: Moran's test, High/Low Clustering (Getis-Ord_General G)
Kolvekova, Liptakova, Strba, Krsak, Sidor, Cehlar, Khouri, Behun (2019) [42]	Regional Tourism Clustering Based on the Three Ps of the Sustainability Services Marketing Matrix: An Example of Central and Eastern European Countries	Period: 2014 Area: 54 regions of Central and Eastern Europe (Czech Republic, Slovakia, Hungary, Poland, Estonia, Lithuania, Latvia, Slovenia, Romania and Bulgaria) Methods: Cluster analysis—Ward's method

Source: [14,31–42].

The scientific publications presented in Table 1 indicate that work is focused on the use of databases in order to develop methods and tools demonstrating the spatial diversity of tourism. The authors use a number of variables to show the spatial diversity of tourism. Some authors define the specialization of tourist regions using indicator and taxonomic methods. Papulova et al. [36] analyzed the economic relations between sub-regions in a coastal area of Greece, and the spatial concentration of economic activities and examination of communities within the sense of socio-economic characteristics, placing emphasis on the analysis of the correlation between employment in the tourism sector and other economic activities. These authors think the geographical allocation of tourist facilities constitutes a broadly applied hint on measuring spatial fluctuations in the tourist industry. It is important because the tourist base constitutes one of the most significant elements of a tourist product that makes it possible to measure it, and data concerning the geographical allocation of the tourist base provide useful elements because of the importance of tourism and its spatial structure. Borzyszkowski et al. [37] carried out an analysis of the spatial diversity of the tourist function development based on the values of Defert's tourist function index (DTFI), which is one of the basic indicators used in tourism geography. The analysis showed considerable differences between the communes in the region examined. This confirms the assumption that the highest tourist function development is typical of seaside communes. DTFI compares the number of tourist beds available in a destination to the total number of residents or hosts in the region (in this article it is the variable X_2). Gawroński and et al. [40] presented an evaluation of the spatial diversity of tourism attractiveness. They believe that an assessment can be made based on the analysis of the statistical data carried out using taxonomic methods (zeroed notarization and the Wrocław taxonomic method).

Świstak and Świątkowska [39] presented an analysis of the spatial diversity of accommodation facilities in Poland and their use by the tourists. The scope of the work included the presentation of the resources and structure of the tourist accommodation base and a general spatial analysis and database on the basis of selected indicators. In the study, the authors used, among others, Defert's tourist function index and the Charvata accommodation density indicator, expressed in the number of tourist beds per 1 km^2 of land (in this paper, the variables X_3 and X_4).

There are also studies on the spatial diversity of tourism using cluster analysis. Lascu et al. [14] compared the level of tourism in the 17 major regions of Spain and identified the key natural, cultural, and dual attractions using a two-step cluster analysis to ascertain the relative importance of the three types of attractions. Rodriguez and Sanchez [41] claimed that the techniques provided by spatial analysis have become a great ally of tourist planning as they allow exhaustive territorial analyses to be carried out. The authors' present study uses these techniques to study the degree of equilibrium in the distribution of places and its level of occupation in a region. Other authors perform cluster analysis with Ward's method. Navarro Chavez et al. [38] used cluster analysis for the analysis of 14 competitive tourism factors for 20 member countries of the Asia-Pacific Economic Cooperation

(APEC). Kolvekova et al. [42] discussed the fusion of 54 regions of Central and Eastern Europe (Czech Republic, Slovakia, Hungary, Poland, Estonia, Lithuania, Latvia, Slovenia, Romania and Bulgaria) into clusters according to the selected tourism indicators which Eurostat uses to evaluate tourism. The authors studied the capacity and occupancy of collective tourist accommodation using mainly numerical data (except nights spent by residents and non-residents per thousand inhabitant and nights spent by residents and non-residents per km^2). This approach, in the case of spatial analysis, may give inconclusive results, because the population and area of regions are different. Therefore, all of the variables used in our article are not numerical values but indicators. The literature presents much information about research in the issue of cluster analysis in tourism. The extensive use of Ward's method in tourism is summarized and discussed in Dwyer et al. [43].

Summing up, what is important from the point of view of the aim of the article is the issue connected with the dependencies of the spatial diversity of tourism. The number of articles on the issue is still small (in particular ones providing a comparative analysis of countries). The issue discussed in the article is a new one and has not been fully recognized from the research point of view till now. An EU-wide study should be considered as a research gap. The use of the division of the analysis into accommodation base, tourist traffic and economic factors is a novelty. This will allow the identification of specific tourist differences between EU countries.

3. Materials and Methods

Cluster analysis is a group of multivariate techniques whose primary purpose is to group objects based on the characteristics they possess. The resulting clusters should exhibit high internal (within-cluster) homogeneity and high external (between-cluster) heterogeneity. Cluster analysis has been used in every research setting imaginable. It can classify different objects: individual people; markets, including the market structure; and analyses of the similarities and differences among new products or country [10]. Therefore, cluster analysis can be used to research in tourism and to show the spatial diversity between countries. The spatial diversity of tourism was verified based on the cluster analysis with the use of Ward's method. It is one of the agglomerative hierarchical clustering methods and is based on the classical criterion of the sum of squares [44]. The division should be carried out in such a way that objects of one group (class) are as similar as possible and those of different classes as different as possible. The measures of similarities or differences are based on the distance between the units [45]. The starting point in this method is matrix D of Euclidean distance d_{ij} between classified objects:

$$d(x, y) = \sqrt{\sum_{i=1}^{p} (x_i - y_i)^2} \tag{1}$$

The algorithm procedure is as follows:

(1) Each O_i object $(i = 1,2, \dots, n)$ is treated as a one-element group;

(2) The distance matrix finds the minimum value: $d_{pq} = min\{d_{ij}\}$;

(3) O_p and O_q objects are treated as one-element groups and A_p and A_q are combined into one two-element group A_r: $A_r = A_p \cup A_q$;

(4) Determination of the distance d_{ir} of the formed A_r group from all other groups A_i;

(5) Repeating steps 2–4 until all objects form one group [10,46].

The general formula for the conversion of the distance matrix while combining groups A_{pi} A_q into a the new group A_r for hierarchical agglomerative methods based on the principle of the central agglomerative procedure takes the following form:

$$d_{ir} = a_p d_{ip} + a_q d_{iq} + b d_{pq} + c[d_{ip} - d_{iq}] \tag{2}$$

where:

d_{ir}—the distance between groups A_i and A_r;

d_{ip}—the distance between groups A_i and A_p;

d_{iq}—the distance between groups A_i and A_q;

d_{pq}—the distance between groups A_p and A_q;

a_p, a_q, b, c—the transformation parameters.

Thus, Ward's method consists of combining such clusters as Ap and Aq, which ensures the minimum sum of squares of the distance from the center of gravity of the new cluster they create. Ward's method aims to obtain rather small clusters and is believed to be very efficient. This method was able to better ascertain the optimal classification than other methods—minimum, maximum and mean. To choose the number of classes, the Cubic Clustering Criterion (CCC) [47] and Pseudo F [48] were used. All the calculations were made with the SAS 9.4 software.

In the case of an analysis of clusters, it is usually proposed to make the classification complete, disjunctive and non-empty. Completeness means that every object belongs to a class. Disjunction means that it belongs to only one class. And non-emptiness requires that each class should contain at least one object. The problem in cluster analysis may result from ensuring completeness in case there are distinct units, dissimilar to others, in the examined cluster [46].

The simplest solution is the creation of one-element classes, which can in fact be interpreted as the specific exclusion of such objects (countries). However, such a situation may result in the erroneous classification of the remaining objects. This is why the article thoroughly analyzes the examined variables first, and then, when the distinct objects are recognized, they are eliminated in the course of clustering countries and treated as separate classes.

In order to verify the spatial diversity of tourism, the authors based the analysis on secondary, non-public data from the United Nations World Tourism Organization (UNWTO) [49] and public data from Eurostat [50]. In order to verify the spatial diversity, the 2017 data were purposefully chosen because this was the latest year for which full data were available at the time of writing. The analysis covers all the EU member states in 2018.

Seven variables were chosen to analyze the spatial diversity of tourism in the EU. These variables are as follows:

X_1—Average length of stay;

X_2—Available capacity (beds per 1000 inhabitants);

X_3—Accommodation for visitors (per 1000 km^2);

X_4—Accommodation in hotels and similar establishments (per 1000 km^2);

X_5—Overnight visitors (tourists) (per 1000 inhabitants);

X_6—Tourism expenditure over GDP (%);

X_7—Tourism receipts over GDP (%).

The descriptive statistics of variables in the EU countries can be found in Table 2.

Table 2. The descriptive statistics of variables.

	X_1	X_2	X_3	X_4	X_5	X_6	X_7
Average	4.00	31.43	132.84	75.44	1.56	2.65	4.98
Median	3.12	24.62	73.03	30.34	1.28	2.40	3.05
Minimum	1.92	8.74	6.20	2.90	0.43	1.10	1.10
Maximum	7.97	92.49	733.33	733.33	4.58	6.00	19.30
Standard deviation	1.96	20.73	156.21	137.21	0.98	1.13	4.39
Coefficient of variation (CV) (%)	49.03	65.95	117.60	181.88	62.98	42.60	88.22

Source: own studies based on UNWTO and Eurostat data [49,50].

The variables were selected on purpose so that it is possible to compare elements of the accommodation base, tourist traffic and economic factors. It should be mentioned that, apart from the substantive criterion, the choice of the variables also resulted from the low mutual correlation of variables (correlation rate below 0.8) (Table 3). This proves the reliability and validity of the variables in the cluster analysis. In addition, all variables were standardized. There are two main benefits from standardization. First, it is much easier to compare variables because they are on the same scale. Second, no difference occurs in the standardized values when only the scale changes. Thus, using standardized variables eliminates the effects due to scale differences across variables and for the same variable as well [10].

Table 3. Pearson's correlation indicators.

	X_1	X_2	X_3	X_4	X_5	X_6	X_7
X_1	1						
X_2	0.50	1					
X_3	0.23	0.54	1				
X_4	0.24	0.64	0.79	1			
X_5	0.28	0.77	0.48	0.57	1		
X_6	0.06	0.25	0.07	0.18	0.33	1	
X_7	0.39	0.65	0.30	0.37	0.74	0.40	1

Source: own studies based on UNWTO and Eurostat data [49,50].

4. Results of the Cluster Analysis

4.1. Spatial Diversity of the Accommodation Base

Accommodation facilities are basic elements of the material-technical base of tourism, since they facilitate the visitors' stay at a destination and constitute a basis for further development of the destination [35]. Figure 1 presents the outcomes of clustering the EU countries with regard to the level of similarity of the accommodation base. The use of Ward's method resulted in the differentiation of five groups of countries that are most similar in terms of accommodation base infrastructure. The first one contains Austria, Cyprus and Greece. This cluster can be labeled as "Very well developed accommodation base". In these countries at that time there was a very large number of beds (amounting to about 70 places per 1000 inhabitants) and the accommodation was mainly in hotels and similar establishments (Table 4).

Table 4. Cluster descriptive characteristics of available capacity (beds per 1000 inhabitants), accommodation for visitors (per 1000 km^2) and accommodation in hotels and similar establishments (per 1000 km^2).

		Indicators			
			X_2	X_3	X_4
		Mean	70.2	126.7	88.6
	Cluster 1	Max	71.0	245.5	147.2
		Min	69.1	60.6	44.9
		CV	1.2%	66.4%	48.6%
		Mean	24.6	150.5	100.0
	Cluster 2	Max	31.4	264.8	178.2
		Min	15.4	85.6	51.8
Ward method		CV	23.9%	39.1%	38.1%
		Mean	22.0	40.3	16.0
	Cluster 3	Max	39.7	125.0	30.6
		Min	8.7	6.2	2.9
		CV	42.9%	75.0%	61.2%
		Mean	32.4	329.4	62.9
	Cluster 4	Max	40.8	363.4	109.8
		Min	18.6	302.6	23.7
		CV	0.3%	0.1%	0.6%
	Malta		92.5	733.3	733.3

Source: own studies based on UNWTO data [49].

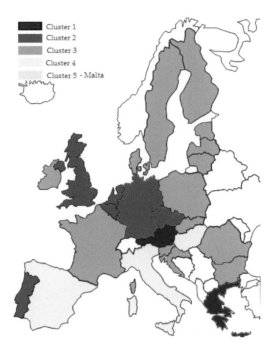

Figure 1. Grouping of countries according to cluster analysis—accommodation base. Source: own studies based on UNWTO data [49].

The second cluster rated as average developed accommodation base. The cluster is composed of Belgium, the Czech Republic, Germany, Luxembourg, The Netherlands, Portugal and the United Kingdom, where the number of beds per 1000 inhabitants ranged between 15.4 and 31.4. In addition, in these countries there was quite a high availability of accommodation in hotels and similar establishments (per 1000 km^2), which on average was 100.

The third cluster contains Bulgaria, Croatia, Denmark, Estonia, Finland, France, Ireland, Latvia, Lithuania, Poland, Romania, Slovakia, Slovenia and Sweden. This cluster can be labeled as "Less developed accommodation base". In these countries, the availability of beds per 1000 inhabitants was at a similar level to the second cluster. However, the availability of accommodation in hotels and similar establishments (per 1000 km^2) was lower; on average it was 16 places with a maximum of 30.

The fourth cluster consists of three countries: Hungary, Italy and Spain, in which the accommodation base is well developed. In these countries, the availability of accommodation for visitors (per 1000 km^2) was 330 on average. The last cluster consists solely of Malta, in which the number of beds was as much as 92 per 1000 inhabitants and the main accommodation was in hotels—733 places per 1000 km^2.

4.2. Spatial Diversity of Tourism Traffic

Figure 2 presents the grouping of EU countries in terms of tourist traffic. The use of Ward's method resulted in the distinction between three groups of countries. The first one contains Austria, Croatia, Cyprus and Malta. These countries were characterized by high tourist traffic and can be labeled as "Long-term travels". The average length of stay was 5.9 days and the number of overnight tourists per 1000 inhabitants was 3.5 persons (Table 5).

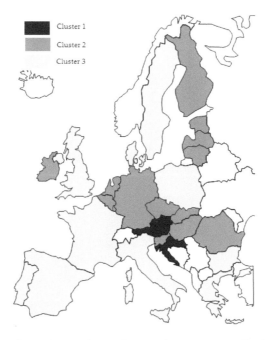

Figure 2. Grouping of countries according to cluster analysis—tourism traffic. Source: own studies based on UNWTO data [49].

Table 5. Cluster descriptive characteristics of average length of stay and overnight visitors (tourists) (per 1000 inhabitants).

		Indicators		
			X_1	X_5
Ward method	Cluster 1	Mean	5.9	3.5
		Max	8.0	4.6
		Min	3.7	2.7
		CV	27.0%	19.9%
	Cluster 2	Mean	2.3	1.3
		Max	2.6	2.4
		Min	1.9	0.4
		CV	11.0%	45.8%
	Cluster 3	Mean	5.6	1.2
		Max	7.4	2.2
		Min	3.6	0.5
		CV	20.9%	43.4%

Source: own studies based on UNWTO data [49].

The second cluster was made up of Belgium, the Czech Republic, Estonia, Finland, Germany, Hungary, Ireland, Latvia, Lithuania, Luxemburg, The Netherlands, Romania, Slovakia and Slovenia. This cluster can be labeled as "Short-term travels". In these countries the average length of stay was the lowest and ranged from 1.9 to 2.6 days. The same was true for the number of overnight tourists per 1000 inhabitants, which averaged 1.3.

The remaining EU countries formed a third cluster, which we described as "Long-term but dispersed tourist traffic". The number of overnight tourists per 1000 inhabitants was also low, as in the case of the second cluster. However, in these countries the average length of stay was 5.6 days.

4.3. Spatial Diversity of Tourism Expenditures and Revenues

The importance of tourism in creating the GDP of a given country is an interesting research issue. Figure 3 presents the grouping of EU countries in terms of tourism-related revenues and expenditure. The use of Ward's method resulted in the distinction between five groups of countries. The first cluster, which we described as "An important role of tourism in the country's GDP", represents Austria, Bulgaria, Greece, Hungary, Portugal, Slovenia and Spain. The group included countries that were characterized by high revenues from tourism, on average 6.2% of GDP (Table 6), while expenditures in these countries was at 2% of GDP.

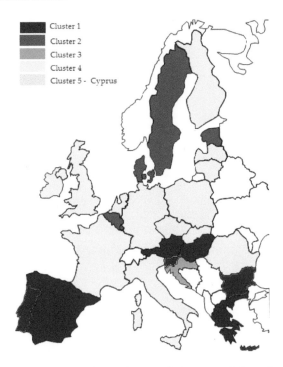

Figure 3. Grouping of countries according to cluster analysis—economic factor. Source: own studies based on Eurostat data [49,50].

The second cluster was made up of the following countries: Belgium, Denmark, Estonia, Luxembourg and Sweden. This cluster can be labeled as "An average role of tourism in the country's GDP". In these countries, revenues and expenditures as part of GDP were at a similar level, on average about 4%.

The third cluster was made up of Croatia and Malta, where tourism revenues as part of GDP were one of the largest and tourism expenditure over GDP was at a low level. This cluster can be labeled as "Tourist countries".

A separate cluster was created by Cyprus, in which revenues accounted for 14.1% and expenditures for 6% of GDP. The other EU countries formed the fifth cluster. In these countries, both revenue and expenditure for tourist purposes accounted for about 2% of GDP. This cluster can be labeled as "Non-tourism countries".

Table 6. Cluster descriptive characteristics of tourism expenditure over GDP (%) and tourism receipts over GDP (%).

		Indicators	X_5	X_6
Ward method	Cluster 1	Mean	2.1	6.1
		Max	2.9	8.1
		Min	1.0	4.4
		CV	26.9%	22.0%
	Cluster 2	Mean	4.0	4.2
		Max	4.8	7.3
		Min	3.0	2.4
		CV	18.8%	50.1%
	Cluster 3	Mean	3.1	16.5
		Max	3.7	19.3
		Min	2.5	13.7
		CV	19.4%	17.0%
	Cluster 4	Mean	2.1	2.2
		Max	2.7	3.2
		Min	1.4	1.1
		CV	19%	32%
	Cyprus		6.0	14.1

Source: own studies based on Eurostat data [49,50].

The groups of countries obtained in the research can be linked to research on measuring the tourism efficiency of European countries by using Data Envelopment Analysis [51]. According to this research, the third and fourth cluster countries were considered effective. In addition, effective countries include: Estonia, Finland, France, Greece, Hungary, Ireland, Latvia, Luxembourg, Poland, Portugal and Spain. Other studies confirm the relations between the income generated by the inhabitants and the competitiveness of tourist destinations [24,25,52].

5. Discussion and Conclusions

The tourism sector is one of the largest and fastest growing industries in the world. Thanks to the generation of employment, export revenues, investments and infrastructure developments, the tourism sector makes serious contributions to the socio-economic process directly and indirectly. The issues concerning the accommodation base, tourist traffic, and expenditures and revenues analyzed in the work cover the main aspects of tourism development. Other authors also pay attention to conducting individual analyses of individual elements of tourism [42]. It must be noticed that the accommodation base is the most important element of tourism management that is of key significance for tourist traffic. First of all, it serves to satisfy the need to sleep, rest and reside. Confirmation of the importance of accommodation facilities can be seen in the fact that hotel services belong to the basic services satisfying tourists' material needs connected with the change of the place of residence and travel as well as a series of other needs of travelers [53]. Therefore, it can be said that there are no grounds for development or even the occurrence of tourist traffic determining revenues from tourism without appropriate tourism management, the main element of which is the accommodation base, which is confirmed in the present research.

The development of tourism is a consequence of complex natural factors, forms of spatial organization, and the effects of human activities [54]. One of the development directions is the use of tourism attractiveness to build competitive advantage and attract tourists [55]. In many regions, tourism has become the sole or key determinant of income, as well as economic and social changes. Countries such as Malta, Croatia and Cyprus, which often form clusters in the spatial diversity analyses herein, can be the examples of that. It is worth noting that the accommodation base in EU countries is more spatially diverse (five clusters) than tourist traffic (three clusters). This may indicate that other factors that have not been studied in this paper also have an impact on tourist traffic. The distinguishing of areas attractive for possible tourism is based on the assessment of the occurrence of, inter alia, the tourism attractions that constitute the aim of tourists' arrivals, and the tourism infrastructure that makes it possible to use those attractions [14,40].

Data on clusters, as presented in this paper, can be used in the effective planning and decision-making for a destination [56] to support sustainable tourism development in a specific country. The data can also be used as a relevant base for potential future cooperation between various countries from one cluster to support tourism competitiveness and sustainable development [57,58]. In some countries, tourism has a good opportunity for joint development, e.g., by introducing a joint offer for tourists. Especially if the countries are located close to each other, there is a chance for tourists to use common tourist assets, such as tourist routes.

Moreover, the results presented in the article may be of application significance, both in scientific and practical terms. They can be useful for:

- Country's authorities—to develop a strategy for tourism development in the country;
- Universities, research institutes and scientists—comparison of obtained results; implementation of projects on tourism development in EU countries; looking for dependencies in the spatial development of regions;
- Organizations (e.g., national, regional and local tourist organizations, tourist associations, tourist clusters) and institutions (e.g., the Ministry of Tourism)—use of the results during trainings, courses, scientific conferences on the development of tourism and its spatial conditions; comparing elements of tourism in different countries;
- Tourist service providers (e.g., hotels, hostels, guesthouses)—defining perspectives for tourism development and tourist traffic (e.g., in areas of strong tourist competition).

Tourism is considered to be an activity that perfectly expresses spatial interaction [36]. Tourism has a heavy impact on local development [59]. Based on the results of clusters it can be determined:

- The spatial diversity of the accommodation base may indicate countries in which it can lead to some estimations of overuse, e.g., laundry, electricity or cosmetics (countries from clusters 1, 4 and Malta). Other authors also pay attention to this [42];
- The spatial diversity of tourist traffic may indicate an increase in the use of tourist and associated infrastructure, such as the transport infrastructure in individual countries [60]. This can also show the level of the impact on sustainable tourism development. On the other hand, countries with more tourist traffic should have this infrastructure more developed (countries from the clusters "Long-term travels" and "Long-term but dispersed tourist traffic");
- The analysis of the spatial differentiation of revenues and expenditure indicated countries specializing in "tourism", which at the time of crises or epidemics may show very large losses in the budget of the state and inhabitants (objects from cluster "Tourist countries").

The importance of the spatial diversity of tourism in terms of the factors analyzed in the article has a great impact on the presentation of tourism development in a given country. Spatial diversity is fundamental for characterizing and carrying out research into tourism in a given area [11]. However, some limitations of the study should be acknowledged:

- It should be highlighted that the more countries or regions the research covers, the more probable it is that it will be more differentiated and it will be more necessary to obtain detailed and comparable spatial-temporal data concerning tourism [9]. This is why the presented issue should be recognized as very broad, with research into it not being fully exhausted. The more the available statistical data from official European data sources on tourism are limited in terms of both the spatial and temporal resolutions, the more it curbs potential analyses and applications relevant for tourism management and policy.

- Use of more tourism indicators in the cluster analysis may result in more accurate outputs. However, in some cases, it may lead to changes within clusters and/or the number of clusters. The limitation in this case is also the lack of comparable data for all countries.

The literature on the subject lacks studies on the spatial diversity of tourism including the variables used (accommodation, tourism, expenditures and revenues from tourism). There is also a lack of spatial studies containing other factors such as tourist seasonality or the recently fashionable issue of innovation in tourism [61–63]). There are dynamic changes taking place in tourism so it is worth upholding the issue and conducting similar research, e.g., covering spatial relationships at lower territorial units (NUTS 2—basic regions for the application of regional policies or NUTS 3—small regions for specific diagnoses).

Author Contributions: Conceptualization, M.R. (Michał Roman), M.R. (Monika Roman), A.N.; data curation, M.R. (Monika Roman), M.R. (Michał Roman); formal analysis, M.R. (Michał Roman), M.R. (Monika Roman); methodology, M.R. (Monika Roman), M.R. (Michał Roman); resources, M.R. (Michał Roman), M.R. (Monika Roman); visualization, A.N., M.R. (Michał Roman), M.R. (Monika Roman); writing—original draft, M.R. (Monika Roman), M.R. (Michał Roman), A.N.; writing—review and editing, M.R. (Monika Roman), M.R. (Michał Roman), A.N. All authors have read and agreed to the published version of the manuscript.

Funding: This research received no external funding.

Acknowledgments: Authors would like to thank reviewers for their helpful and constructive comments and suggestions that greatly contributed to improving the final version of this paper.

Conflicts of Interest: The authors declare no conflict of interest.

References

1. World Tourism Organization (UNWTO). *World Tourism Barometer*; World Tourism Organization: Madrid, Spain, 2017; Volume 15, pp. 1–2. Available online: https://www.e-unwto.org/doi/pdf/10.18111/wtobarometereng.2017.15.6.1 (accessed on 10 December 2019).
2. World Bank Group. *Tourism for Development. 20 Reasons Sustainable Tourism Counts for Development*; Public Disclosure Authorized. Knowledge Series; International Finance Corporation, World Bank Group: Washington, DC, USA, 2017; p. 8. Available online: http://documents.worldbank.org/curated/en/558121506324624240/pdf/119954-WP-PUBLIC-SustainableTourismDevelopment.pdf (accessed on 10 December 2019).
3. Hawkins, D.; Mann, S. The World Bank's Role in Tourism Development. *Ann. Tour. Res.* **2007**, *34*, 348–363. [CrossRef]
4. Santos, A.; Cincera, M. Tourism demand, low cost carriers and European institutions: The case of Brussels. *J. Transp. Geogr.* **2018**, *73*, 163–171. [CrossRef]
5. Juul, M. *Tourism and the European Union. Recent Trends and Policy Developments*; European Parliamentary Research Service: Brussels, Belgium, 2015; p. 1.
6. Weston, R.; Guia, J.; Mihalič, T.; Prats, L.; Blasco, D.; Ferrer-Roca, N.; Lawler, M.; Jarratt, D. *Research for TRAN Committee—European Tourism: Recent Developments and Future Challenges*; European Parliament, Policy Department for Structural and Cohesion Policies: Brussels, Belgium, 2019; p. 11.
7. Anastasiadou, C. Tourism and the European Union. In *Tourism in the New Europe: The Challenges and Opportunities of EU Enlargement*; Hall, D., Smith, M., Marciszewska, B., Eds.; CABI Publishing: Wallingford, UK, 2006; pp. 20–31.
8. Romão, J.; Guerreiro, J.; Rodrigues, P.M.M. Territory and sustainable tourism development: A space-time analysis on European regions. *Region* **2017**, *4*, 1–17. [CrossRef]
9. Batista e Silva, F.; Herrera, M.A.M.; Rosina, K.; Barranco, R.R.; Freire, S.; Schiavina, M. Analysing spatiotemporal patterns of tourism in Europe at High-Resolution with conventional and big data sources. *Tour. Manag.* **2018**, *68*, 101–115. [CrossRef]
10. Hair, J.; Black, W.; Babin, B.; Anderson, R.; Tatham, R. *Multivariate Data Analysis*; Prentice-Hall: Upper Saddle River, NJ, USA, 1998; pp. 417–440.
11. Zarębski, P.; Kwiatkowski, G.; Malchrowicz-Mośko, E.; Oklevik, O. Tourism Investment Gaps in Poland. *Sustainability* **2019**, *11*, 6188. [CrossRef]

12. Pina, I.P.A.; Delfa, M.T.D. Rural tourism demand by type of accommodation. *Tour. Manag.* **2005**, *26*, 951–959. [CrossRef]

13. Wall, G.; Dudych, D.; Hutchinson, J. Point pattern analyses of accommodation in Toronto. *Ann. Tour. Res.* **1985**, *12*, 603–618. [CrossRef]

14. Lascu, D.N.; Manrai, L.A.; Manrai, A.K.; Gan, A. A cluster analysis of tourist attractions in Spain. Natural and cultural traits and implications for global tourism. *Eur. J. Manag. Bus. Econ.* **2018**, *27*, 218–230. [CrossRef]

15. Navrátil, J.; Švec, R.; Pícha, K.; Doležalová, H. The Location of Tourist Accommodation Facilities: A Case Study of the Šumava Mts. and South Bohemia Tourist Regions (Czech Republic). *Morav. Geogr. Rep.* **2012**, *20*, 50–63.

16. Ritchie, J.R.B.; Crouch, G.I. *The Competitive Destination: A Sustainable Tourism Perspective*; CABI Publishing: Oxon, UK, 2003.

17. Goeldner, C.R.; Ritchie, J.R.B. *Tourism: Principles, Practices, Philosophies*; Wiley: New York, NY, USA, 2009.

18. Bégin, S. The geography of a tourist business: Hotel distribution and urban development in Xiamen, China. *Tour. Geogr.* **2000**, *2*, 448–471. [CrossRef]

19. Shoval, N.; Mckercher, B.; NG, E.; Birenboim, A. Hotel location and tourist activity in cities. *Ann. Tour. Res.* **2011**, *38*, 1594–1612. [CrossRef]

20. Roman, M.; Górecka, A.; Roman, M. *Wykorzystanie Transportu Pasażerskiego w Rozwoju Turystyki (The Use of Passenger Transport in Tourism Development)*; Wydawnictwo SGGW: Warsaw, Poland, 2018; pp. 13–15. Available online: https://witrynawiejska.org.pl/data/Transport%20w%20turystyce.pdf (accessed on 10 December 2019).

21. Enright, M.J.; Newton, J. Tourism destination competitiveness: A quantitative approach. *Tour. Manag.* **2004**, *25*, 777–788. [CrossRef]

22. Das, J.; Dirienzo, C.E. Tourism competitiveness and the role of fractionalization. *Int. J. Tour. Res.* **2012**, *14*, 285–297. [CrossRef]

23. Fuchs, M.; Hoepken, W.; Lexhagen, M. Big data analytics for knowledge generation in tourism destinations—A case from Sweden. *J. Destin. Mark. Manag.* **2014**, *3*, 198–209. [CrossRef]

24. Garcia, C.F.; Valverde, I.M.; Mascuñano, P.J.; Gimeno, V.M. Quality Implications of the Use of Big Data in Tourism Statistics: Three Exploratory Examples. In Proceedings of the European Conference on Quality in Official Statistics (Q2016), Madrid, Spain, 31 May–3 June 2016; Volume 11.

25. Miah, S.J.; Vu, H.Q.; Gammack, J.; McGrath, M. A Big Data Analytics Method for Tourist Behaviour Analysis. *Inf. Manag.* **2017**, *54*, 771–785. [CrossRef]

26. Dokmeci, V.; Balta, N. The evolution and distribution of hotels in Istanbul. *Eur. Plan. Stud.* **1999**, *7*, 99–109. [CrossRef]

27. Urtasun, A.; Gutierrez, I. Hotel location in tourism cities: Madrid 1936–1998. *Ann. Tour. Res.* **2006**, *33*, 382–402. [CrossRef]

28. Egan, D.J.; Nield, K. Towards a theory of intraurban hotel location. *Urban Stud.* **2000**, *37*, 611–621. [CrossRef]

29. Shoval, N. The geography of hotels in cities: An empirical validation of a forgotten theory. *Tour. Geogr.* **2006**, *8*, 56–75. [CrossRef]

30. Xiao, H.; Smith, S.L.J. Case studies in tourism research: A state-of-the-art analysis. *Tour. Manag.* **2006**, *27*, 738–749. [CrossRef]

31. Soybali, H.H. Temporal and Spatial Aspects of Tourism in Turkey. Ph.D. Thesis, Bournemouth University, Bournemouth, UK, 2005.

32. Raun, J.; Ahas, R.; Tiru, M. Measuring tourism destinations using mobile tracking data. *Tour. Manag.* **2016**, *57*, 202–212. [CrossRef]

33. Peng, X.; Huang, Z. A Novel Popular Tourist Attraction Discovering Approach Based on Geo-Tagged Social Media Big Data. *ISPRS Int. J. Geo-Inf.* **2017**, *6*, 216. [CrossRef]

34. Del Vecchio, P.; Mele, G.; Ndou, V.; Secundo, G. Open Innovation and Social Big Data for Sustainability: Evidence from the Tourism Industry. *Sustainability* **2018**, *10*, 3215. [CrossRef]

35. Guilarte, Y.P.; Quintans, D.B. Using Big Data to Measure Tourist Sustainability: Myth or Reality. *Sustainability* **2019**, *11*, 5641. [CrossRef]

36. Papapavlou-Ioakeimidou, S.; Rodolakis, N.; Kalfakakou, R. Spatial structure of tourist supply and relations between sub-regions: A case study in a coastal region. In Proceedings of the Conference Paper 46th Congress of the European Regional Science Association (ERSA): Enlargement, Southern Europe and the Mediterranean, University of Thessaly—Department of Planning and Regional Development, Volos, Greece, 30 August–3 September 2006.

37. Borzyszkowski, J.; Marczak, M.; Zarębski, P. Spatial diversity of tourist function development: The municipalities of Poland's West Pomerania province. *Acta Geogr. Slov.* **2016**, *56*, 267–276. [CrossRef]

38. Navarro Chavez, J.C.L.; Zamora Torres, A.I.; Cano Torres, M. Hierarchical Cluster Analysis of Tourism for Mexico and the Asia-Pacific Economic Cooperation (APEC) Countries. *Tur. Anal.* **2016**, *27*, 235–255. [CrossRef]

39. Świstak, E.; Świątkowska, M. Spatial Diversity of Accommodation as a Determinant of Tourism in Poland. *Econ. Probl. Tour.* **2018**, *2*, 201–210. [CrossRef]

40. Gawroński, K.; Król, K.; Gawrońska, G.; Leśniara, N. Spatial diversity of tourism attractiveness of the Nowy Sącz district, using the Wrocław taxonomic method. *Geomat. Landmanag. Landsc.* **2019**, *2*, 37–54. [CrossRef]

41. Rodriguez Rangel, M.C.; Sanchez Rivero, M. Spatial Imbalance Between Tourist Supply and Demand: The Identification of Spatial Clusters in Extremadura, Spain. *Sustainability* **2019**, *12*, 1651. [CrossRef]

42. Kolvekova, G.; Liptakova, E.; Strba, L.; Krsak, B.; Sidor, C.; Cehlar, M.; Khouri, S.; Behun, M. Regional Tourism Clustering Based on the Three Ps of the Sustainability Services Marketing Matrix: An Example of Central and Eastern European Countries. *Sustainability* **2019**, *11*, 400. [CrossRef]

43. Dwyer, L.; Gill, A.; Seetaram, N. *Handbook of Research Methods in Tourism: Quantitative and Qualitative Approaches*; Edward Elgar Publishing: Cheltenham, UK, 2012; pp. 212–226.

44. Ward, J.H. Hierarchical Grouping to Optimize an Objective Function. *J. Am. Stat. Assoc.* **1963**, *58*, 236–244. [CrossRef]

45. Murtagh, F. Ward's Hierarchical Agglomerative Clustering Method: Which Algorithms Implement Ward's Criterion? *J. Classif.* **2014**, *31*, 274–295. [CrossRef]

46. Roman, M.; Roman, M. The similarity of the structure of foreign trade in dairy products in the European Union. In Proceedings of the 27th International Scientific Conference Agrarian Perspectives, Prague, Czech Republic, 19–20 September 2018; pp. 297–303.

47. Sarle, W.S. *Cubic Clustering Criterion*; Technical Report A-108; SAS Institute Inc.: Cary, NC, USA, 1983.

48. Calinski, T.; Harabasz, J.A. Dendrite Method for Cluster Analysis. *Commun. Stat. Theory Methods* **1974**, *3*, 1–27. [CrossRef]

49. UNWTO. Tourism Statistics. 2017. Available online: https://www.e-unwto.org/action/doSearch?ConceptID=1070&target=topic (accessed on 1 September 2019).

50. Eurostat. Tourism Statistics. 2017. Available online: https://ec.europa.eu/eurostat/statistics-explained/images/8/88/Travel_receipts_and_expenditure_in_balance_of_payments%2C_2012%E2%80%932017.png (accessed on 1 December 2019).

51. Soysal-Kurt, H. Measuring Tourism Efficiency of European Countries by Using Data Envelopment Analysis. *Eur. Sci. J.* **2017**, *13*, 31–49. [CrossRef]

52. Jackman, M.; Lorde, T.; Lowe, S.; Alleyne, A. Evaluating tourism competitiveness of small island developing states: A revealed comparative advantage approach. *Anatolia* **2011**, *22*, 350–360. [CrossRef]

53. Knowles, T. *Zarządzanie Hotelarstwem i Gastronomią (Hotel and Catering Management)*; Wydawnictwo PWE: Warszawa, Poland, 2001.

54. Ntibanyurwa, A. Tourism as a factor of development. *Sustain. Tour.* **2006**, *97*, 73–84.

55. Kang, S.; Kim, J.; Nicholls, S. National tourism policy and spatial patterns of domestic tourism in South Korea. *J. Travel Res.* **2014**, *53*, 791–804. [CrossRef]

56. Bhatia, A.K. *International Tourism Management*; Sterling Publishers Pvt. Ltd.: New Delhi, India, 2001; p. 539.

57. Bramwell, B.; Lane, B. *Tourism Collaboration and Partnerships: Politics, Practice and Sustainability*; Channel View Publications: Clevedon, UK, 2000; p. 351.

58. Capone, F. Tourist desinations, clusters, and competitiveness: An introduction. In *Tourist Clusters, Destinations and Competitiveness: Theoretical Issues and Empirical Evidences*; Capone, F., Ed.; Routledge: Abingdon, UK, 2016; pp. 1–12.

59. Da Cunha, S.K.; da Cunha, J.C. Tourism cluster competitiveness and sustainability: Proposal for a systemic model to measure the impact of tourism on local development. *Bar Braz. Admin. Rev.* **2005**, *2*, 47–62. [CrossRef]
60. Roman, M.; Roman, M. Bicycle Transport as an Opportunity to Develop Urban Tourism—Warsaw Example. *Procedia Soc. Behav. Sci.* **2014**, *151*, 295–301. [CrossRef]
61. Hjalager, A. A review of innovation research in tourism. *Tour. Manag.* **2010**, *31*, 1–12. [CrossRef]
62. Hu, M.M.; Horn, J.S.; Sun, Y.H. Hospitality teams: Knowledge sharing and service innovation performance. *Tour. Manag.* **2009**, *30*, 41–50. [CrossRef]
63. Hall, C.M.; Williams, A.M. *Tourism and Innovation*; Routledge: London, UK, 2008.

Article

Evaluating the Impact of Air Pollution on China's Inbound Tourism: A Gravity Model Approach

Boyang Xu and Daxin Dong *

School of Business Administration, Southwestern University of Finance and Economics, Chengdu 611130, China; xuboyang@smail.swufe.edu.cn
* Correspondence: dongdaxin@swufe.edu.cn

Received: 9 January 2020; Accepted: 11 February 2020; Published: 15 February 2020

Abstract: China's inbound tourism grew very slowly in recent years. This study modelled China's inbound tourism based on a gravity model with province-level inbound tourist arrivals data from 13 countries of origin between 2010 and 2016. It was found that air pollution in tourist destinations and origin regions both had significant negative impacts on China's inbound tourism. On average, if the concentration of particulate matter with a diameter of 2.5 micrometers or less ($PM_{2.5}$) in China and foreign countries increased by 1 $\mu g/m^3$, inbound tourist arrivals would decline by approximately 1.7% and 3.8%, respectively. The effect of pollution in destination regions is explained by the importance of clean air as a favored characteristic of tourist attractions. The effect of pollution in tourist origin countries is explained by more awareness of and concern about air pollution by potential tourists if they live in more polluted countries. Further analysis showed that the impact of air pollution in destination regions was larger for tourists coming from more polluted and Asian countries, and visiting less polluted and more popular destinations. This study has a clear policy implication: improving air quality can be considered as a straightforward and effective way to promote inbound tourism in China. If air quality in China can be substantially improved in the future, inbound tourist arrivals have the potential to rise by at least tens of millions of person-times.

Keywords: inbound tourism; China; air pollution; $PM_{2.5}$; gravity model

1. Introduction

Every year, numerous travelers from all over the world visit China for its beautiful scenery, renowned world heritage sites, and mysterious oriental culture. The expansion of the tourism industry has greatly benefited several relevant industries in China, such as tourism product manufacturing, transportation, hotels, and retail businesses [1]. Overall, the tourism industry has effectively promoted macroeconomic growth in many Chinese regions. According to a report released by China's Ministry of Culture and Tourism [2], in 2018, the tourism sector's total contribution to China's gross domestic product (GDP) was 9940 billion CNY, accounting for 11.0% of GDP. Additionally, the tourism sector contributed roughly 28.3 million jobs directly and 51.7 million jobs indirectly. These two numbers together accounted for 10.3% of total employment in China. The World Travel and Tourism Council forecasted that in 2028 the total economic contribution of tourism in China could reach 18,462 billion CNY, as much as 12.9% of GDP. The contribution to job creation was forecasted to be 116.5 million in total, as much as 14.7% of total employment in the coming decade [3].

However, aside from its substantial growth in the past few decades, tourism in China still has problems that need to be dealt with. One of the most obvious problems is the huge difference between the levels of inbound and domestic tourism. Figure 1 shows the number of inbound and domestic tourist arrivals in China between 2010 and 2018. It can be seen from the figure that the growth of inbound tourist arrivals has remained stagnant in recent years. Since 2010, the number of inbound tourist arrivals vacillated between 128 and 141 million person-times. It even decreased in several years (e.g., the annual growth rate was −2.5% in 2013). In contrast, during the same period, the number of domestic tourist arrivals rose from 2103 to 5540 million person-times with an average annual growth rate of 12.9%. Concerning the revenues from tourism industries, the inbound tourism market in China is also much smaller than domestic tourism, though not shown in the graph. According to the official data, from 2010 to 2018, the annual inbound tourism receipts increased from 46 to 127 billion USD (i.e., from 310 to 841 billion CNY) while domestic tourism receipts grew from 1258 to 5128 billion CNY.

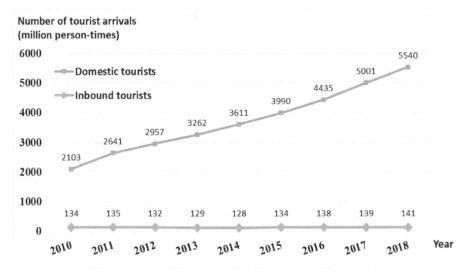

Figure 1. Number of inbound vs. domestic tourist arrivals in China (2010–2018). Data source: Yearbook of China Tourism Statistics published by the National Bureau of Statistics of China.

The development of China's inbound tourism not only lags behind domestic tourism, but also far behind the average level in the world. Figure 2 shows the ratios of inbound tourist arrivals to local population in China and some other countries. (In the graph, we only demonstrate the circumstances in other four Asian countries, including India, Japan, South Korea, and Thailand, which have evident geographical or cultural similarities to China. The essential finding would not be changed if we take into account other countries for comparison.) It is apparent that the ratio in China is much lower than that in many other countries. For instance, in 2016, the ratios in South Korea and Thailand were around 34% and 47%, respectively. However, in China, the ratio was only slightly more than 4%. The world average ratio was around 17%, approximately four times the ratio in China. Additionally, from the perspective of inbound tourism receipts, China is still far behind other large economies. According to data provided by the World Bank's World Development Indicators (WDI) dataset, in 2016, the international tourism receipts-to-GDP ratio in China was only 0.4%, much less than Japan's 0.7%, USA's 1.3%, and France's 2.5%.

In order to find effective strategies for promoting China's inbound tourism, it is important to evaluate the causes of stagnation in inbound tourism growth. There is no doubt that air quality is a crucial factor in the selection of tourist destinations [4–8]. Tourists care about air quality for at least two crucial reasons. First, air pollution causes considerable health risks. The medical literature has reported that air pollution is closely correlated with the incidence of mental and emotional depression, and respiratory and cardiovascular diseases [9–11]. Second, severe air pollution significantly impairs the visibility of air in scenic spots. This will heavily reduce the aesthetic enjoyment and pleasure obtained by tourists, and lower their willingness to travel and visit [12,13]. Therefore, it is expected that air pollution would have a negative influence on the number of tourist arrivals.

Inbound Tourist Arrivals/Population

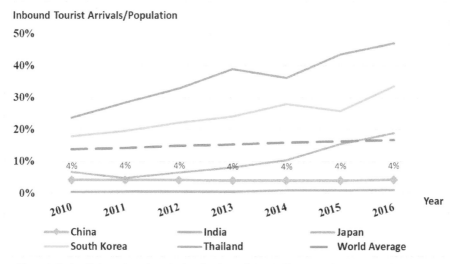

Figure 2. Ratio of inbound tourist arrivals to local population in China vs. other countries (2010–2016). Data source: World Bank's World Development Indicators (WDI) dataset. Statistics shown in this graph are only for overnight visitors.

In recent years, China suffered severe haze problems much more frequently than before, which showed a deterioration of air quality. According to the 2018 China Environment Bulletin published by the Ministry of Ecology and Environment of China [14], 217 out of 338 cities in China failed to meet the preferred standard of the air quality index (AQI). The air pollution problem in China is indeed severe compared to many other countries in the world. Figure 3 shows the severity of air pollution, measured by the proportion of population exposed to particulate matter with a diameter of 2.5 micrometers or less ($PM_{2.5}$) pollution levels exceeding World Health Organization (WHO) Interim Target-1 value (i.e., 35 $\mu g/m^3$), in different countries. The higher the proportion, the severer the air pollution. In 2016, 81% of Chinese residents were exposed to $PM_{2.5}$ pollution levels exceeding WHO Interim Target-1 value. This proportion was substantially higher than the world average of 51%. Many countries with developed inbound tourism industries had low levels of air pollution. For instance, the value was 0% in Japan and South Korea, and 3% in Thailand. The haze problem not only affects the daily lives of local residents, but also substantially decreases the willingness of tourists to visit the destination. One impressive example is that, in 2013, due to the severe smog problem, the number of foreign visitors to Beijing declined by roughly half in the first three quarters of the year [15]. Combining Figures 2 and 3 together, we can also observe a negative relationship between air pollution and tourist arrivals from the cross-country comparison. Particularly, China and India have high levels of air pollution and low levels of tourist arrivals-to-population ratio. In contrast, Japan, South Korea, and Thailand have low levels of pollution and high levels of tourism development. Although the figures suggest some preliminary evidence about the adverse effect of air pollution on China's inbound tourism, the graphical observations are not sufficient to accurately evaluate the impact of air pollution. A quantitative assessment based on statistical methods is required.

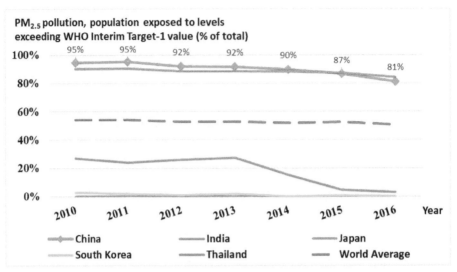

Figure 3. Severity of air pollution in China vs. other countries (2010–2016). Data source: World Bank's World Development Indicators (WDI) dataset. Abbreviations: $PM_{2.5}$, particulate matter with a diameter of 2.5 micrometers or less; WHO, World Health Organization.

The purpose of this study was to assess the impact of air pollution on China's inbound tourism. Although several previous studies have empirically investigated the same research topic, there was no consensus on the magnitude of the impact of air pollution. For example, Liu et al. [16] used $PM_{2.5}$ to measure the degree of air pollution in 17 undeveloped provinces in China during 2005–2015, and reported that air pollution had no statistically significant effect on inbound tourist arrivals. Differently, a study by Tang et al. [17] indicated a significant and large impact of air pollution. They focused on Beijing City, and reported that the number of inbound tourists from major origin countries would decline by around 2%, if the AQI in Beijing rose by 1%. Given the large contribution of tourism to regional economic development (e.g., [1,18–20]), understanding the extent to which air pollution influences tourism is important. If the impact of air pollution is really large, communities, industrial sectors, and governments should consider clean air as a priority in tourism development strategies and make large collaborative efforts to mitigate pollution. If the impact is small, policy-makers might need to focus on other factors, such as tourism advertising and infrastructure construction, in order to promote local tourism industries. In addition, a precise estimation of the impact of air pollution will improve the reliability and accuracy of tourism demand forecasting, and hence facilitate the management and marketing of local tourism resources in practice.

This study contributes to the literature in several aspects. First, this paper utilized a gravity model with province-level data to estimate the influence of air pollution on inbound tourism in China. By containing a wide set of control variables suggested by the literature and taking the possible endogeneity issue into account in the regression analysis, this study attempted to provide a more accurate and reliable estimate. Second, this study explored possible heterogeneities among different tourist groups, which have not been analyzed in previous literature. Particularly, it was found that inbound tourists coming from different origin countries and visiting different destination regions responded to air pollution dissimilarly. Overall, according to the study results, it can be inferred that, if the air quality in China can be substantially improved, inbound tourist arrivals have the potential to rise by at least tens of millions of person-times. This study demonstrates that there is a bright market prospect for China's inbound tourism.

The rest of the paper is organized as follows. Section 2 presents a literature review and develops the hypotheses. Section 3 describes the empirical model and data. Section 4 reports the estimation results based on the empirical model. Section 5 discusses the results and associated implications. Finally, Section 6 concludes the paper and talks about directions for future studies.

2. Literature Review and Hypothesis Development

Intuitively, a contaminated environment impedes the willingness of potential tourists to visit. Based on the relevant literature, the mechanisms through which air pollution affects tourism can be roughly summarized as follows. First, air pollution poses great health risks to tourists [21,22]. For instance, air pollution is directly correlated with the exacerbation of asthma, higher incidence of cardiovascular diseases, and increase in mortality [9,11,23]. Second, air pollution impairs the visibility of air in tourist attractions. This matter harms the aesthetic features of sceneries and tourist experiences, and sometimes causes traffic delays. As a result, tourists tend to have negative impressions and the destination images are damaged [12,13,24]. In addition, air pollution possibly has subtle impacts on the psychological status and behaviors of tourists, though they may not realize that. For instance, a recent study by Zhang et al. [25] reported that tourists who perceive severe air pollution in a destination are more likely to be suspicious of local service suppliers. Medical research also reported that air pollution causes more occurrences of mental and emotional troubles such as depression [10], which would reduce the happiness obtained from travelling and leisure activities. Overall, the literature indicated that air pollution could exert adverse impacts on tourists both physically and psychologically. It is reasonable to argue that air quality is a critical influential factor in tourism development.

2.1. Impact of Air Pollution in China

A set of studies have quantitatively revealed the harm of local air pollution to inbound tourism in China. The studies included Becken et al. [24], Deng et al. [26], Dong et al. [27], Tang et al. [17], Xu and Reed [28], Xu et al. [29], Zhou et al. [30], and Zhou et al. [31] on different districts in Mainland China; Cheung and Law [32] and Law and Cheung [33] on the Hong Kong SAR of China; and Chen et al. [34] on the Sun Moon Lake scenic area in the Taiwan Province of China.

Several studies inspected potential tourists' intention to visit China. For example, Becken et al. [24] surveyed hundreds of American and Australian residents about their contemporary views on China as a travel destination. Their findings showed that potential travelers expressed negative views about travel risks in China caused by poor air quality. Xu and Reed [28] suggested that people's perception of pollution levels substantially impeded tourism, by using Google Trends data as a proxy for tourism demand.

Some studies estimated the impact of air pollution on the actual level of inbound tourism. For instance, for one single scenic spot, Sun Moon Lake, Chen et al. [34] stressed the negative effect of air pollution on the business cycle of tourism demand, and reported that the monthly number of visitors would decrease by 25,725 person-times if the number of days with air pollution increased by one day during peak times. Using panel data on 31 Chinese provinces during 2001–2013, Deng et al. [26] reported that industrial waste gas emission had a significant negative correlation with tourist arrivals in different provinces. Dong et al. [27] found that the concentration of particulate matter with a diameter of 10 micrometers or less (PM_{10}) significantly reduced both inbound tourist arrivals and tourism receipts, based on data for 274 cities during 2009–2012. Moreover, they reported that the estimated impact was stronger after controlling for endogeneity in the econometric analysis. Tang et al. [17] quantified the impact of air quality on inbound tourism in Beijing, and found that air pollution, measured by AQI, had a negative effect on tourist arrivals in the long run, but not in the short run.

Following the findings in previous studies, the first hypothesis in this study was established as follows:

Hypothesis 1. *Air pollution in China negatively affects its inbound tourism.*

Obviously, this hypothesis is not novel, as it has been tested in several previous studies. However, most of those studies did not distinguish inbound tourists according to their countries of origin, and hence did not include the characteristics of tourist origin countries and the interactive factors between origin and destination regions as explanatory variables in the econometric analysis. In consequence, important explanatory variables might be neglected and so-called "omitted variable bias" might cause the estimated effect of air pollution to be insufficiently accurate and reliable. Therefore, re-estimating the impact of air pollution on tourism within a gravity model, which explicitly controls for variables reflecting the features of origin regions and origin–destination interactions, is valuable.

2.2. Impact of Air Pollution in Tourist Origin Countries

It is notable that tourism might be affected by air pollution not only in destination areas, but also in tourist origin regions. Based on a sample covering 11 Chinese cities, Wang et al. [35] reported that air pollution in China stimulated Chinese residents' outbound tourism demand. Given that the air pollution problem is severe in China relative to many other countries, this demand-inducement effect of local air pollution on outbound tourism reported by Wang et al. [35] is convincing, as Chinese people have many options for outbound travel destinations with good air quality. However, the same effect might not occur when the focus is on tourist flows from foreign countries to China. Even though the pollution in foreign countries stimulates the outbound tourism demand of foreign tourists, they may not choose China as a preferred travel destination because they would like to visit places with good air quality. Therefore, it was conjectured that the air pollution in foreign tourist origin countries might not have a positive impact on China's inbound tourism.

Even worse, potential tourists living in foreign countries may have less preference for China as a destination if the air quality in their home countries deteriorates. This is because local air pollution raises residents' awareness of and concern about the pollution problem, which has been confirmed by previous environmental literature. For example, Deguen et al. [36] interviewed around 2500 inhabitants in France to examine the association between air pollution and public perception of air quality. They reported that the measure of air quality perception (including sensory perceptions, symptoms and risk perception) significantly increased with the local air pollution level. Similar findings about the positive correlation between local air pollution and inhabitants' awareness of and concern about pollution were also reported by some other studies, such as Atari et al. [37] in Canada, Moffatt et al. [38] in the UK, and Oglesby et al. [39] in Switzerland among others [40,41]. Nowadays, the usage of Internet even amplifies the air pollution risk perception of people [42]. In a nutshell, if the degree of air pollution in tourists' origin countries increases, on average, tourists probably care more about pollution and become less willing to visit China. Following this logic, the second hypothesis in this study was formulated as follows:

Hypothesis 2. *Air pollution in foreign tourist origin countries negatively affects China's inbound tourism.*

3. Empirical Model and Data

3.1. Model

In order to provide a precise evaluation of the impact of air pollution on tourism, the empirical analysis should carefully control for other determinants of tourism. Tourist flows can be well modelled using the gravity model, which has been widely used in the international trade literature. As discussed in previous literature (e.g., [43]), the general form of a typical gravity model used in tourism research could be expressed by the following formula: $T_{ij} = f(Destination_i, Origin_j, Interaction_{ij})$, where T_{ij} denotes the number of tourist visits to destination region i from origin region j; $Destination_i$ refers to the features of the destination that act as forces pulling tourists to region i (e.g., clean environment, famous scenic spots, attractive culture); $Origin_j$ refers to the features of the origin region that act as forces pushing tourists from region j (e.g., large population size, high disposable income); and $Interaction_{ij}$ denotes the interactive factors that determine the costs for tourists from origin j to visit destination i (e.g., geographic distance, convenience of applying for a visa). The gravity model has been used in previous studies to explore the determinants of tourism. For instance, Huang et al. [44], Xu et al. [45], and Yang and Wong [46] investigated inbound tourism flows to China.

In this paper, in order to estimate the impact of air pollution on inbound tourism in different Chinese provinces, the following gravity model in a linear form was used:

$$T_{ijt} = \eta\, AirPollution_{it} + \varphi\, AirPollution_{jt} + Destination_{it}\alpha$$
$$+ Origin_{jt}\beta + Interaction_{ijt}\gamma + s_i + u_j + v_t + \varepsilon_{ijt},$$

(1)

where T_{ijt} is the dependent variable, the number of inbound tourist arrivals (in person-times) in China's province i from country j in period t. Here, "inbound tourist" refers to the tourist who is not a resident of Mainland China. $AirPollution_{it}$ and $AirPollution_{jt}$ are the degree of air pollution in province i and country j, respectively. $Destination_{it}$ is a vector containing a set of variables capturing the characteristics of destination province i. $Origin_{jt}$ is a vector containing the variables measuring the features of origin country j. $Interaction_{ijt}$ is a vector containing the variables describing the interactive relationship between province i and country j. s_i is the province-fixed effect; u_j is the country-fixed effect; and v_t is the time-fixed effect. ε_{ijt} is the error term. The dependent variable is log-transformed to address the scaling problem. Thus, variations in tourist arrivals are expressed in percentage changes. η, φ, α, β, and γ are coefficients to be estimated.

3.2. Selection of Explanatory Variables

3.2.1. Air Pollution

In this study, the degree of air pollution was measured by the degree of $PM_{2.5}$ concentration in ambient air. $PM_{2.5}$ is one of the most significant air pollutants, well known by the public. Previous studies have reported that $PM_{2.5}$ heavily harms public health and the tourism experience (e.g., [29,47–52]). Thus, in Equation (1), the variables $AirPollution_{it}$ and $AirPollution_{jt}$ refer to the annual average density of $PM_{2.5}$ pollutant ($\mu g/m^3$). According to Hypotheses 1 and 2, we expected that these two variables had negative coefficients.

3.2.2. Destination Features

The vector $Destination_{it}$ in Equation (1) contains the following variables for province i in year t: $ln(Population)_{it}$, $ln(GDPpc)_{it}$, $ln(Scenic)_{it}$, $ln(Hotel)_{it}$, $Hospital_{it}$, $Transport_{it}$, $Urban_{it}$, $GDPgr_{it}$, $Structure_{it}$, $Temperature_{it}$, and $Rain_{it}$.

$ln(Population)_{it}$ and $ln(GDPpc)_{it}$ are the logarithmic values of population and real GDP per capita, respectively. Previous studies suggested that the scale of destination economy is a determinant of cross-border tourism volume [53,54]. Ceteris paribus, a bigger economy is correlated with larger tourism volume compared to a smaller economy. The economic scale is typically measured by the size of GDP, which can be decomposed into GDP per capita multiplied by population. GDP per capita can be considered as an indicator of economic development level and people's income level. Countries with higher GDP per capita usually enjoy better infrastructure and more developed transportation networks, and have abilities to provide services with higher quality. All of these attributes help constitute a favored tourism destination [55]. We expected that larger population and higher income level were associated with more inbound tourist arrivals.

$ln(Scenic)_{it}$ refers to the logarithmic value of the number of 4A- and 5A-rated scenic spots, classified by the China National Tourism Administration. Because 5A spots are usually considered to be much more attractive than 4A spots, one 5A spot was assumed to be equal to two 4A spots. $ln(Hotel)_{it}$ is the logarithmic value of the number of star-rated hotels. The number of scenic spots is a proxy for the attractiveness of the destination region. The number of hotels indicates the capacity of providing accommodation services. Apparently, these two variables were expected to be positively correlated with tourist arrivals.

$Hospital_{it}$ is the ratio of the number of health-care workers to local population. This variable is a proxy for the abundance of public hygiene infrastructure, which provides a component of tourism services. As many foreign tourists stay in China for days or even weeks, the availability of public health services might be a concern. $Transport_{it}$ is a variable reflecting the convenience of transportation, measured by the length of road per capita. Since the transportation system is responsible for transporting travelers and relevant tourist products, its infrastructure should be seen as one of the most vital bases for tourism services. Convenient transportation infrastructure will increase the possibility that international travelers will visit. In contrast, terrible traffic conditions will leave a negative impression on foreign visitors, hurt the tourist experience, and limit the expansion of tourism. In previous studies, such as those by Khadaroo and Seetanah [53] and Zheng et al. [56], it was widely confirmed that transportation infrastructure is a significant determinant of tourism development. These two variables, measuring hospital and transportation availability, were supposed to facilitate inbound tourism.

$Urban_{it}$ is the urbanization rate, measured by the proportion of urban population in total population. $GDPgr_{it}$ is the GDP growth rate. These two variables were used to describe social and macroeconomic status. As tourism is a part of the aggregate socioeconomic system, it is probably relevant to these two variables. $Structure_{it}$ is the industrial structure, with the non-agricultural value added as a share of GDP as proxy. It was expected that the process of industrial updating was positively correlated with the development of tourism.

$Temperature_{it}$ and $Rain_{it}$ refer to the annual average temperature and proportion of rainy days. These two variables might be relevant to the number of tourist arrivals because tourism is a weather-dependent industry.

3.2.3. Origin Features

The vector $Origin_{jt}$ in Equation (1) contains the following variables for country j in year t: $ln(Population)_{jt}$, $ln(GDPpc)_{jt}$, $Transport_{jt}$, $Urban_{jt}$, and $GDPgr_{jt}$.

$ln(Population)_{jt}$ is the logarithmic value of population size. $ln(GDPpc)_{jt}$ is the logarithmic value of GDP per capita. The scale of origin country may be a crucial determinant of cross-border tourism volume [53,54]. Generally speaking, a big country has larger tourism volume compared to a small country. The economic scale can be measured by the size of GDP, which equals GDP per capita multiplied by population. A higher GDP per capita level indicates a higher level of personal income, on average, implying that more people can afford international travels. A larger population base is associated with a greater scale of population mobility. We expected that these two variables had positive correlations with the number of tourists visiting China.

$Transport_{jt}$ reflects the convenience of air transport, measured by the ratio of the number of registered carrier departures to local population. The transportation system is responsible for transporting travelers and tourist products. Transportation infrastructure is one of the most vital bases for tourism activities. Since most international tourists need to travel long distances from their origin countries to China, the convenience of air transport in their countries is a crucial concern. We supposed that this variable had a positive effect on tourist arrivals in China.

$Urban_{jt}$ is the urbanization rate, and $GDPgr_{jt}$ is the GDP growth rate. We used them as control variables to represent the basic social and macroeconomic status in tourists' home countries. We did not impose any prior expectation on the sign of their coefficients.

3.2.4. Interaction Variables

The vector $Interaction_{ijt}$ in Equation (1) contains the following variables: $ln(ER)_{ijt}$, $ln(Distance)_{ij}$, $TradeOpen_{ijt}$, and $VisaFree_{ijt}$.

$ln(ER)_{ijt}$ is the logarithmic value of the relative exchange rate between Chinese currency and foreign currency adjusted by price level. It was calculated according to the formula: $ln(ER)_{ijt} = ln[(CPI_{it}/E_{it})/(CPI_{jt}/E_{jt})]$, where CPI is the consumer price index (value in 2010 = 100) and E is the exchange rate of the local currency against the US dollar (value in 2010 = 100). The relative price of tourism products and services between origin and destination countries influences tourists' decisions [57–59]. The price factor demonstrates the relative cost of staying in the destination country compared to staying in the origin country. Two major elements of tourists' expenditures are the costs of travel and living [60,61]. The consumer price index together with the exchange rate are key indices used to evaluate the cost. We expected that the relative price negatively affected the tourist arrivals in China.

$ln(Distance)_{ij}$ is the logarithmic value of the geographic distance between the capital city of province i and the capital of country j. The distance between origin and destination countries should be taken into account. The geographical distance between two regions directly affects the cost of travel. International tourists usually depart from and arrive in big cities because of the good infrastructure and convenient transportation in those cities. Thus, researchers often use the distance between capital cities of origin and destination countries as a proxy for intercountry distance. Besides geographic distance, it was found in the literature that cultural distance might also play a role in shaping tourism demand [62]. For instance, Yang and Wong [46] reported that cultural distance had a negative effect on inbound tourism flow into China. Because of the lack of data, we did not include the cultural distance in our model. The variable of geographic distance was expected to be negative correlated with the dependent variable.

$TradeOpen_{ijt}$ refers to the degree of international trade openness, calculated by $TradeOpen_{ijt} = Trade_{ijt}/GDP_{jt}$, where $Trade_{ijt}$ is the volume of international trade between province i and country j and GDP_{jt} is the GDP of country j. The factor of trade flows can be used to assess the intensity of economic interactions between two regions. The more intensive the economic relationship, the more business tourists there are traveling between regions. Thus, the relative trade volume is a meaningful variable that can be utilized as a proxy for the closeness of intercountry economic relationship and partially explain the volume of tourism flow [44,45]. Because of its great size in terms of macroeconomy and international trade, China is one of the most important business partners for many countries. Obviously, the variable of trade flows cannot be omitted in research on tourists into China. It was expected that, if the degree of trade openness was high, the number of cross-border tourists would also be large.

$VisaFree_{ijt}$ is a dummy variable indicating whether there is a 72-h visa-free policy for tourists from country j to the capital city of province i. Its value is equal to 1 if the policy was implemented, and 0 otherwise. As a sign of the relationship between different countries, tourism liberalization policies also play an important role in tourism development. Liberalization policies provide convenience for potential visitors and present a welcome attitude to tourists. Arita et al. [63] found that Approved Destination Status (ADS), which allows government-approved travel agencies to obtain visas to ADS destinations in bulk, resulted in a significant increase in the number of cross-border tourists. Gil-Pareja et al. [64] reported that tourism-related agreements had a significant impact on international tourism inflow. For many ordinary tourists, the process of applying for a visa is time-consuming. Thus, a visa-free policy might significantly stimulate people's intention to visit.

3.3. Data

The sample covered 30 provinces in Mainland China, excluding Tibet. Tibet was not included because of the unavailability of weather-relevant data. Tourist arrivals data at the province level were available for 13 origin countries: Australia, Canada, France, Germany, Japan, South Korea, Malaysia, Philippines, Russia, Singapore, Thailand, the United Kingdom, and the United States. The number of tourist arrivals from those 13 countries accounted for more than half of total foreign tourist arrivals in China. The sample period covered seven years, spanning from 2010 to 2016.

The PM$_{2.5}$ data in different Chinese provinces were obtained from the Chinese Research Data Services Platform (CNRDS), available at https://www.cnrds.com. The data of tourist arrivals and the destination regions' economic and social features were derived from the database provide by the EPS China Data, which was accessed at http://www.epschinadata.com. The weather data were obtained from the China Meteorological Data Service Center, accessed at http://data.cma.cn/en. The data for variables in different foreign countries were publicly available from the World Bank's World Development Indicators (WDI) dataset at http://datatopics.worldbank.org/world-development-indicators.

The data of the interaction variables were constructed by combining several data sources. The variable of relative exchange rate required information about the exchange rate and price level. The exchange rate data mainly came from the WDI dataset. Since WDI does not report the exchange rate for Euro Zone countries, the exchange rate data for France and Germany were obtained from the website of the Federal Reserve Bank of St. Louis at https://fred.stlouisfed.org. CPI data in the foreign countries were obtained from the WDI. CPI data in different Chinese provinces were obtained from the EPS database. The values of the distances between different regions were calculated based on longitude and latitude information supplied by the World Cities Database, available at https://simplemaps.com/data/world-cities. Information about trade openness required data at both the province and country level, which were available from the EPS and WDI, respectively. The data for 72-h visa-free policy were collected from news reports published by the official mass media.

Summary statistics of the variables are reported in Table 1. The table shows that the study samples were highly diversified, including regions with different levels of air pollution and degrees of tourism development. The final dataset used in regression analyses was comprised of 23 variables with 2651 observations in total.

Table 1. Summary statistics.

	Variable	Definition	Mean	SD	Min	Max
Tourist arrivals	$ln(Arrivals)_{ij}$	Inbound tourist arrivals (person-times)	10.264	1.757	3.367	14.245
Air pollution	$AirPollution_i$	PM$_{2.5}$ concentration ($\mu g/m^3$)	30.754	17.212	3.260	82.420
	$AirPollution_j$	PM$_{2.5}$ concentration ($\mu g/m^3$)	16.316	6.821	6.549	31.610
Destination features	$ln(Population)_i$	Population (10,000 persons)	8.113	0.843	5.704	9.306
	$ln(GDPpc)_i$	GDP per capita (in constant 2010 USD)	8.624	0.430	7.576	9.626
	$ln(Scenic)_i$	Number of 4A- and 5A-rated scenic spots	4.291	0.704	2.398	5.517
	$ln(Hotel)_i$	Number of star-rated hotels	5.713	0.624	4.007	6.916
	$Hospital_i$	Number of health-care workers (per 10,000 residents)	73.112	13.835	44.336	137.810
	$Transport_i$	Length of road (km per 10,000 residents)	42.521	39.854	5.149	248.024
	$Urban_i$	Urbanization rate (%)	54.434	13.727	22.670	89.600
	$GDPgr_i$	Annual GDP growth rate (%)	10.142	2.782	−2.500	17.400
	$Structure_i$	Share of non-agricultural value added in GDP (%)	89.687	5.112	73.800	99.610
	$Temperature_i$	Annual average temperature (°C)	13.733	5.518	1.791	25.800
	$Rain_i$	Annual proportion of rainy days	0.305	0.100	0.097	0.555
Origin features	$ln(Population)_j$	Population	17.878	0.962	15.440	19.593
	$ln(GDPpc)_j$	GDP per capita (in constant 2010 USD)	10.355	0.610	8.627	11.347
	$Transport_j$	Number of registered carrier departures per capita	0.016	0.011	0.002	0.038
	$Urban_j$	Urbanization rate (%)	76.786	14.782	43.856	100
	$GDPgr_j$	Annual GDP growth rate (%)	3.088	2.330	−2.308	14.526
Interaction variables	$ln(ER)_{ij}$	Relative exchange rate adjusted by price level	0.117	0.129	−0.055	0.551
	$ln(Distance)_{ij}$	Distance (km)	8.505	0.699	6.329	9.506
	$TradeOpen_{ij}$	Ratio of bilateral trade volume to GDP	0.003	0.010	0	0.117
	$VisaFree_{ij}$	Dummy variable for 72-h visa-free policy	0.310	0.463	0	1

Abbreviations: SD, standard deviation; Min, minimum; Max, maximum.

4. Results

This section reports the estimation results. First, based on the gravity model with province-level data, the important influence of air pollution on China's inbound tourism was identified. Then, a set of robustness checks were conducted. After that, the heterogeneities among different tourist groups were explored.

4.1. Main Result

The regression results for Equation (1) are listed in Table 2. The table shows the impacts of different factors on China's inbound tourism. Column (i) shows the baseline regression result. Air pollution in local provinces substantially harmed inbound tourism. The estimated coefficient for the variable $AirPollution_i$ is -0.017, statistically significant at the 1% level. The coefficient implies that, if $PM_{2.5}$ concentration rose by 1 $\mu g/m^3$, inbound tourism arrivals would decline by 1.7%. Thus, Hypothesis 1 in this study is supported. Given that the average scale of inbound tourist arrivals in China between 2010 and 2016 was 133 million person-times per year, this number indicates that, if the country could take effective actions to reduce $PM_{2.5}$ by 1 $\mu g/m^3$, annual inbound tourist arrivals would increase by 2.261 million person-times. This is indeed a large benefit.

Table 2. Impact of air pollution on China's inbound tourism estimated at the province level.

		Estimated Coefficient			
		Baseline Model	Robustness Analysis		
	Variable		Use AQI	IV-2SLS Estimation	IV-GMM Estimation
		(i)	(ii)	(iii)	(iv)
Air pollution	$AirPollution_i$	−0.017 ***	−0.014 ***	−0.050 *	−0.053 *
	$AirPollution_j$	−0.038 *	−0.027 *	−0.039 *	−0.040 *
Destination features	$ln(Population)_i$	−2.315	−2.409	−3.320 *	−3.659 **
	$ln(GDPpc)_i$	2.021 ***	1.992 ***	1.795 ***	1.754 ***
	$ln(Scenic)_i$	0.290 *	0.296 *	0.367 **	0.391 **
	$ln(Hotel)_i$	0.264 *	0.261 *	0.190	0.195
	$Hospital_i$	0.003	0.003	−0.006	−0.008
	$Transport_i$	0.036 ***	0.036 ***	0.040 ***	0.041 ***
	$Urban_i$	−0.092 ***	−0.094 ***	−0.117 ***	−0.120 ***
	$GDPgr_i$	−0.048 ***	−0.048 ***	−0.041 **	−0.039 **
	$Structure_i$	0.117 ***	0.117 ***	0.118 ***	0.113 ***
	$Temperature_i$	−0.035	−0.034	−0.038	−0.040
	$Rain_i$	0.538	0.555	0.854	0.892
Origin features	$ln(Population)_j$	0.727	0.732	0.776	0.760
	$ln(GDPpc)_j$	−0.909	−0.91	−0.922	−0.978
	$Transport_j$	27.240 **	27.185 **	26.679 **	26.397 **
	$Urban_j$	0.004	0.004	0.005	0.003
	$GDPgr_j$	−0.0004	−0.0004	−0.0003	−0.002
Interaction variables	$ln(ER)_{ij}$	−0.518 *	−0.518 *	−0.516 *	−0.491
	$ln(Distance)_{ij}$	−1.340 ***	−1.340 ***	−1.341 ***	−1.341 ***
	$TradeOpen_{ij}$	4.891 ***	4.882 ***	4.731 ***	4.709 ***
	$VisaFree_{ij}$	0.069	0.067	0.049	0.053
Province-fixed effect		Yes	Yes	Yes	Yes
Country-fixed effect		Yes	Yes	Yes	Yes
Time-fixed effect		Yes	Yes	Yes	Yes
Observations		2651	2651	2651	2651
R^2		0.819	0.819	0.817	0.816
Cragg-Donald Wald F-statistic		-	-	48.431 **	48.431 **
Kleibergen-Paap rk Wald F-statistic		-	-	48.519 **	48.519 **
Hansen J-statistic		-	-	1.141	1.141

Statistical significance: * $p < 10\%$, ** $p < 5\%$, *** $p < 1\%$. Abbreviations: AQI, air quality index; IV, instrumental variable; 2SLS, two-stage least squares; GMM, general method of moments.

It is notable that the degree of air pollution in tourist origin countries also had an obvious impact on tourist arrivals, as suggested by the estimated coefficient of $AirPollution_j$, which is -0.038 and statistically significant. This finding is not consistent with the finding by Wang et al. [35] that local air pollution stimulated outbound tourism. They reported that Chinese residents tended to have an increased demand for outbound tourism when local air quality became worse. What they found was not detected for tourists from foreign countries to China. The estimate in this study indicates that, on average, if $PM_{2.5}$ density in potential tourists' home countries increased by 1 $\mu g/m^3$, the actual number of tourists visiting China would decline by 3.8%, equal to a decline of 5.054 million person-times per year. Thus, Hypothesis 2 in this study is confirmed.

The estimated coefficients of the control variables are also reported in the table. The coefficient of $ln(Population)_i$ is not statistically significant, indicating that inbound tourism is not sensitive to the local population size. The coefficient of $ln(GDPpc)_i$ is significantly positive, indicating that expansion of inbound tourism is accompanied by overall economic development. The variables $ln(Scenic)_i$ and $ln(Hotel)_i$ both have significant positive coefficients, reflecting the straightforward opinion that more scenic spots and hotels are associated with a larger scale of tourism. The variables used as proxies for the abundance of infrastructure, $Hospital_i$ and $Transport_i$, both have positive coefficients, though the coefficient of $Hospital_i$ is not statistically significant. $Urban_i$ and $GDPgr_i$ both have significantly negative coefficients, implying that rapid urbanization and GDP growth actually do not increase the attractiveness of China to foreign tourists. $Structure_i$, the indicator for industrial structure, has a significantly positive coefficient, which was expected. The variables for weather, $Temperature_i$ and $Rain_i$, do not demonstrate any statistically significant impact.

The variables describing the characteristics of origin countries generally do not have a significant impact on inbound tourism in China. An exception is the variable $Transport_j$, whose coefficient is positive and significant at the 5% level. This indicates that international tourists' decision to visit China is affected by the convenience of cross-country transportation.

The signs of interaction variables are consistent with the economic intuition. $ln(ER)_{ij}$ has a statistically significant negative coefficient, indicating that an increase in the relative price of tourism in China would reduce the number of inbound tourist arrivals. The coefficient of $ln(Distance)_{ij}$ is significantly negative, indicating a strong negative impact of travel distance. $TradeOpen_{ij}$ is positively correlated with tourist arrivals, revealing that the trade linkage between two regions is associated with people's mobility. As expected, $VisaFree_{ij}$ has a positive coefficient, though not statistically significant.

4.2. Robustness Analysis

This subsection describes several robustness checks that were conducted to inspect the robustness of the baseline estimation results. First, we inspected whether the estimate was robust to the selection of air pollution indicator. Previously, the level of $PM_{2.5}$ concentration in ambient air was utilized to measure the degree of air pollution. Although $PM_{2.5}$ is one of the most significant air pollutants in daily life, people sometimes check the AQI value rather than $PM_{2.5}$ density to judge the severity of pollution. AQI has a nonlinear monotonic relationship with the physical density of air pollutants, and is also a widely used indicator of air pollution. Column (ii) of Table 2 reports the estimated coefficients if $PM_{2.5}$ was replaced by the corresponding AQI value calculated based on the Chinese official standard. This time, the coefficient of $AirPollution_i$ is -0.014, close to the value of -0.017 reported in column (i). The coefficient of $AirPollution_j$ is -0.027, not far from the value of -0.038 reported in column (i). The results indicate that our estimation was not sensitive to the selection of index used to measure the degree of air pollution.

Next, the endogeneity issue in econometric regression was taken into account. Previous studies, such as Dong et al. [27], suggested paying attention to the possible endogeneity problem when estimating the impact of air pollution on tourism because environmental quality and tourism might have reciprocal interactions with each other [65]. The instrumental variable (IV) approach is an effective method to tackle the potential endogeneity problem. Two meteorological indicators, wind speed and vapor pressure, were used as instrumental variables. Valid instrument variables should satisfy two conditions: they should be strongly correlated to the endogenous explanatory variable, and they should not directly affect the dependent variable, except through their link with the endogenous variable. The meteorological and environmental literature confirmed that meteorological conditions are strongly relevant to the degree of air pollution (e.g., [66–68]). There is no obvious reason to believe that tourists' visiting behaviors are sensitive to those meteorological indicators (as long as they are within normal ranges), except the relationship between air pollution and meteorological conditions. Thus, both conditions for the selection of IVs were satisfied.

Column (iii) reports the two-stage least squares (2SLS) IV estimation results. The estimated coefficient of $AirPollution_i$ is -0.050, which is statistically significant and even larger than the coefficient in the baseline regression shown in column (i). The corresponding Cragg–Donald Wald F-statistic and Kleibergen–Paap rk Wald F-statistic are both statistically significant, indicating that the selected IVs were not "weak IVs". The Hansen J-statistic is not statistically significant, indicating that the regression model was not overidentified. Overall, these statistics imply that the IVs were properly used in the estimation. In order to further inspect the IV estimation results, the general method of moments (GMM) estimation was applied. The results, shown in column (iv), provide a statistically significant coefficient of -0.053 for $AirPollution_i$. Therefore, combining columns (iii) and (iv) together, the previous finding that air pollution harms China's inbound tourism is still supported after the potential endogeneity issue is explicitly addressed. In addition, it is easy to see that the finding about the negative effect of air pollution in tourist origin countries is robust. As demonstrated in columns (iii) and (iv), the estimated coefficients of $AirPollution_j$ are -0.039 and -0.040, respectively, very close to the value of -0.038 reported in column (i).

4.3. Heterogeneities among Different Tourist Groups

Different types of inbound tourists may respond to air pollution in dissimilar ways. Considering this, tourists were classified into groups by the characteristics of their origin countries and destination regions, and their heterogeneous responses to air pollution were analyzed. Because the air pollution in tourists' origin countries is out of China's control, in this subsection, we focus on the heterogeneous responses of tourists to the air pollution within China. The analysis was based on Equation (2):

$$T_{ijt} = \eta_1 AirPollution_{it} + \eta_2 AirPollution_{it} \times D + \varphi AirPollution_{jt}$$
$$+ Destination_{it}\alpha + Origin_{jt}\beta + Interaction_{ijt}\gamma + s_i + u_j + v_t + \varepsilon_{ijt}. \tag{2}$$

Equation (2) was revised from Equation (1) by adding the interactive term $AirPollution_{it} \times D$. Here, D is a dummy variable equal to 1 or 0, depending on the classification of tourists. For the tourist group with $D = 1$, the impact of air pollution in China is measured by the coefficient $\eta_1 + \eta_2$; for the tourist group with $D = 0$, the impact is measured by the coefficient η_1.

First, tourists were classified according to the degree of air pollution in their origin countries. This classification makes sense because the basic logic behind this study is that people will compare the air quality in candidate destinations with that in their home country and, ceteris paribus, will be more willing to visit places with better air quality. Consistent with this logic, if the degree of air pollution in tourists' origin country is high, potential tourists may be highly concerned about the pollution problem, and be very responsive to the air pollution in China. To verify this viewpoint, we set up one "high-pollution" country group and one "low-pollution" country group. The dummy variable was defined such that $D_j^{HighPollution} = 1$ if the mean air pollution level in country j during the sample period was above the sample average, and $D_j^{HighPollution} = 0$, otherwise. The estimate results are reported in column (i) of Table 3. The estimated coefficients of $AirPollution_i$ and $AirPollution_i \times D_j^{HighPollution}$ are -0.014 and -0.006, respectively. Both coefficients are statistically significant. Therefore, it was found that, if PM$_{2.5}$ pollution increased by 1 μg/m^3, the number of tourists from "low-pollution" and "high-pollution" countries would decline by 1.4% and 2.0% ($= 0.014 + 0.006$), respectively. Indeed, as expected, tourists from more polluted countries were more responsive to China's air pollution.

Second, the influence of air pollution on tourists from Asian and non-Asian countries was examined. The majority of inbound tourists to China come from Asian regions. Asian and non-Asian tourists may react to air pollution differently. To investigate this, we set the dummy variable such that $D_j^{AsianCountries} = 1$ if tourist origin country j is in Asia, and $D_j^{AsianCountries} = 0$, otherwise. (We classified Russia as an Asian country because it shares very long common national boundaries with China.) As reported in column (ii) of Table 3, the estimated coefficient of $AirPollution_i$ is -0.014, and the coefficient of $AirPollution_i \times D_j^{AsianCountries}$ is -0.005. Both are statistically significant. Thus, it was found that China's air pollution has a larger negative impact on Asian tourists than on non-Asian tourists.

Table 3. Heterogeneous impact of air pollution on China's inbound tourism estimated at the province level.

	Variable	Estimated Coefficient			
		(i)	(ii)	(iii)	(iv)
Air pollution	$AirPollution_i$	−0.014 **	−0.014 **	−0.011 *	0.006
	$AirPollution_i \times D_j^{HighPollution}$	−0.006 ***			
	$AirPollution_i \times D_j^{AsianCountries}$		−0.005 ***		
	$AirPollution_i \times D_i^{LowPollution}$			−0.035 **	
	$AirPollution_i \times D_i^{PopularDestinations}$				−0.040 ***
	$AirPollution_j$	−0.038 *	−0.038 *	−0.038 *	−0.038 *
Destination features	$\ln(Population)_i$	−2.314	−2.312	−2.902 *	−2.775 *
	$\ln(GDPpc)_i$	2.022 ***	2.023 ***	1.725 ***	2.230 ***
	$\ln(Scenic)_i$	0.289 *	0.289 *	0.309 *	0.225
	$\ln(Hotel)_i$	0.263 *	0.264 *	0.282 **	0.291 **
	$Hospital_i$	0.003	0.004	0.00005	0.001
	$Transport_i$	0.036 ***	0.036 ***	0.037 ***	0.035 ***
	$Urban_i$	−0.092 ***	−0.093 ***	−0.095 ***	−0.088 ***
	$GDPgr_i$	−0.048 ***	−0.048 ***	−0.040 **	−0.044 **
	$Structure_i$	0.117 ***	0.117 ***	0.117 ***	0.097 ***
	$Temperature_i$	−0.035	−0.035	−0.031	−0.055
	$Rain_i$	0.539	0.539	0.603	0.269
Origin features	$\ln(Population)_j$	0.701	0.722	0.721	0.689
	$\ln(GDPpc)_j$	−0.915	−0.899	−0.903	−0.920
	$Transport_j$	27.371 **	27.315 **	27.387 **	27.613 **
	$Urban_j$	0.004	0.004	0.004	0.004
	$GDPgr_j$	−0.0004	−0.0002	−0.0004	−0.0005
Interaction variables	$\ln(ER)_{ij}$	−0.528 *	−0.515 *	−0.512 *	−0.532 *
	$\ln(Distance)_{ij}$	−1.336 ***	−1.356 ***	−1.340 ***	−1.340 ***
	$TradeOpen_{ij}$	6.394 ***	5.953 ***	4.844 ***	4.860 ***
	$VisaFree_{ij}$	0.069	0.066	0.073	0.079
Province-fixed effect		Yes	Yes	Yes	Yes
Country-fixed effect		Yes	Yes	Yes	Yes
Time-fixed effect		Yes	Yes	Yes	Yes
Observations		2651	2651	2651	2651
R^2		0.820	0.820	0.820	0.820

Statistical significance: * $p < 10\%$, ** $p < 5\%$, *** $p < 1\%$.

Third, tourists were classified according to the air pollution level in their visiting destinations. We set up one "high-pollution" province group and one "low-pollution" province group. The dummy variable was defined such that $D_i^{LowPollution} = 1$ if the mean air pollution level in Chinese province i during the sample period was below the sample average, and $D_i^{LowPollution} = 0$, otherwise.

The estimation results are reported in column (iii) of Table 3. The coefficient of $AirPollution_i$ is -0.011, and the coefficient of $AirPollution_i \times D_i^{LowPollution}$ is -0.035. Both are statistically significant. Thus, we essentially detected a nonlinear effect of air pollution on China's inbound tourism. In "high-pollution" and "low-pollution" provinces, if $PM_{2.5}$ concentration rose by 1 μg/m^3, the number of inbound tourist arrivals would decline by 1.1% and 4.6% ($= 0.011 + 0.035$), respectively. In other words, tourists who decide to visit more polluted areas are less sensitive to the variations of air pollution, and those that choose to visit less polluted areas care much more about pollution.

Lastly, tourists were grouped according to the degree of popularity of their visiting destinations. We considered one "popular destinations" province group and one "less popular destinations" province group. We defined the dummy variable such that $D_i^{PopularDestiantions} = 1$ if the mean number of annual inbound visitors to province i during the sample period was above the sample average, and $D_i^{PopularDestinations} = 0$, otherwise. As demonstrated in column (iv) of Table 3, the estimated coefficient of $AirPollution_i$ is not statistically significant, and the coefficient of $AirPollution_i \times D_i^{PopularDestination}$ is -0.040 and significant at the 1% level. Thus, it was found that tourists visiting popular Chinese destinations are sensitive to air quality, but tourists who choose to visit less popular destinations are not responsive to air pollution. Indeed, if a foreign tourist decided to travel to a Chinese region that was not visited by many people, the tourist would probably have an extraordinary interest or reason, e.g., for the purpose of business or conference. In this circumstance, air quality may not be a major concern.

In summary, the heterogeneity analysis shows that the magnitude of tourists' responses to air pollution in China is dependent on the characteristics of their origin and destination regions. The impact of air pollution in China is larger for travelers coming from more polluted and Asian countries, and visiting less polluted and more popular destinations.

5. Discussion and Implications

This study emphasizes the importance of good air quality for inbound tourism development. While this point has been confirmed by previous literature, this study aimed to estimate the impact of air pollution on the basis of a wide sample by using a gravity model, in which the features of destinations, origin regions, and their interactive relationship were explicitly modelled. According to the estimation results, if $PM_{2.5}$ concentration in China rose by 1 μg/m^3, inbound tourist arrivals would decline by approximately 1.7%. Hypothesis 1 is strongly supported. This result confirms the importance of a clean environment as a favored characteristic of tourist attractions as argued in the literature, such as by Goodwin [4], Hu and Wall [5], Mihalič [6], Zhang et al. [7], and Zhang et al. [8].

An interesting finding of this study is that, if $PM_{2.5}$ in tourist origin countries increased by 1 μg/m^3, tourist arrivals in China would drop by 3.8%. This large impact has not been noted in previous studies. Environmental studies, such as those by Atari et al. [37], Dong et al. [40], and Moffatt et al. [38], reported that the existence of local air pollution would raise residents' awareness of and concern about the pollution problem. Therefore, if air quality in their home countries got worse, potential tourists living in foreign countries would be less willing to choose China as a tourism destination. The estimation in this study confirms Hypothesis 2. Although this finding has no direct practical implication for China's tourism development because China cannot change the level of air pollution in foreign countries, it reminds researchers that air pollution in tourist origin regions is an explanatory variable in tourism demand analysis that cannot be ignored.

It is notable that the estimated magnitude of the impact of air pollution in China is different from that reported in previous studies. Table 4 briefly summarizes several previous studies on the impact of air pollution in China on inbound tourist arrivals. There are five columns in the table. The first column, "Literature", lists the authors' names. The second column, "Area Studied", and third column, "Period Covered" provide information about the sample regions and periods studied. Different air pollutants were used in previous studies to represent the degree of air pollution. The fourth column of the table, "Air Pollutant", lists the names of air pollution indicators. The last column,

"Estimated Effect", reports the estimated response of inbound tourist arrivals to a 1 $\mu g/m^3$ increase in air pollutant concentration.

Table 4. Estimated response of inbound tourist arrivals to a 1 $\mu g/m^3$ increase in air pollutant concentration in China, as reported in previous studies.

Literature	Area Studied	Period Covered	Air Pollutant	Estimated Effect
Dong et al. [27]	274 cities in China	2009–2012		−0.56%
Xu et al. [29]	337 cities in China	2007–2016	PM_{10}	insignificant
Zhou et al. [31]	Beijing, China	2005–2016		−0.33%
Liu et al. [16]	17 provinces in China	2005–2015	$PM_{2.5}$	insignificant
Xu et al. [29]	337 cities in China	2007–2016		−1.23%

For instance, according to the study by Dong et al. [27], who investigated 274 cities in China for the period 2009–2012, if PM_{10} concentration in ambient air increased by 1 $\mu g/m^3$, inbound tourist arrivals would decline by 0.56%. Zhou et al. [31] focused on Beijing City, and reported that, if PM_{10} density increased by 1 $\mu g/m^3$, inbound tourist arrivals in Beijing would decline by 0.33%. Differently from these two studies, Xu et al. [29] reported that the response of inbound tourist arrivals to PM_{10} pollution was not significant statistically, based on a sample covering 337 cities. However, they found that inbound tourists were sensitive to $PM_{2.5}$ pollution. The estimated effect of a 1 $\mu g/m^3$ rise in $PM_{2.5}$ concentration on tourist arrivals was −1.23%. But this finding was not supported by Liu et al. [16], whose study did not report a statistically significant impact of $PM_{2.5}$ pollution on tourism. Overall, these previous studies have not provided a consensus on the magnitude of the impact of air pollution on inbound tourism in China.

Although the core finding of this study on the harmful influence of air pollution in China is qualitatively consistent with the findings of Dong et al. [27], Xu et al. [29], and Zhou et al. [31], the estimated effect of air pollution in this study is quantitatively different from that reported in previous studies. Particularly, the estimated negative impact is much stronger than that reported by Liu et al. [16] and Xu et al. [29], who also took $PM_{2.5}$ as the indicator of air pollution. Since this study utilized a sample covering almost all Chinese regions and focused on recent years, the results may better reflect the general situation in China in the recent period.

The estimation results in this study enables a quantitative evaluation of the potential of promoting inbound tourism by improving air quality. According to the estimation, if $PM_{2.5}$ density could be reduced by 1 $\mu g/m^3$, inbound tourist arrivals would rise by 1.7%. This impact is substantial. For instance, if $PM_{2.5}$ density can be reduced by 10 $\mu g/m^3$, which is not an unrealistic target, it is expected that inbound tourist arrivals would rise by around 17%. In 2016, the number of annual inbound tourist arrivals was 138 million person-times. An increase of 17% represents 23.46 million person-times. Obviously, improving air quality should be considered as a practical and effective way to promote China's inbound tourism. If air quality in China can be substantially improved in the future, inbound tourist arrivals could potentially increase by at least tens of millions of person-times.

As reported in the section on heterogeneity analysis of different tourist groups, inbound tourists are more sensitive to air pollution in less polluted and more popular destinations. This finding indicates that air quality is a critically important factor of sustainable development in tourism-dependent areas. Because many scenic spots in less polluted areas are famous for their natural landscape, air pollution will substantially reduce the attractiveness or even destroy the beauty of these spots. Since popular destinations are representative of China and preferred options for most international travelers, their ability to attract tourists largely determines China's position in the world tourism market. Thus, particular emphasis should be placed on pollution control in currently less polluted and more popular tourist destinations, in order to improve the attractiveness and competitiveness of China's tourism.

Based on the results of this research, two practical implications can be drawn for China's inbound tourism. First, from the perspective of industrial policy, it is urgent to implement environmental regulations effectively to ensure that the environment can be improved in the future. This is especially crucial in districts whose economies are largely dependent on tourism. The local governments in those districts should prioritize the issue of air quality improvement. Second, from the perspective of tourism marketing, in order to attract more international tourists, China's destination image should be repaired from the negative influence of air pollution. It is valuable to inform potential foreign tourists that there are attractive places with good air quality and the air quality is getting better. The tourism sector needs to have supportive policies and conduct strong tourism destination marketing campaigns, such as participating in international tourism exhibitions and forums.

In fact, in the past few years, China has implemented a comprehensive and complicated set of policies to reduce air pollution, including many environmental laws and standards, environmental action plans proposed by the central and local governments, and specific and detailed regulatory measures on the production and economic activities [69,70]. China has achieved some substantial success in air pollution reduction, especially concerning SO_2 and NO_x emissions. However, so far, PM concentrations remain high, and haze remains a severe problem in many areas [69,71]. It is necessary to promote research on the sources of PM pollutants, and apply new technologies and methods to further reduce emissions. Improving air quality will generate great benefits. More tourists will be attracted to boost the economy, and local residents' life and public health will also be ameliorated.

6. Conclusions and Directions for Future Studies

In this study, we explored the negative effects of air pollution on inbound tourist arrivals in China, based on a gravity model using data of province-level inbound tourist arrivals from 13 origin countries during the period 2010–2016. The estimation results show that, on average, if $PM_{2.5}$ concentration in China increased by 1 $\mu g/m^3$, inbound tourist arrivals would decline by approximately 1.7%. This verifies Hypothesis 1, confirming that clean air is an important element of attractive tourist destinations. This finding generates a clear policy implication: China's inbound tourism can be substantially expanded by implementing environmental protection policies. In addition, it was found that, if $PM_{2.5}$ concentration in tourist origin countries rose by 1 $\mu g/m^3$, inbound tourist arrivals in China would decline by roughly 3.8%. This supports Hypothesis 2, which can be explained by potential tourists' increased perception of and concern about air pollution in response to the pollution problems in their home countries. This finding indicates that an accurate modelling of tourism demand should also take into account the influence of pollution in regions where tourists come from.

This study was restricted by several limitations that could be addressed in the future. First, this study focused on air pollution and neglected other types of pollution such as water pollution and solid waste. Although air pollution has a severe impact on tourism, as reported by this study, other kinds of pollution might also have a substantial influence (e.g., [72–74]). Taking into account multiple pollution categories would help provide a more comprehensive understanding of the environment–tourism nexus. In the future, researchers can consider different pollution types as independent variables in one regression model, and compare their estimated impacts. This will help identify the relative importance of different pollutants and facilitate the design of efficient policies. Second, this study evaluated the benefits of improving air quality to boost tourism, but did not assess the costs of air pollution reduction. Obviously, actions to improve air quality are not free. For instance, some environment-friendly production processes should be adopted and some air-cleaning equipment needs to be installed. In the future, a detailed cost–benefit analysis would provide valuable suggestions for tourism policy-makers. This requires the researchers to collect detailed information about the costs and benefits of pollution reduction. As it is difficult to obtain sufficient data for a wide geographic area, researchers may start from the analysis on a specific small region, such as one scenic spot.

Author Contributions: Conceptualization, data curation, formal analysis, funding acquisition, methodology, and original draft preparation, D.D.; literature review, review and editing, software, and validation, B.X. All authors have read and agreed to the published version of the manuscript.

Funding: This research was funded by the Fundamental Research Funds for the Central Universities (Grant No. JBK1809054).

Acknowledgments: The authors are grateful to the editors and three anonymous referees for their comments and suggestions.

Conflicts of Interest: The authors declare no conflict of interest.

References

1. Zhang, L.; Gao, J. Exploring the effects of international tourism on China's economic growth, energy consumption and environmental pollution: Evidence from a regional panel analysis. *Renew. Sustain. Energy Rev.* **2016**, *53*, 225–234. [CrossRef]

2. Ministry of Culture and Tourism of the PRC. Basic Situation of Tourism Market in 2018 (in Chinese). 2019. Available online: http://zwgk.mct.gov.cn/auto255/201902/t20190212_837271.html (accessed on 15 November 2019).

3. World Travel and Tourism Council. Travel and Tourism: Economic Impact 2018—China. 2018. Available online: https://www.chinatravelnews.com/images/201803/3e373c28a7e45f2b.pdf (accessed on 15 November 2019).

4. Goodwin, H. Tourism and the Environment. *Biologist* **1995**, *42*, 129–133.

5. Hu, W.; Wall, G. Environmental Management, Environmental Image and the Competitive Tourist Attraction. *J. Sustain. Tour.* **2005**, *13*, 617–635. [CrossRef]

6. Mihalič, T. Environmental management of a tourist destination: A factor of tourism competitiveness. *Tour. Manag.* **2000**, *21*, 65–78. [CrossRef]

7. Zhang, H.; Gu, C.l.; Gu, L.W.; Zhang, Y. The evaluation of tourism destination competitiveness by TOPSIS & information entropy—A case in the Yangtze River Delta of China. *Tour. Manag.* **2011**, *32*, 443–451. [CrossRef]

8. Zhang, A.; Zhong, L.; Xu, Y.; Wang, H.; Dang, L. Tourists' Perception of Haze Pollution and the Potential Impacts on Travel: Reshaping the Features of Tourism Seasonality in Beijing, China. *Sustainability* **2015**, *7*, 2397–2414. [CrossRef]

9. Hadley, M.B.; Vedanthan, R.; Fuster, V. Air pollution and cardiovascular disease: A window of opportunity. *Nat. Rev. Cardiol.* **2018**, *15*, 193–194. [CrossRef]

10. Szyszkowicz, M.; Kousha, T.; Kingsbury, M.; Colman, I. Air Pollution and Emergency Department Visits for Depression: A Multicity Case-Crossover Study. *Environ. Health Insights* **2016**, *10*, 155–161. [CrossRef]

11. Trasande, L.; Thurston, G.D. The role of air pollution in asthma and other pediatric morbidities. *J. Allergy Clin. Immunol.* **2005**, *115*, 689–699. [CrossRef] [PubMed]

12. Mace, B.L.; Bell, P.A.; Loomis, R.J. Visibility and Natural Quiet in National Parks and Wilderness Areas: Psychological Considerations. *Environ. Behav.* **2004**, *36*, 5–31. [CrossRef]

13. Poudyal, N.C.; Paudel, B.; Green, G.T. Estimating the Impact of Impaired Visibility on the Demand for Visits to National Parks. *Tour. Econ.* **2013**, *19*, 433–452. [CrossRef]

14. Ministry of Ecology and Environment of the PRC. 2018 China Ecology and Environment Bulletin (in Chinese). 2019. Available online: http://www.mee.gov.cn/home/jrtt_1/201905/t20190529_704841.shtml (accessed on 15 November 2019) .

15. Wall Street Journal. Pollution Halves Visitors to Beijing. 2013. Available online: https://blogs.wsj.com/chinarealtime/2013/10/31/beijing-air-pollution-drives-50-drop-in-visitors/ (accessed on 15 November 2019) .

16. Liu, J.; Pan, H.; Zheng, S. Tourism Development, Environment and Policies: Differences between Domestic and International Tourists. *Sustainability* **2019**, *11*, 1390. [CrossRef]

17. Tang, J.; Yuan, X.; Ramos, V.; Sriboonchitta, S. Does air pollution decrease inbound tourist arrivals? The case of Beijing. *Asia Pac. J. Tour. Res.* **2019**, *24*, 597–605. [CrossRef]

18. Brida, J.G.; Cortes-Jimenez, I.; Pulina, M. Has the tourism-led growth hypothesis been validated? A literature review. *Curr. Issues Tour.* **2016**, *19*, 394–430. [CrossRef]

19. Li, K.X.; Jin, M.; Shi, W. Tourism as an important impetus to promoting economic growth: A critical review. *Tour. Manag. Perspect.* **2018**, *26*, 135–142. [CrossRef]
20. Paramati, S.R.; Alam, M.S.; Chen, C.F. The Effects of Tourism on Economic Growth and CO2 Emissions: A Comparison between Developed and Developing Economies. *J. Travel Res.* **2016**, *56*, 712–724. [CrossRef]
21. Guindi, M.N.; Flaherty, G.T.; Byrne, M. Every breath you take: How does air pollution affect the international traveller? *J. Travel Med.* **2018**, *25*, tay021. [CrossRef]
22. Pant, P.; Huynh, W.; Peltier, R.E. Exposure to air pollutants in Vietnam: Assessing potential risk for tourists. *J. Environ. Sci.* **2018**, *73*, 147–154. [CrossRef]
23. Lu, F.; Xu, D.; Cheng, Y.; Dong, S.; Guo, C.; Jiang, X.; Zheng, X. Systematic review and meta-analysis of the adverse health effects of ambient PM2.5 and PM10 pollution in the Chinese population. *Environ. Res.* **2015**, *136*, 196–204. [CrossRef] [PubMed]
24. Becken, S.; Jin, X.; Zhang, C.; Gao, J. Urban air pollution in China: Destination image and risk perceptions. *J. Sustain. Tour.* **2017**, *25*, 130–147. [CrossRef]
25. Zhang, K.; Hou, Y.; Li, G.; Huang, Y. Tourists and Air Pollution: How and Why Air Pollution Magnifies Tourists' Suspicion of Service Providers. *J. Travel Res.* **2019**. [CrossRef]
26. Deng, T.; Li, X.; Ma, M. Evaluating impact of air pollution on China's inbound tourism industry: A spatial econometric approach. *Asia Pac. J. Tour. Res.* **2017**, *22*, 771–780. [CrossRef]
27. Dong, D.; Xu, X.; Wong, Y.F. Estimating the Impact of Air Pollution on Inbound Tourism in China: An Analysis Based on Regression Discontinuity Design. *Sustainability* **2019**, *11*. [CrossRef]
28. Xu, X.; Reed, M. Perceived pollution and inbound tourism in China. *Tour. Manag. Perspect.* **2017**, *21*, 109–112. [CrossRef]
29. Xu, X.; Dong, D.; Wang, Y.; Wang, S. The Impacts of Different Air Pollutants on Domestic and Inbound Tourism in China. *Int. J. Environ. Res. Public Health* **2019**, *16*, 5127. [CrossRef]
30. Zhou, B.; Qu, H.; Du, X.; Yang, B.; Liu, F. Air Quality and Inbound Tourism in China. *Tour. Anal.* **2018**, *23*, 159–164. [CrossRef]
31. Zhou, X.; Santana Jiménez, Y.; Pérez Rodríguez, J.V.; Hernández, J.M. Air pollution and tourism demand: A case study of Beijing, China. *Int. J. Tour. Res.* **2019**, *21*, 747–757. [CrossRef]
32. Cheung, C.; Law, R. The impact of air quality on tourism: The case of Hong Kong. *Pac. Tour. Rev.* **2001**, *5*, 69–74.
33. Law, R.; Cheung, C. Air Quality in Hong Kong: A Study of the Perception of International Visitors. *J. Sustain. Tour.* **2007**, *15*, 390–401. [CrossRef]
34. Chen, C.M.; Lin, Y.L.; Hsu, C.L. Does air pollution drive away tourists? A case study of the Sun Moon Lake National Scenic Area, Taiwan. *Transp. Res. Part D Transp. Environ.* **2017**, *53*, 398–402. [CrossRef]
35. Wang, L.; Fang, B.; Law, R. Effect of air quality in the place of origin on outbound tourism demand: Disposable income as a moderator. *Tour. Manag.* **2018**, *68*, 152–161. [CrossRef]
36. Deguen, S.; Pédrono, G.; Ségala, C.; Mesbah, M. Association Between Pollution and Public Perception of Air Quality-SEQAP, a Risk Perception Study in France. *Epidemiology* **2008**, *19*, S216.
37. Atari, D.O.; Luginaah, I.N.; Fung, K. The Relationship between Odour Annoyance Scores and Modelled Ambient Air Pollution in Sarnia, "Chemical Valley", Ontario. *Int. J. Environ. Res. Public Health* **2009**, *6*. [CrossRef]
38. Moffatt, S.; Phillimore, P.; Bhopal, R.; Foy, C. 'If this is what it's doing to our washing, what is it doing to our lungs?' Industrial pollution and public understanding in North-East England. *Soc. Sci. Med.* **1995**, *41*, 883–891. [CrossRef]
39. Oglesby, L.; Künzli, N.; Monn, C.; Schindler, C.; Ackermann-Liebrich, U.; Leuenberger, P.; the SAPALDIA Team. Validity of Annoyance Scores for Estimation of Long Term Air Pollution Exposure in Epidemiologic Studies : The Swiss Study on Air Pollution and Lung Diseases in Adults (SAPALDIA). *Am. J. Epidemiol.* **2000**, *152*, 75–83. [CrossRef]
40. Dong, D.; Xu, X.; Xu, W.; Xie, J. The Relationship Between the Actual Level of Air Pollution and Residents' Concern about Air Pollution: Evidence from Shanghai, China. *Int. J. Environ. Res. Public Health* **2019**, *16*, 4784. [CrossRef]
41. Pu, S.; Shao, Z.; Fang, M.; Yang, L.; Liu, R.; Bi, J.; Ma, Z. Spatial distribution of the public's risk perception for air pollution: A nationwide study in China. *Sci. Total Environ.* **2019**, *655*, 454–462. [CrossRef]

42. Guo, Y.; Li, Y. Online amplification of air pollution risk perception: The moderating role of affect in information. *Inf. Commun. Soc.* **2018**, *21*, 80–93. [CrossRef]

43. Morley, C.; Rosselló, J.; Santana-Gallego, M. Gravity models for tourism demand: Theory and use. *Ann. Tour. Res.* **2014**, *48*. [CrossRef]

44. Huang, X.; Han, Y.; Gong, X.; Liu, X. Does the belt and road initiative stimulate China's inbound tourist market? An empirical study using the gravity model with a DID method. *Tour. Econ.* **2019**. [CrossRef]

45. Xu, L.; Wang, S.; Li, J.; Tang, L.; Shao, Y. Modelling international tourism flows to China: A panel data analysis with the gravity model. *Tour. Econ.* **2019**, *25*, 1047–1069. [CrossRef]

46. Yang, Y.; Wong, K.K.F. The influence of cultural distance on China inbound tourism flows: A panel data gravity model approach. *Asian Geogr.* **2012**, *29*, 21–37. [CrossRef]

47. Barregard, L.; Molnàr, P.; Jonson, E.J.; Stockfelt, L. Impact on Population Health of Baltic Shipping Emissions. *Int. J. Environ. Res. Public Health* **2019**, *16*. [CrossRef] [PubMed]

48. Colacci, A.; Vaccari, M.; Mascolo, G.M.; Rotondo, F.; Morandi, E.; Quercioli, D.; Perdichizzi, S.; Zanzi, C.; Serra, S.; Poluzzi, V.; et al. Alternative Testing Methods for Predicting Health Risk from Environmental Exposures. *Sustainability* **2014**, *6*, 5265–5283. [CrossRef]

49. Săndică, A.M.; Dudian, M.; Ştefănescu, A. Air Pollution and Human Development in Europe: A New Index Using Principal Component Analysis. *Sustainability* **2018**, *10*, 312. [CrossRef]

50. Song, C.; He, J.; Wu, L.; Jin, T.; Chen, X.; Li, R.; Ren, P.; Zhang, L.; Mao, H. Health burden attributable to ambient PM2.5 in China. *Environ. Pollut.* **2017**, *223*, 575–586. [CrossRef]

51. Xu, D.; Huang, Z.; Hou, G.; Zhang, C. The spatial spillover effects of haze pollution on inbound tourism: evidence from mid-eastern China. *Tour. Geogr.* **2019**. [CrossRef]

52. Yin, H.; Pizzol, M.; Xu, L. External costs of PM2.5 pollution in Beijing, China: Uncertainty analysis of multiple health impacts and costs. *Environ. Pollut.* **2017**, *226*, 356–369. [CrossRef]

53. Khadaroo, J.; Seetanah, B. The role of transport infrastructure in international tourism development: A gravity model approach. *Tour. Manag.* **2008**, *29*, 831–840. [CrossRef]

54. Santeramo, F.G.; Morelli, M. Modelling tourism flows through gravity models: A quantile regression approach. *Curr. Issues Tour.* **2016**, *19*, 1077–1083. [CrossRef]

55. Zamparini, L.; Vergori, A.S.; Arima, S. Assessing the determinants of local tourism demand: A simultaneous equations model for the Italian provinces. *Tour. Econ.* **2017**, *23*, 981–992. [CrossRef]

56. Zheng, Q.; Kuang, Y.; Huang, N. Coordinated Development between Urban Tourism Economy and Transport in the Pearl River Delta, China. *Sustainability* **2016**, *8*, 1338. [CrossRef]

57. Mangion, M.L.; Durbarry, R.; Sinclair, M.T. Tourism Competitiveness: Price and Quality. *Tour. Econ.* **2005**, *11*, 45–68. [CrossRef]

58. Seetanah, B.; Sannassee, R.; Rojid, S. The impact of relative prices on tourism demand for Mauritius: An empirical analysis. *Dev. South. Afr.* **2015**, *32*, 363–376. [CrossRef]

59. Vogt, M.G.; Wittayakorn, C. Determinants of the demand for Thailand's exports of tourism. *Appl. Econ.* **1998**, *30*, 711–715. [CrossRef]

60. Dwyer, L.; Forsyth, P.; Rao, P. The price competitiveness of travel and tourism: A comparison of 19 destinations. *Tour. Manag.* **2000**, *21*, 9–22. [CrossRef]

61. Martin, C.A.; Witt, S.F. Substitute prices in models of tourism demand. *Ann. Tour. Res.* **1988**, *15*, 255–268. [CrossRef]

62. Ahn, M.J.; McKercher, B. The Effect of Cultural Distance on Tourism: A Study of International Visitors to Hong Kong. *Asia Pac. J. Tour. Res.* **2015**, *20*, 94–113. [CrossRef]

63. Arita, S.; Edmonds, C.; Croix, S.L.; Mak, J. Impact of Approved Destination Status on Chinese Travel Abroad: An Econometric Analysis. *Tour. Econ.* **2011**, *17*, 983–996. [CrossRef]

64. Gil-Pareja, S.; Llorca-Vivero, R.; Martínez-Serrano, J.A. The impact of embassies and consulates on tourism. *Tour. Manag.* **2007**, *28*, 355–360. [CrossRef]

65. Holden, A. The environment-tourism nexus: Influence of market ethics. *Ann. Tour. Res.* **2009**, *36*, 373–389. [CrossRef]

66. Hien, P.D.; Bac, V.T.; Tham, H.C.; Nhan, D.D.; Vinh, L.D. Influence of meteorological conditions on PM2.5 and PM2.5–10 concentrations during the monsoon season in Hanoi, Vietnam. *Atmos. Environ.* **2002**, *36*, 3473–3484. [CrossRef]

67. Koutrakis, P.; Sax, S.N.; Sarnat, J.A.; Coull, B.; Demokritou, P.; Demokritou, P.; Oyola, P.; Garcia, J.; Gramsch, E. Analysis of PM10, PM2.5, and PM2.5–10 Concentrations in Santiago, Chile, from 1989 to 2001. *J. Air Waste Manag. Assoc.* **2005**, *55*, 342–351. [CrossRef]

68. Wang, J.; Ogawa, S. Effects of Meteorological Conditions on PM2.5 Concentrations in Nagasaki, Japan. *Int. J. Environ. Res. Public Health* **2015**, *12*, 9089–9101. [CrossRef]

69. Jin, Y.; Andersson, H.; Zhang, S. Air Pollution Control Policies in China: A Retrospective and Prospects. *Int. J. Environ. Res. Public Health* **2016**, *13*, 1219. [CrossRef]

70. Yang, W.; Yuan, G.; Han, J. Is China's air pollution control policy effective? Evidence from Yangtze River Delta cities. *J. Clean. Prod.* **2019**, *220*, 110–133. [CrossRef]

71. Zeng, Y.; Cao, Y.; Qiao, X.; Seyler, B.C.; Tang, Y. Air pollution reduction in China: Recent success but great challenge for the future. *Sci. Total Environ.* **2019**, *663*, 329–337. [CrossRef]

72. Jang, Y.C.; Hong, S.; Lee, J.; Lee, M.J.; Shim, W.J. Estimation of lost tourism revenue in Geoje Island from the 2011 marine debris pollution event in South Korea. *Mar. Pollut. Bull.* **2014**, *81*, 49–54. [CrossRef] [PubMed]

73. Krelling, A.P.; Williams, A.T.; Turra, A. Differences in perception and reaction of tourist groups to beach marine debris that can influence a loss of tourism revenue in coastal areas. *Mar. Policy* **2017**, *85*, 87–99. [CrossRef]

74. Williams, A.T.; Rangel-Buitrago, N.G.; Anfuso, G.; Cervantes, O.; Botero, C.M. Litter impacts on scenery and tourism on the Colombian north Caribbean coast. *Tour. Manag.* **2016**, *55*, 209–224. [CrossRef]

MDPI

St. Alban-Anlage 66

4052 Basel

Switzerland

Tel. +41 61 683 77 34

Fax +41 61 302 89 18

www.mdpi.com

Sustainability Editorial Office

E-mail: sustainability@mdpi.com

www.mdpi.com/journal/sustainability

Lightning Source UK Ltd.
Milton Keynes UK
UKHW050802011220
374381UK00003B/350